Myth, Rhetoric, and Fiction

Myth, Rhetoric, and Fiction

A Reading of Longus's
Daphnis and Chloe

Bruce D. MacQueen

University of Nebraska Press
Lincoln and London

The paper in this book
meets the minimum
requirements of American
National Standard for
Information Sciences –
Permanence of Paper
for Printed Library Materials,
ANSI Z39.48–1984.

Library of Congress
Cataloging-in-Publication Data

MacQueen, Bruce D.
Myth, rhetoric, and fiction:
a reading of Longus's
Daphnis and Chloe /
Bruce D. MacQueen.
p. cm. Includes
bibliographical references (p.
ISBN 0-8032-3137-7 (alk. paper)
1. Longus. Daphnis and Chloe.
2. Daphnis (Greek mythology)
in literature.
3. Rhetoric, Ancient.
I. Title. PA4229.L9M28   1990
883'.01 – dc20
90-12054   CIP

Publication of this book was
assisted by a grant from
The Andrew W. Mellon Foundation

To
Mrs. Esther Eubanks,
and to
the memory of
Mr. George W. Eubanks

Contents

Part two
Encountering the Tradition

Preface

This study of Longus's *Daphnis and Chloe* began, oddly enough, as a digression from a projected book on Sallust, the first of the great Roman historians. This may seem, at first, a curious sort of digression, but it was not unmotivated. It can be explained, and probably should be: after all, the Greek word ἀρχή (*archê*), which means "beginning," also means something like "organizing principle" (cf. "hier*archy*"), an inextricable part of the nature of any entity. The critical problems that first motivated this now very lengthy digression from Sallust have never entirely ceased to shape its course. Thus a brief summary of certain historiographical issues, in relation to which the aims of this study of Longus developed, may prove to be of some use.

Anyone who must rely on Sallust as a source for Catiline's conspiracy, or the war against Jugurtha, can testify that Sallust is sometimes careless with his facts. Not only is he occasionally confused about chronology and geography, but he also invents incidents and puts sometimes unwarranted constructions on the actions and motives of his characters. In short, he is anything but scrupulously objective; and on such grounds as these, he has more than once been accused of crossing that (putatively) sharp line that ought to separate history from fiction. To use his own words, Sallust seems to have written "ficta pro falsis" (roughly, "lies and falsehoods").[1]

This seems to need explaining. Indeed, many and various are the explanations adduced over the last 150 years for this "fictionalization" of historical data. Some scholars have argued that it results from simple mendacity on Sallust's part; others, that a certain tendentiousness is responsible; yet others, that he had no clear concept of how history is supposed to be written. Thus Sallust is either lying (for partisan political purposes), suborning history for some ulterior purpose (Stoic philosophy, usually), or writing rhetorical showpieces disguised as history. Almost all the existing scholarly work on Sallust is based, whether explicitly or not, on one or another of these premises.[2]

Some readers will quickly perceive something fundamentally wrong with the whole critical stance reflected in these various hypotheses. Sallust has been misinterpreted, because he has been read in the wrong way, which is to say in a way that fails to recognize how fundamentally his mode of composition (his "textuality," as some modern critics would say) differs from what we usually associate with historiography. This difference cannot be reduced to a relative degree of sophistication or explained away in terms of the evolution of historical methods. It is not that Sallust would have been more objective if only he had known how. On the contrary, the fundamental subjectivity of his narrative is central to and implicit in his whole literary project. His texts, unlike those of a modern historian, are not strictly or simply referential, either in intent or in execution; they do not succeed in accurately reproducing the events of the past precisely because they do not really intend to do so.[3] Sallust means, in other words, both more and other than what he says. It is this disjunction between what is said and what is meant, rather than the elegance or sophistication of Sallust's prose style, which puts the *Bellum Catilinae* and the *Bellum Iugurthinum* squarely in the category of literature, where modern historiography, by contrast, does not usually belong.

It need hardly be said that raising the issue of literariness in the works of Sallust opens a theoretical can of worms. To say that Sallust might have had certain political or philosophical prejudices or predilections, which may have colored his treatment of particular historical persons or events, is one thing; it is quite another to argue, as here, that Sallust's narratives actually represent or signify other events than those related, events which are never explicitly mentioned. This does not mean, of course, that either of his two monographs is an allegory, in the strictest sense of the term, but rather that there is a subtext (or interpretant), in terms of which the text is properly read. Sallust is preoccupied with the collective trauma of the Roman revolution and uses the stories of Catiline and Jugurtha to make several clear and compelling (but implicit) statements about his own times. What would be the "signified" in the work of a modern historian (that is, the story actually told, the matter at hand, *res gestae*) has thus become the "signifier," and the real meaning of the text is at one remove from the literal.

From a narratological perspective, then, Sallust has more in common with a novelist, whose narrative almost always points beyond itself, than with the modern historian, whose aims are more nearly scientific and whose works are always directly and strictly referential. The modern historian's narrative, whether or not it aims at or achieves some kind of scientific objectivity, claims to be about the real world, about what really happened. This claim necessarily raises the issue of accurate representation, and thus subjects the narrative to the test of truth, a test which it may either pass or fail, in various ways and to various extents. By contrast, however, the conventions implicit in the very existence of literary fiction allow the novelist to forgo this test of truth by conceding from the outset that his story is, in the strict referential sense, false. This concession, which amounts to some sort of tacit agreement between the author and the reader that the incidents and characters about to be described are not real, allows the novelist to aim at another kind of truth, of a sort that can never, or with difficulty, be reached through the discursive representation of reality.

Sallust could not, of course, claim such a license. Even the relatively more literary (and less scientific) conventions of ancient historiography would never allow Sallust to take this radical step of conceding (referential) falsehood for the sake of truth of another sort. The ancient historian may not have been required to be objective, or even always strictly accurate, but he was not free to indulge in wholesale literary invention. Then again, neither was anyone else in antiquity, with the exception (and that rather narrowly circumscribed) of the comic poet.[4] Thus Sallust's artistic dilemma lay in his need to reconcile the requisite degree of reference to actual facts with his desire to signify something other and greater than those facts. The resulting tension creates a historical narrative with a significance for its audience and its times not to be found explicitly stated anywhere in the text. Whatever of fiction there may be in Sallust's monographs, then, is not mendacity, but rather an alternative means of signification; and that is why the reader will have to approach Sallust with a different set of presuppositions than he or she would use to read even the most tendentious modern historian.

The continued pursuit of this line of thought naturally led, in a series of logical steps, to the study of the ancient novel, where one might expect to find fiction in its own right. To some extent, indeed, this search for "pure" fiction in ancient prose literature resulted from a certain frustration: my efforts to establish a critical basis for a "novelistic" reading of Sallust's monographs seemed to be stymied by the lack of any consensus on the meaning of the terms involved. While trying to define "fiction," then, and discuss its role in ancient historiography, I came to realize how very little I knew about the origin and nature of fiction in the ancient world. As I began to research this issue further, I slowly came to the uncomfortable realization that much of this critical territory is still terra incognita. The scholarly debate over the origins of prose fiction in antiquity was set firmly on the wrong track by Erwin Rohde in 1876, and has, for the most part, never since succeeded in contributing more light than heat to the problem.[5] The books and articles I read provided very little help in either defining fiction or in tracing the development of the theory of fiction (as opposed to its technique) in ancient literature.

Classicists, as a rule, are not trained to read novels. This should not be surprising: the novel was always something of an unwelcome parvenu on the ancient literary scene.[6] If Thucydides and Cicero are held up as the paradigms of Greek and Latin prose style, respectively, few in the classical academic tradition, ancient or modern, will hold a brief for Apuleius or Longus. Many a modern work on ancient fiction contains somewhere in it the almost obligatory disclaimer, a denial that the ancient novels have any real literary value, an apology for wasting one's precious time studying them.[7] Many seem to share, implicitly or otherwise, the attitude of the ancient critics, who either took no notice of novels at all, or relegated them to the backwaters of historiography. We speak, to be sure, of poetic fiction, the rhetoricians' *plasma* (πλάσμα); but by this we do not mean "fiction" in quite the same sense that the latter term has when applied to, for example, *Moll Flanders*. *Plasma* more nearly means "poetic license" than "fiction" and thus has little or nothing to do with the creation of fictitious narratives in prose. Any prose writer who, like Sallust, employs "plasmatic license" in the writing of prose narratives is likely to be tagged a liar; and serious scholarship on works of which one morally disapproves is all but impossible.

For my own part, I had already made the acquaintance of the Greek novel, and of *Daphnis and Chloe*, while a graduate student at the University of Iowa, where a course on the Greek novel was required for the Ph.D. degree. Like many first readers, I was struck at the time by the modernity of Longus's narrative technique, which seemed to me incongruous in a work of classical literature. So when I found myself, several years later, grappling with the meaning and function of literary fiction, it seemed only natural to turn to Longus. The result is the present study.

Thus explained, the path that leads from Sallust to Longus, though seldom trodden, is not perhaps as circuitous, even tortuous, as it may have seemed initially, even to me. What began as a digression, an effort to solve a problem in ancient historiography, has taken on a life and interest of its own. I remain, as will be seen, interested in the relationship between historiography and the novel, although my understanding of that relationship is not now what it was at first. Unlike Edward Schwartz, who likewise digressed into the ancient novel from ancient history, I do not believe that the novel is a lineal descendant of (debased) historiography.[8] Chariton's *Chaereas and Callirhoe* is not merely the illegitimate offspring of Xenophon's *Cyropaideia*; the relationship is far more subtle and complex than that. The ancient novel has a history of its own, worthy of interest on its own merits. And any attempt to interpret that history will have to come to terms with that least "historical" of all the ancient novels, Longus's *Daphnis and Chloe*.

THE CENTRAL QUESTIONS

All this is not to say that any new study of *Daphnis and Chloe*, regardless of its particular genesis, requires apology. No one can seriously contend that the interpretive possibilities of Longus's novel have been exhausted. Goethe, for example, opined that it would take "ein ganzes Buch" to say everything that one ought to say about Longus.[9] Still, there has been no great rush to meet Goethe's challenge; the scholarly bibliography on *Daphnis and Chloe*, while not negligible, remains modest. We now have, at long last, M. D. Reeve's Teubner edition of *Daphnis and Chloe*, which will be used hereinafter for all references to the text; but while William McCulloh and R. L. Hunter have written good and useful books on Longus, neither has exhausted the subject.[10] They have told us a great deal about the author and date, the sources and antecedents, the language, style, and ambience of *Daphnis and Chloe*—in sum, everything that the reader may want to know, except what *Daphnis and Chloe* really means, if indeed it turns out to mean anything at all.

To say that these questions remain unanswered does not necessarily mean, however, that they are as yet unasked. There has in fact been at least one sustained and comprehensive effort to interpret *Daphnis and Chloe*: to wit, the allegorical readings put forward by Karl Kerényi, Reinhold Merkelbach, and H. H. O. Chalk.[11] This "mystery-text" thesis is now mostly discredited; but it remains not only the best-known effort to interpret (rather than merely to describe) *Daphnis and Chloe* but almost the only one.[12] It has been refuted, for the most part, but not replaced. An unspoken consensus among scholars seems to hold that *Daphnis and Chloe*, if it is not an allegory of initiation into the rites of Dionysus or Eros or Isis, must then, faute de mieux, be no more than what it seems to be: a charming story about two incredibly naive young pastoral lovers named Daphnis and Chloe. In the pages that follow, I shall attempt to show that this implicit choice between a novel with a religious subtext and a novel with nothing to offer but the pleasure of reading it, substantial though that may be, is a false dilemma. There are other possibilities, only some of which have been explored here.

From this last argument an important disclaimer follows. One of the constant seductions of literary scholarship is the desire to say the last word on something, to write a study so grand and so profound that it will supersede what went before and preclude any future rivals. Much otherwise good work, perhaps especially in the classics, has been vitiated by an invalid claim of privilege and authority. This book, for a variety of reasons, does not purport to be the definitive critical study of Longus. It may not be a critical study at all, if Hunter's *Study of Daphnis and Chloe* is properly so called. The latter is an impressive accumulation of information, exhaustively annotated, about every salient feature of *Daphnis and Chloe*. Its second chapter is thus revealingly entitled, "The Constituent Elements." The procedure is distinctly Aristotelian: to explain a thing, divide it up into its constituent parts, its μέρη, and learn whatever can be learned about each one.[13] While this is a good and useful way of approaching a literary text, it is not the only way. The present study has different goals, which require different means; it has concerned itself first with what is in the text, not where it came from, and second with its reaction to the various traditions of which it is a part. And a tradition is not quite the same thing as a pedigree.

Daphnis and Chloe is a novel. While it is not perhaps a direct or significant progenitor of the modern novel—Heliodorus may have been more influential in the development of the novel in Europe—it is certainly a sign of great changes in the intellectual and literary life of the West. It marks the beginning of the passage from the classical world to the modern. That this happens in the work of a writer who may as well have been anonymous, whose work apparently found little audience in its own time, may have caused its importance to be overlooked both from the perspective of classicists and from that of their counterparts in the modern literatures. Even if *Daphnis and Chloe* failed to produce literary progeny, it was, nonetheless, a revolution in and of itself. And precisely because it is both ancient and modern, it has something to offer, not only to the classicist, within whose academic province both its language and its position in literary history place it, but also to the student and critic of the modern novel. Note well: the present study will not argue that Longus is the forgotten "Father of the Novel"; a logically unbridgeable gap separates *Daphnis and Chloe* from whatever modern work one may choose to call "the first novel."[14] Even the fact that editions and translations of Longus were published and read during the formative years of the early French novel does not really bridge that gap. What will be argued here is that the ancient world, for reasons that upon scrutiny may seem rather familiar, produced at least one work of prose fiction that is an analogue, if not a homologue, of the modern novel. That perception may be of some interest to students of the latter.

Any such undertaking as this always runs the risk of falling between two stools, by failing to be rigorous enough to suit the specialist, while alienating the nonspecialist with various bits of arcana. Whether or not I have succeeded in steering a safe course between Scylla and Charybdis must necessarily be the judgment of others. Certain mechanical features of this book are to be explained, however, in terms of this intention. Thus all passages from ancient authors are quoted in the original languages (primarily Greek), but a translation is provided in the body of the text so that Greekless readers (and I hope there may be more than a few) will not have to interrupt their reading to glance at a footnote or an appendix, or, even worse, try to find a translation or a translator elsewhere. (Unless otherwise noted, all translations are my own.) This practice will sometimes seem cumbersome, especially to those who do not need it, but I would rather be tiresome to a few than incomprehensible to some portion of an audience I would really like to reach. I have also chosen not to avoid certain subjects and arguments which may perhaps overtax the nonclassicist reader from time to time; but I have also sometimes included fuller explanations and identifications than might be necessary for a readership entirely composed of classicists. One perhaps unfortunate (though unavoidable) result of this is an unusually large number of explanatory notes. But without them, however unfashionable they may be, the flow of argument would be subject to frequent interruptions, either for explanations unnecessary for the classicist, or arguments too detailed for the nonclassicist. In this situation, recourse to explanatory notes is clearly the lesser of two (or three) evils.

Recently the Modern Language Association has published a new style sheet, setting out a radically different mode of bibliographical citation. This I have assiduously ignored. Notes herein will generally follow the familiar format of the *Chicago Manual of Style*. A complete bibliography of secondary scholarship and of editions, commentaries, and translations of *Daphnis and Chloe* can be found at the end of the book.

ACKNOWLEDGMENTS

Many different people have contributed to the completion of this book, some knowingly, others not. Donald Jackson of the University of Iowa taught the class on the Greek novel where I first read *Daphnis and Chloe*; his skeptical attitude toward the received wisdom on the ancient novel, and his sympathetic reception of my first attempts to analyze the structure of *Daphnis and Chloe*, were enormously helpful and stimulating. Many of my former colleagues in the Department of Foreign Languages and Literatures at Purdue University listened with patience and sympathy as I grappled with the critical problems posed by a study such as this; all of them taught me a great deal. Allan Pasco, in particular, challenged me to call Longus a novelist; and Djelal Kadir had much of value to say about my notions of rings and mirrors, and the relationship between them. More recently, my colleagues here at the University of Dallas have pushed me in other directions. I would especially like to thank William Frank, of the Department of Philosophy, for challenging my diffidence about approaching various of the philosophical issues raised in this book.

Those readers who know my mentor, Roger Hornsby, will be able to see from whom I learned to read and write.

The Andrew W. Mellon Foundation made it possible for me to spend the 1984/1985 academic year at Harvard University as a Faculty Fellow, delving into the almost inexhaustible resources of the Widener Library. Without that fellowship, and particularly without the patient support of Richard M. Hunt, director of the Mellon program, this book could never have been written. And I must finally thank my wife, Eleanor, and my two sons, John David and Jeffrey Michael, for their unflagging patience and encouragement during the trials that inevitably attend any such undertaking as this; if they had given up, I would have, too.

Chapter 1

The Problem of Interpretation

What is Longus's *Daphnis and Chloe* about? There is something tricky, difficult, elusive, in that apparently simple word "about," something which makes an answer harder to come by the closer one looks at the question. *Daphnis and Chloe* is "about" a love affair between a goatherd named Daphnis and a shepherdess named Chloe, who are exposed as infants, but miraculously found and suckled by animal mothers; who are then discovered and adopted by the families of local herdsmen; whose adoptive fathers, at the command of Eros, put them to work tending their respective flocks; who fall in love, as we somehow suspected they would; who are, however, too naive to know exactly what has happened to them, until a series of events, and the intervention of two older people, teach them what they must know; who pass through various ordeals and adventures, ranging from attempted rapes and kidnaps to the advent of rival suitors, as their love ripens, until at last their true identities are revealed; whereupon they are first reunited with their real parents, and then married, to live happily ever after.

This will serve as a synopsis of the major incidents; but someone might reasonably object that, while it certainly lists all the essentials of the plot, it rather leaves out much that seems very important about *Daphnis and Chloe*. For one thing, very little of what happens in the middle two books of the novel found a place in that synopsis, an omission which ought to give us pause. So then, it seems necessary to reconsider, and to answer the question on another level. *Daphnis and Chloe* is really "about" the initiation of an innocent young boy and an equally innocent young girl into the mysteries of love and sex, all in the (usually) charming ambience of a simple pastoral life in the countryside of Lesbos. Or it is "about" the innocence of country people, as contrasted to the depravity of city folk. Or it is "about" the benevolence of Eros, and the special favor he shows to young lovers.

These answers seem better than the first one, as far as they go, but no serious reader is likely to be entirely satisfied with them. After even the lengthiest synopsis of the plot, or characterization of the novel's central themes or ambience, it is still possible, even necessary, to ask again what *Daphnis and Chloe* is about. If a typical class of college undergraduates were to be asked what *Moby Dick* is about, for example, some of them might well answer that it is "about" life on a whaling ship in the nineteenth century; others, that it is "about" the one-legged captain of a whaling ship, who sets out to pursue a white whale, and who leads his ship and all but one of his crew to destruction in the course of his search for revenge. But such observations, even if germane, provide only the most rudimentary beginning of a satisfactory answer, a starting point, at best, for further investigation and deeper reflection. Let us concede that there is a place for "book reports" in the education of young readers; still, these are the things of childhood, so to speak, usually best left behind in the transition to the university. Something beyond a "book report" is clearly called for if, on being asked what *Moby Dick* is about, one means to give an intelligent answer. One senses that such a book requires (and deserves) more than a synopsis or a description.

What it demands, in a word, is interpretation. To venture that *Moby Dick* is "about" obsession, or the human soul in conflict with inscrutable nature, or civilization crippled by its confrontation with the untamed, or what-have-you, is to interpret it, for good or ill. Interpretation, then, is precisely that "something beyond" which seems needful when one reads a great book. Here, in fact, may lie the key to a useful definition of literature itself, in that any text which seems to demand some effort on the reader's part to interpret it is by that very token literary. In other words, what distinguishes a literary text from a nonliterary text is not so much a degree of quality or value but rather the hermeneutical posture assumed by the text in question. We read literature on the assumption that it has something to teach us, else we are wasting precious time; but very often this teaching, because it goes on beneath the most literal level of meaning, requires a certain explication, which the text itself does not provide. The critic, or the critical reader, will have to do more than to decipher the words on a page. Learning to read, in reality, is a task that often seems mastered but seldom really is.

This is not to say, of course, that every book we read needs to be interpreted, or can be, in the same way that we ordinarily speak of "interpreting" a literary text. Everyone, no doubt, has read books of which the only possible interpretation is a synopsis of the plot. We may amuse ourselves by reading Agatha Christie murder mysteries, for example, but we are unlikely to feel that they need to be interpreted, or that they have anything in particular to teach, unless it be the manners and morals of England between the wars. They are worth reading once, perhaps, but are then put aside. They do not provoke questions, once the identity of the murderer has been revealed; no one reads *Ten Little Indians* expecting to find therein answers to the deepest enigmas of the human soul.[1] We read a computer manual, on the other hand, for no other reason than to learn something which it purports to teach us; but precisely because whatever lessons it contains are right on the surface, interpretation ought to be unnecessary. When it is necessary, in such cases, we are inclined to ascribe that to a fault in the manual, and rightly so. Of such books, the cardinal virtue of their teaching is clarity, above all; profundity is likely to be no more than a nuisance in such a text, and very possibly a serious hindrance. We can speak of a software manual as "literature" only because the latter term has in recent years come to mean anything written and published.

Now some readers, to be sure, may think that *Daphnis and*

Chloe has rather more in common with an Agatha Christie novel, in these terms, than with so "serious" a book as *Moby Dick,* and so reject as pointless the whole project of interpreting it. Others may do so on broader theoretical grounds, responsive to a certain contemporary diffidence about the very possibility of "deeper" meanings in literary texts; both the noun "meaning" and the adjective "deeper" are unfashionable, the word "interpretation" is suspect, and there are those who seem not quite sure that the term "literary" has any content. But χαιρόντων, as the Greeks would say: "May they fare well." The first premise of this book, before we proceed any further, is that some texts have meanings, which extend beyond the stories they tell, and which can be talked about intelligently and with profit.[2] The second premise is that *Daphnis and Chloe* is such a text. Like *Moby Dick,* it has something more to say to its readers, then and now, than what appears in any synopsis of its plot: that is, it stands in need of interpretation.

This is not really an altogether new or unprecedented observation to make about *Daphnis and Chloe.* To judge from recorded responses, few readers have finished Longus's novel without some sense, however vague, that there is something of value embedded in this text, worth the digging out. Longus seems to merit, even require, second thoughts. We may find the traces of such a reaction, not only in a certain proliferation of scholarly efforts to explain what *Daphnis and Chloe* is about, but even in the way the text has been received by readers not given to learned disquisitions on its meaning. Goethe, for example, on reading a copy given him by Eckermann, was moved to exclaim, "Man müsste ein ganzes Buch schreiben, um alle grosse Verdienste dieses Gedichts nach Werden zu schätzen" (One would have to write an entire book, in order to do justice to all the great virtues of this poem).[3] Ravel wrote a beautiful ballet suite called *Daphnis and Chloe;* and such well-known artists as Chagall and Mailliot have not thought their talents wasted in drawing illustrations for deluxe editions.[4] It seems clear enough, in sum, that Longus is capable of touching a responsive chord within many readers, if not most. And this at least implies, if it does not prove, that *Daphnis and Chloe* is about something at least a little more important, or profound, or resonant, than the charming little tale which constitutes its plot. To go even a little further: one senses that there is some sort of truth that Longus means to teach us through his novel, a truth which is something other than, and greater than, the accurate depiction of the lives of two really rather impossible characters. For the fictionality (in a sense, untruthfulness) of his plot does not preclude Longus from saying something true; in fact, it may be that this very element of fiction, of collusive untruth, is essential to expressing whatever truth Longus is out to teach. But this is somewhat in anticipation of matters best left for later; for the moment, suffice it to say that we need not begin this study of *Daphnis and Chloe* in a spirit of apology, as some have done before.[5] The project of interpreting this novel will stand on its own merits.

No one should be misled, at this point, into thinking that it will be easy to say what *Daphnis and Chloe* is about, in any deeper sense of "about." On this issue, recorded opinions are many and diverse. To some, the whole novel has seemed to be an allegory of initiation into a cult, of Isis or Dionysus or Eros; its plot is a liturgy, and its characters are catechumens.[6] Another scholar has argued that Longus meant to write an allegory of love itself, largely informed by Plato's teachings in the *Symposium* and *Phaedrus*.[7] Searching for allegorical referents is surely one way to find something worthwhile ($\sigma\pi o v\delta a\hat{\imath}ov$), in *Daphnis and Chloe*, but it is not the only way, and perhaps not the best way at that. Allegorizing can be a dangerous business. That may be why neither of the two books on *Daphnis and Chloe* written in English has much to say about allegory strictly so called, though both accept—as one is all but compelled to accept—that both religion and Platonic philosophy have a role to play.[8] To William McCulloh, the essence of *Daphnis and Chloe* is what he calls its "hybrid virtues," the blending of the numinous and the romantic in a pastoral setting; to R. L. Hunter, on the other hand, what exiguous virtues the text possesses are the result of its style and technique, and particularly of its rhetorical sophistication.[9] One wonders, in fact, on reading both these books, as valuable as they are, whether both men have read the same text. We are still a long way from knowing what *Daphnis and Chloe* is about.

One might adduce, no doubt, any number of reasons why *Daphnis and Chloe* has elicited so many and such different interpretations. Despite the easy grace of Longus's style, this is a complex text, in which nothing, or almost nothing, is as simple as it seems. But some of the interpretational difficulties are, in a sense, outside the text itself. The very act of asking what *Daphnis and Chloe* is *about* necessarily involves a presumption that we know what it *is*. This question, too, has an easy answer, which ultimately fails to satisfy. By convention, *Daphnis and Chloe* is most often assigned to the genre variously called "Greek novel" or "Greek romance." Four other works that seem to belong to the same genre have survived intact, and every indication is that there were others, probably many, which did not survive; from time to time fragments of some of them are rescued from the sands of Egypt.

All in all, this may not be the best company for Longus, an author with manifest literary aspirations, to be keeping. In antiquity, prose fiction, as a genre, was never even dignified with a name of its own, which is at least part of the reason modern scholars have had such a hard time deciding what to call it. The ancient grammarians who speak for the literary establishment of their times either never even mention the novels or consign them to the backwaters of historiography.[10] These texts belong to the periphery of literary history, a footnote, as it were, to the long sad twilight of pagan antiquity, their very appearance a symptom, if not somehow a cause, of the decline of the classical world. Classical scholars have occasionally taken an interest in them, even men of such stature as Erwin Rohde and Edward Schwartz in the last century and B. E. Perry in this; but even these have approached their subject with an essentially antiquarian interest, not unmixed with a certain slightly veiled disdain.[11] The five extant Greek novels have seldom been thought worthy of study on their own account, as living literary texts rather than as artifacts, and have no place in anyone's "core" curriculum—not even, for the most part, in graduate programs in the classics.[12] If we are out to interpret *Daphnis and Chloe*, then, the mere assertion that it is a Greek novel (or romance) will not, in the present state of our knowledge, equip us with many useful presuppositions, and may rather serve to handicap us with worse-than-useless prejudices.

Even if that were not the case, however, even if the label "Greek novel" had some interpretive content in a general way, we would still be constrained to ask what *Daphnis and Chloe* actually is. *Daphnis and Chloe* sometimes seems to belong to the same genre as *Chaereas and Callirhoe* and the rest only faute de mieux, for no other reason than that it is an extended prose narrative in Greek and is concerned with the love between two attractive young people. Anyone who has read all five of the extant ancient Greek novels is very likely to conclude, even if the error of over-stating the sameness of the other novels (or romances) is scrupulously avoided, that the other four have rather more in common with each other than any of them has with *Daphnis and Chloe*.[13] Viewed from one perspective, in fact, the latter's plot, setting, and ambience are distinctly anomalous. What we shall see, however, is that there are other (and probably better) ways of looking at the matter. The separateness of *Daphnis and Chloe* can be (and has been) overstated, and there are good reasons to think of it as belonging to the genre "ancient Greek novel," as representing, in fact, a further stage in its coming to maturity and establishing a tradition of its own. Still, there would be no need to dwell on the point if it were self-evident. To the genre as it has been defined in and through the great critical edifices erected by Rohde and Perry, *Daphnis and Chloe* must be peripheral. We can learn little from it about the origin of the genre, which has been the main interest of those who have heretofore busied themselves with the Greek novel. This is, in sum, a peripheral text in a peripheral genre, and that is a sure prescription for neglect and misunderstanding.

What is more, we know nothing of the man Longus; even that he was a man and that his name was "Longus" cannot be proven. Though it is possible to establish a very approximate floruit for Longus, little is certain beyond that he probably wrote in the period between the last years of the Antonines and the fall of the Severi (roughly A.D. 175–235).[14] For all practical purposes, *Daphnis and Chloe* might as well be anonymous. No author before the twelfth century alludes to or mentions Longus, which means that we cannot measure the contemporary impact of *Daphnis and Chloe*—or rather, we are forced to admit that it may well have had none. Its virtues, in sum, seem to be solitary ones; it appears as a diversion, or a digression, from the literary history of later pagan antiquity.

Perhaps the best way of summarizing all these problems is to say that *Daphnis and Chloe* comes to us as a text without a context. Now the word "context," of course, can mean many different things; but we can keep our bearings here if we recall and meditate upon the etymological connection between the two words at issue. The context of a literary text is, in the broadest sense, that into which and with which it is "woven." [15] What constitutes the context of a work in any more specific sense depends entirely upon the point of view, the angle of approach. One might be tempted to say that any text has not one context, but many contexts: historical, cultural, philosophical, political, and, perhaps most important, literary. For one of the salient facts about a literary text is its relation to other literary texts, and in a special way to those of its own tradition.

The precise meaning of the word "tradition" is, if anything, even more elusive than that of "context" and thus in need of clarification before we go any further. [16] A literary text, when published, takes its place in the economy of a certain literary tradition, from which it receives much of its form, its sense of decorum, its conventions, and many of its themes. Seldom, if ever, is a text produced entirely de novo; if it were, its intended readers would have no way of knowing how to read it. Conversely, it is precisely ignorance of its traditions that often makes a text from a remote place or time difficult for a particular reader to understand. To be sure, a given author in a given text may choose to reject or alter some part of the tradition in its received form; but it is essential to realize that the tradition in such an instance is not being ignored. No writer who wishes to be understood on any but the most superficial level can avoid entering into the economy of tradition, in one way or another. Such encounters with tradition may take a thousand forms; they may even be resented and resisted; but in the end they cannot be bypassed. And as most readers are doubtless aware, this is especially true of ancient literature, where innovation in form and content had a small place, if any, in the canon of literary virtues.

Tradition operates, of course, on several levels. The word itself can be reduced to stems meaning "to hand across" (that is, "to hand down," in contemporary English idiom). The genus "tradition" is thus fundamentally "that which has been received," while the different species are to be differentiated on the basis of source: one asks, in other words, "From whom has it been received?" In a very specific way, then, one may speak of the tradition of a particular genre, in which case "the tradition" means the work of one's predecessors in a particular form of composition. Encountering the tradition would then entail encountering the whole set of assumptions and presuppositions which emerge from a consideration of these works. On a larger scale, too, no author can be entirely unaffected by the whole corpus of the literature read and written by the culture in which and for which the new text is written. This, again, may be especially true of ancient Greek and Latin literature, where the influence of Homer, Plato, and a hundred others was all but inescapable.

Insofar as various traditions inform various aspects of *Daphnis and Chloe,* as they must, it may be possible for us to learn rather a lot about the context of this novel. As for "context" in any other sense, however, the dearth of solid information will provide no few problems. When we set out to interpret a Greek tragedy, we know enough about its author, its times, and the Greek stage in the fifth century B.C. (no matter how enigmatic or debatable the origins of the genre itself) to get some sense of our bearings when we are immersed in the text itself. Even if there are in fact no patent topical allusions in *Oedipus the King,* for example, it still helps to know that the play was written in the context of Periclean Athens about the time of the great plague. In the same way, one can hardly conceive of an interpretation of Virgil's *Aeneid* without some reference to the Augustan realities within which Virgil lived and wrote. But when the immediate historical context of a work is less clear. the text is in some danger of being read, as it were, in a vacuum. It is not surprising, then, that those who have set out to interpret *Daphnis and Chloe* have tended to concentrate on supposed allegory, or on the stylistic texture of the novel, both of which can be discussed without having to pin down the context very precisely, or scarcely deal with it at all. Qua allegory, *Daphnis and Chloe* could as easily be (late) Hellenistic as imperial; qua rhetorical exercise, it could as well be Byzantine, as in fact it was once thought to be. Neither approach would be seriously affected if *Daphnis and Chloe*'s putative date of composition were raised or lowered by two centuries.

By now the complexity of the issues involved in all this should be clear. We cannot properly ask what *Daphnis and Chloe* is about without involving ourselves in other issues. We shall have to travel τὴν μακροτέραν ὁδὸν, as Plato says, "by the longer way"; but that is not necessarily a bad thing.[17] The τέλος, the goal, is to find out what *Daphnis and Chloe* is about; to do that, we shall have to find out what it is; and to do that, we shall have to put this text into some sort of context. That, in a nutshell, is the program of this book. Thus stated, it seems an impossibly ambitious program, rather as though we had committed ourselves to a close reading of *Daphnis and Chloe and* a history of the ancient novel *and* a cultural history of late antiquity. Fortunately, however, it is Longus himself who provides us with a way of keeping our inquiries within bounds. For if we are attentive to what Longus says, we shall discover that he has much to say about the various traditions within which he writes. The text itself reveals to the attentive reader that Longus is quite sensitive to what we may call the "tradition" of the ancient Greek novel and to certain strains in the much larger and grander tradition of ancient Greek literature generally. Nor should we be misled into supposing that the apparent timelessness of his story means that he cannot or will not read the signs of the times. Indeed, the primary contention of this book is precisely that Longus's real intention in *Daphnis and Chloe* is to confront certain traditions, and to reflect on them, even at the moment when they are about to give way to something new.

There are, then, two major lines of inquiry, which will be pursued to a certain point, after which it will be possible to bring them together. We shall begin, in part I, by looking carefully at how *Daphnis and Chloe* is put together. What is new in the present study, on this level, is a detailed analysis of the narrative structure of *Daphnis and Chloe,* in which lies, as it seems, the key to its interpretation.[18] The structure sorts out what is central from what is peripheral and allows us to see much more clearly how Longus means to engage in an extended conversation with various literary traditions through a systematic exploration of the themes of rhetoric and myth. The second line of inquiry, in part I, concerns Longus's reaction to the traditions, larger and smaller, within which he writes. We shall see how Longus simultaneously appropriates and subverts the conventions of the ancient Greek novel; how he situates himself in that tradition, especially as that tradition in turn attempts to situate itself vis-à-vis the much older tradition of historiography; and finally how Longus uses the pastoral to put some distance between himself and both traditions, the novel and historiography, and between himself and his culture. This will lead to a synthesis, in the last chapter, where we shall see how both lines of inquiry, the narrative structure of *Daphnis and Chloe* and Longus's conversation with tradition, finally converge.

Daphnis and Chloe has been called "the last great creation in pagan Greek literature," which indeed it is.[19] But it is more than that. It is also a masterpiece, perhaps *the* masterpiece, of what is in fact the first postclassical literary genre. As such, *Daphnis and Chloe* contains deep and subtle reflections on the classical heritage. It is, in fact, pervaded with an appreciation of the past, but precisely as past, a closed book, a finished monument. There is a precious insight here into the pagan world at the dawn of the Christian era. If the study of any literary text really requires a justification, then let this be ours: that *Daphnis and Chloe* is both the last and the first, on the boundary between one world and another. We ourselves, who may very well be living in just such an in-between time, are perhaps in a better position to understand and appreciate what Longus has to say than were those of an earlier age, when things seemed clearer and the line between the true and the false, between illusion and reality, seemed easier to draw. With all these things in mind, then, let us proceed.

PART I

The Structure of
Daphnis and Chloe

Chapter 2

The Prologue

That no small degree of deliberateness and craft has gone into the construction of *Daphnis and Chloe* has always been manifest to those with eyes to see. Even the casual reader can hardly fail to notice the elaborate narrative architecture of this novel, revealed in the patterned recurrence of particular words, images, and themes; one feels it, too, in the harmonies and disharmonies between the characters' feelings and actions, on the one hand, and the cycle of the seasons, on the other. Even the unhurried pace with which the episodes follow one another suggests that the development of the story is not purely sequential. But then, Longus makes that clear enough from the very beginning. Early in the Prologue, Longus tells us that he wrote this book in the grips of a πόθος . . . ἀντιγράψαι τῇ γραφῇ, "a longing to write something in response to the painting"; and in that all-but-untranslatable play between the two senses of the Greek {graph-} morpheme—to wit, "draw" and "write"—is an implicit justification of the search for structure. For structure, in a literary text, is precisely that which lends a spatial, even pictorial dimension to something that we ordinarily think of as existing in one dimension only, from beginning to end. Longus explains his manner of composition, then, in a way that should predispose us to look at his work as we look at a painting: not along one line only, but back and forth, up and down. What we see in one part of the painting may cause us to look again at what we have already seen and understand it differently.[1]

The inherent probability that the structure of *Daphnis and Chloe* is worth investigating has not escaped the notice of previous scholars. On the contrary, a quick search through the secondary literature on *Daphnis and Chloe* will discover no lack of previous efforts to delineate its structure. Indeed, so many ostensibly conflicting models are already available to the assiduous scholar that there may seem to be no compelling need to add another one here and now. If what follows were to be offered as a rival to the work of previous scholars, as though they were all deluded, and here, at last, was the definitive truth of the matter, then there would be something undeniably hubristic about the whole enterprise. But such an attitude would be naive and grounded on a false premise: namely, that the structure of *Daphnis and Chloe* is, as it were, a "puzzle," to which there is only one correct "solution." But that is simply wrong. Any work of art, literary or otherwise, that could be reduced to one simple structural principle is hardly likely to merit more than passing attention. This is manifestly not true of *Daphnis and Chloe*.

Most (if not all) of the models that have been advanced before now are grounded on valid perceptions. They can be accepted on their own terms, for good and sufficient reasons, without precluding further labors along the same lines. Thus the new model that will be put forward in these next chapters is not inherently antagonistic to its predecessors, however different it may be from them in detail. That must be understood from the beginning. The rich texture of *Daphnis and Chloe* results in large part from the interplay, not to say tension, between a variety of interwoven and inlaid patterns. Each structural model brings some of these patterns into the foreground and pushes others back, so that each has something to teach us, unique, valuable, and partial. For that matter, the sum total of old and new models may well prove to be only a fraction of the whole picture.

Of all the various efforts to trace the structure of *Daphnis and Chloe*, one of the oldest and best known is based on Longus's use of the changing seasons to control the exposition and development of the plot. This particular model is especially favored, for perhaps obvious reasons, by those who see initiation into the mysteries as Longus's primary subtext.[2] The eternal recurrence of decay and regeneration in the seasons of the year has always been a potent symbol of the parallel cycle of birth and death, and of the attendant hope of immortality. To all this Longus is clearly profoundly sensitive. Descriptions of the seasons receive considerable play and prominence; and, throughout the novel, Daphnis and Chloe are often portrayed responding empathetically to the changes in the natural world around them.[3] It would be as difficult as it is unnecessary, then, to gainsay the thematic importance of the seasons, or to dismantle the structural model that emerges from tracing the interplay between the seasons and the development of the plot. Problems arise only when too much is made of it.[4]

A rather different structural model can be developed from that pregnant phrase in the prologue, ἀντιγράψαι τῇ γραφῇ ("to write in response to the painting"), which at least implies that Daphnis and Chloe is an extended ecphrasis, a painting in words. The first-person narrator tells us that he once saw a painting displayed in a grove of the nymphs on Lesbos and was inspired by it, as he says, to write Daphnis and Chloe. That the novel he has constructed on this basis might have structural components in common with painting is a reasonable enough supposition and has occured to more than a few readers. Otto Weinrich, following certain suggestions made by R. Reitzenstein, propounded a scheme whereby the whole action of Daphnis and Chloe consists of twelve episodes, each episode being a triptych; each of these, in turn, consists of the same three elements recurring in the same order: (1) a description of the setting, (2) an incident or action, and (3) the reaction of Daphnis and Chloe to that incident or action.[5] To deny that some such rhythm as this seems to recur throughout the novel, or that it is there by design, would be, again, both unnecessary and perverse. Every major incident in the novel is preceeded by a description of the locale, the season, or both, and is followed by a description of the two lovers, separately or together, reacting to or reflecting upon what has happened. As Weinrich (and M. C. Mittelstadt) have pointed out,

this procedure seems to be based on the style of narrative painting that was au courant in Longus's day.[6]

To Joseph Kestner, in fact, it seems clear that a certain dialectic between painting and writing and a systematic exploration
by Longus of the relationship between the temporal and the spatial dimensions of all art informs *Daphnis and Chloe* from start to
finish.[7] His structural model begins by identifying certain scenes
in books 1 through 4 as "ecphrastic"; the recurrence of ecphrasis, then, connects all of these scenes thematically to the prologue and thus binds the whole novel together. In the first three
books, Kestner sees the three etiological myths, the "included
narratives," as miniature ecphrases, which remind the reader
that the whole of the novel is itself an ecphrasis.[8] The paired "recognition" scenes centered on the two protagonists are, Kestner
goes on to say, the "ecphrases" of book 4, which once again recall
(and fulfill) the hints and promises of the prologue and thus give
the whole novel a spatial as well as temporal dimension.

Kestner's model, though it shares with that of Mittelstadt and
Weinrich the premise that *Daphnis and Chloe* is structured rather
like a painting, is distinctly different from theirs in detail. The
latter saw the descriptions and set-pieces as frames for the central action, while Kestner has, at least by implication, reversed
the relative structural importance of episodes and images. Kestner, unlike the others, has also built his model on the assumption that the four books into which the text is divided are the
basic architectural units. This would be a dangerous assumption
for many classical authors, who are often not themselves responsible for the division of their longer works into books;[9] but
Longus, oddly enough, goes out of his way to tell us in the prologue that his novel consists of four books. τέτταρας βίβλους
ἐξεπονησάμην, he says, "I worked out four books" (prologue 3).

The three etiological myths, then, which Kestner removed
from the periphery to the center of his model, also provide a
point of departure for several other important discussions of the
literary architecture of *Daphnis and Chloe*, though none of these
presents us with a complete structural model. In the same year
that Kestner's article appeared in *Classical World*, Stavros Deligiorgis wrote an article for *Philological Quarterly*, in which he

showed how Longus uses the patterned reduplication of incidents within the main action of the novel to create a sort of frame around each of these included narratives.[10] The care and elaboration with which Longus does this suggests that these three tales are not at all the aimless digressions they sometimes seem to be, but rather control the thematic development of the whole novel. Quite recently, Marios Philippides has gone on to show in some detail how closely these three apparent digressions are connected with the psychological development of the novel, and especially with the two lovers' erotic education.[11]

On the basis of what has been learned so far, it becomes possible for us to proceed in a manner not dissimilar to the way a scientist goes about solving a problem in the natural sciences: that is, by formulating certain hypotheses and then attempting to verify them by observation. The most salient such hypotheses for the present purposes are these:

1. We shall assume here that the three *aitia* figure prominently in the structure of the novel, since the thematic importance of these enclosed narratives, and the techniques Longus uses to frame them, have already been partially demonstrated by Deligiorgis and others.

2. We observe, too, that all three of these stories are found in roughly the same position (to wit, from two-thirds to three-quarters of the way through) in each book: Phatta, the dove, in book 1; Syrinx, the reed-flute, in book 2; and Echo in book 3. This implies that in any architectural scheme centered on the myths, the individual books will be the main constitutive elements.

3. We shall have to address a dilemma raised by the last hypothesis: namely, that a model based exclusively on the *aitia* of the first three books leaves out the prologue and the final book, neither of which appears to contain an *aition*. But if Kestner is correct in arguing that there is an integral connection between the *aitia* and the Prologue, the matter will need to be carefully investigated.

THE STRUCTURE OF THE PROLOGUE

Let us begin, then, by looking closely at how the Prologue is constructed.

Ἐν Λέσβῳ θηρῶν ἐν ἄλσει Νυμφῶν θέαμα εἶδον κάλλιστον ὧν
εἶδον, εἰκόνος γραφήν, ἱστορίαν ἔρωτος. καλὸν μὲν καὶ τὸ ἄλσος,
πολύδενδρον, ἀνθηρόν, κατάρρυτον· μία πηγὴ πάντα ἔτρεφε, καὶ
τὰ ἄνθη καὶ τὰ δένδρα· ἀλλ' ἡ γραφὴ τερπνοτέρα καὶ τέχνην
ἔχουσα περιττὴν καὶ τύχην ἐρωτικήν, ὥστε πολλοὶ καὶ τῶν ξένων
ἤεσαν, τῶν μὲν Νυμφῶν ἱκέται, τῆς δὲ εἰκόνος θεαταί. γυναῖκες
ἐπ' αὐτῆς τίκτουσαι καὶ ἄλλαι σπαργάνοις κοσμοῦσαι, παιδία
ἐκκείμενα, ποίμνια τρέφοντα, ποιμένες ἀναιρούμενοι, νέοι συν-
τιθέμενοι, λῃστῶν καταδρομή, πολεμίων ἐμβολή, πολλὰ ἄλλα
καὶ πάντα ἐρωτικά. ἰδόντα με καὶ θαυμάσαντα πόθος ἔσχεν ἀντιγράψαι τῇ γραφῇ, καὶ ἀναζητησάμενος ἐξηγητὴν τῆς εἰκόνος
τέτταρας βίβλους ἐξεπονησάμην, ἀνάθημα μὲν Ἔρωτι καὶ Νύμφαις καὶ Πανί, κτῆμα δὲ τερπνὸν πᾶσιν ἀνθρώποις, ὃ καὶ νο-
σοῦντα ἰάσεται καὶ λυπούμενον παραμυθήσεται, τὸν ἐρασθέντα
ἀναμνήσει, τὸν οὐκ ἐρασθέντα προπαιδεύσει. πάντως γὰρ οὐ-
δεὶς Ἔρωτα ἔφυγεν ἢ φεύξεται μέχρις ἂν κάλλος ᾖ καὶ ὀφθαλμοὶ
βλέπωσιν. ἡμῖν δὲ ὁ θεὸς παράσχοι σωφρονοῦσι τὰ τῶν ἄλλων
γραφεῖν.

(While hunting in Lesbos, in a grove of the nymphs, I saw the
most beautiful sight I have ever seen: a painting of an image, a
story of love. Now the grove was beautiful, with lots of trees, and
flowers, and streams running down; one spring fed everything,
the flowers and the trees. But the painting gave even more pleasure, since it manifested both surpassing skill and an erotic subject; and so many came, even foreigners, drawn by its reputation,
to pray [lit., "as pray-ers"] to the nymphs and to see [lit., "as see-
ers" or "watchers" of] the painting. There were women on it giving birth, and others wrapping [babies] in blankets; there were
exposed infants, sheep nursing them, shepherds picking them
up, young people put together, a pirate raid, an enemy invasion,
and many other things, all erotic. When I saw this, I was amazed,
and a longing to respond in writing to the painting seized me; and
after I had sought out someone to interpret the painting, I worked
out [these] four books, an offering to Eros, the nymphs, and Pan,
and a delightful possession for all humanity, which will heal the
sick and comfort the grieving, remind anyone who has loved, and
instruct [in advance] anyone who has not loved. For the fact is that
no one has ever escaped Eros, or will escape him, so long as

beauty exists and eyes see. May the god allow us, so long as we are
prudent, to write about the things of others.)

This prologue seems to stand quite outside the rest of the
novel, much like a prologue from a comedy of Terence, or one
of Cicero's philosophical essays; among other things, the first-
person narrator, speaking here in the authorial persona, never
speaks again. But hardly a word or phrase of this entire prologue fails to have some thematic resonance for the whole novel.
Hunting will recur, as will springs, trees, and flowers. Indeed, a
significant part of the action of *Daphnis and Chloe* is foreshadowed
by the series of images that Longus says he saw on the painting,
so that the reader will find an incident to correspond to every
image Longus lists.

Just at this point, however, some caution is necessary. Closer
scrutiny of the third sentence will show that it contains both more
and less than meets the eye: more thematic prefiguration, but less
actual foreshadowing of the plot. A careful examination of the
order in which Longus mentions the painted scenes is instructive
in this regard, and corrective. The sequence of images implies a
series of incidents presented in a perfectly logical and chronological order. When we move into the body of the novel, however, we find the plot unfolding in quite another way. The first
two images that Longus mentions in the prologue are "women
giving birth" and "other women wrapping [babies] in blankets";
but we shall not be told of the manner and place of either Daphnis's or Chloe's birth, or how they came to be exposed, until very
near the end of the novel. The next three images ("sheep nursing them, shepherds picking them up, young people put together") correspond very closely to the events of the first eight
chapters in book 1, while the mention of a pirate incursion looks
forward to the pirate raid near the end of that same book. The
"enemy invasion" anticipates the Methymnean expedition in the
middle of book 2. But all the rest of *Daphnis and Chloe* is apparently subsumed in the vague πολλὰ ἄλλα καὶ πάντα ἐρωτικά
("many other things, all erotic"). The erotic education of Daphnis
and Chloe, which occupies most of our attention throughout the
novel, is scarcely mentioned; and the various divine interven-

tions are also apparently missing from the painting. So where did the rest of the story come from? Ostensibly, perhaps, from the "exegete," whom we may suppose to have told Longus the whole story, filling in the omitted details; but there are problems with so facile an answer. Is this a story that the author heard from some anonymous "exegete," or is it an extended ecphrasis, as the phrase ἀντιγράψαι τῇ γραφῇ ("to respond in writing to the painting") seems to imply?

The two answers are, if not mutually exclusive, at least hard to reconcile. Retelling a story that one has heard from someone else is one thing, something that in fact occurs every time a Greek author tells a myth. Describing a work of plastic art is quite another, even if one follows the ancient ecphrastic technique of reconstructing the "story" that seems to underlie the painting or statue at hand.[12] It is certainly true that in each case there is a "given," with reference to which the truthfulness of the text might be measured; but the nature of the given in an ecphrasis is altogether different from that of a myth. The veracity of a story depends first on the teller, and then on the person who told him the story, and the person who told *him*, and so forth. A story can thus be rooted either in what actually happened on a certain day in a certain place (in which case it belongs to history), or in tradition (in which case it is a myth), neither of which is really subject to the control of an individual author. A work of art, on the other hand, has an objective existence, usually contemporary (which is to say, that it still exists), as the result of a single act of creation. The author in each case must therefore adopt a fundamentally different posture toward his material; conversely, the reader enters the discourse with different expectations and presuppositions.

Is *Daphnis and Chloe* a story, then, or an ecphrasis? Longus provides no obvious solution to this problem; but the beginning of a resolution may well come from the whole issue of structure, which, as we have already seen, is first raised by the implicit dialectic between the temporal and the spatial in the prologue.[13] This is a structured narrative. It is also fiction, a created story, neither myth nor history, nor a mediation between them, but a tertium quid. Thus it is a created thing, like a painting; but it is also a story, which moves through time and consists of persons and events. So by the time we get to the last word of the prologue, γραφεῖν, there is no way to be sure whether this time it means "to paint" or "to write," whether Longus is a painter of words or a writer of images—a pregnant uncertainty which is never fully resolved.

Taken as a whole, however, the prologue does more than to foreshadow and prefigure the themes and preoccupations of *Daphnis and Chloe*. It also prefigures the architecture of each book; it is, in fact, a miniature of a very particular schema, one which is replicated on a larger scale, as we shall see, in each of the four books. A careful analysis, then, is clearly in order.

A strong hint as to what is in store can be found in the second sentence of the prologue, which contains an elaborate chiasmus, schematized as follows:

καλὸν μὲν καὶ τὸ ἄλσος,

    πολύδενδρον, (trees)

        ἀνθηρόν, (flowers)

            κατάρρυτον· (water)

            μία πηγὴ πάντα ἔτρεφε, (water)

        καὶ τὰ ἄνθη (flowers)

    καὶ τὰ δένδρα· (trees)

At first, this seems to be little more than a trope, albeit a rather elaborate example thereof, with its "double layering." There is more to this than meets the eye, however. This double chiasmus is, in fact, the first occurence of a structural motif, which has a certain resemblance to the rhetorical figure called chiasmus but which is actually far more elaborate. On the one hand, we shall see that things in *Daphnis and Chloe* tend to happen twice; on the other, we shall also see that these reduplicated items occur first in a certain sequence and then recur in reverse order: in other words, like "trees-flowers-water-water-flowers-trees." The latter series is thus a specular image (that is, reversed, or mirror, image) of the first. Specularity, we are about to discover, is the architectural leitmotif of the whole novel.

The prologue falls roughly into two parts: first, the author's encounter with a painting, and second, his writing *Daphnis and Chloe* as a way of reacting to that encounter.[14] At the center of each of these two parts is an antithesis, carefully phrased with the particles μὲν ("on the one hand") and δὲ ("on the other hand"). The sentences that precede and follow these two antitheses, considered from a thematic perspective, tend to mirror each other, one on one. The result is a pattern, roughly as follows:

Aggression (hunting)

    A painting in a grove (context)

        Religion and art ("to worship . . . to see")

    The images on the painting (content)

Eroticism ("all of it erotic")

Possession and amazement ("amazed . . . longing")

    Storytelling (the exegete, the four books)

        Religion and art ("an offering . . . a possession")

    The value of storytelling (healing and teaching)

Prudence ("so long as we remain σώφρονες")

The author introduces himself as a hunter, the first occurence of this recurrent motif. (Other hunters, as we shall see, will include the Methymnean youths and Daphnis, all of whom are thus connected by this theme to the author himself.[15]) What motivates the connection posited here between hunting and Eros, then, should be obvious: a certain innate masculine aggression is an indivisible component of Eros, whose familiar bow, after all, is not that of the warrior but of the hunter. Thus, it seems, the first half of the prologue begins and ends with erotic aggression. Inside the outer frame thus composed, and just outside of the antithesis which lies at the center of the first half of the prologue, is the actual ecphrasis of the painting in the grove. First, its setting is described, and then something is said of its technical excellence (hence the label "context"); this is balanced, then, by the detailed description of the images.

At the center of all this is what might seem to be a certain confusion of motives:[16] people come from all over, to worship the nymphs (that is, to acknowledge the numinous) and to see the painting (that is, to gratify the senses by looking at a thing of beauty). This is, however, considerably less of a paradox than it seems, though it is couched in the μὲν . . . δὲ phraseology that Greek characteristically uses for antitheses. The word for "seeing" used here, θεαταί, comes from the verb θεάομαι, which is used of attendance at a religious service, or at a dramatic presentation (which, let us remember, often amounts to the same in ancient Greece).[17] From the same base are derived the English words "theatre" and "theory." Clearly, this is no ordinary seeing. Those who come to see the painting are not merely gazing at a thing of beauty; when Longus does talk about that sort of seeing later in the prologue, he uses a different verb, βλέπω. There is an interaction with the thing perceived implied in the use of θεαταί, which really means something more like "watch" than merely "see."[18]

This sense of "seeing" qua "watching" is also, though in a perverse manner, implied in the only other passage in all of *Daphnis and Chloe* in which the noun θεατής is used: at 4.11, where the parasitic pederast Gnathon excuses himself from attending Astylus on the hunt, and instead goes to where Daphnis is tending his goats, λόγῳ μὲν τῶν αἰγῶν, τὸ δ᾽ ἀληθὲς Δάφνιδος . . . θεατής ("on the pretext of [seeing] the goats, though in fact he came to watch [lit., 'to be a watcher of'] Daphnis"). The fact that θεατής occurs again in a "μὲν . . . δὲ" clause, in a context where motives seem to be tangled, can hardly be accidental, and may even suggest that the prologue will need to be reread later, in the light of book 4. But then again, that is precisely the point of structure in a literary text, to force us to make just such backward and forward moves as these.

The other term of the antithesis, ἱκέται ("pray-ers" or "suppliants"), is no less ambiguous and ambivalent, since it is no more exclusively a sacred word than θεαταί is exclusively profane. Longus uses the cognate verb ἱκετεύω of a sexually predatory male, Dorcon, who appeals for help when he is beset by the dogs (1.21); this is, in fact, the very next occurrence in the novel of a cognate of ἱκέτης. Later on, a captured grasshopper sings ὅμοιον ἱκέτῃ ("like a suppliant" [1.26]). Gnathon, who was the only other θεατής, is also a suppliant: after he learns who Daphnis really is, he takes refuge in the temple of Dionysus, where he waits in fear, day and night, ὥσπερ ἱκέτης ("as though he were a suppliant" [4.25]). This last passage leads inexorably to a startling observation: that one man, the pederast Gnathon, is the only human being in all of *Daphnis and Chloe*, after the prologue, who is called either a "watcher" or a "suppliant," and he is called both. But again, it is only when we have worked through the rest of the novel and come back to the prologue that we shall be in a position to understand what this might mean.

In the second half of the prologue a similar schema applies. As he looks at the painting, Longus is enthralled, amazed, and a πόθος, a "passionate longing," seizes him. This is highly erotic language, even more obviously so in Greek than in English.[19] The author has lost his objectivity; he is compelled to respond. In so doing, however, he must regain that lost objectivity in order to create something that will be a possession for others. Thus he ends the prologue with a prayer for σωφροσύνη, *sophrosyne*, that untranslatable (and very classical) quality of dispassion, moderation, prudence, objectivity. He must put some distance between himself and his subject, τὰ τῶν ἄλλων, the things of others, before he can write/paint (γράφειν) them. Thus πόθος and σωφροσύνη stand at the beginning and the end of the second half, rather as hunting and Eros served as a sort of frame for the first.

The means by which Longus's lost objectivity can be regained is made clear by what lies just within the frame thus formed: storytelling. Longus frees himself from his πόθος, his longing, by writing a story. The verb he uses to denote his act of writing is unusual and instructive: ἐξεπονησάμην, he says, literally, "I worked out." The verb ἐκπονέω so thoroughly connotes hard labor that it can sometimes mean "to be exhausted" (cf. Latin *con-*

ficio). Ἔγραψα ("I wrote"), or ἐποίησα ("I made"; the verb from which "poem" and all its cognates come) would have been ordinary diction; the historians, and some of the other Greek novelists, use the verb συγγράφω. Πόνος is labor, hard work, struggle. The exegete made the task possible, it seems, but he did not make it easy.

Balancing and answering Longus's depiction of his toils is his vision of the great promise attendant on his πόνος. The story that Longus tells will heal the sick and comfort the afflicted. Here the verb for "comfort," παραμυθήσεται, is especially interesting. Literally, it means to "speak" (-μυθ-) "beside" (παρα-). The use of the {myth-} morpheme invokes (in a typically allusive-elusive way) the whole concept of myth, with which, as we shall see, so much of *Daphnis and Chloe* is concerned. Underlying the literal meaning of παραμυθέω, then, is the image of one sitting beside the bed, telling stories intended to cheer the one who is ill. Though nothing exactly like this happens in *Daphnis and Chloe*, one may still note that stories (μῦθοι) are told throughout the novel to distract or entertain the hearer—though we shall eventually learn that there is teaching going on as well, *sub rosa*.

The center of this second half of the prologue is occupied by the dual role to be fulfilled by *Daphnis and Chloe* itself. There is again a blending of the sacred and the profane, expressed in a "μὲν . . . δὲ" construction; and again, much can be learned by following the career of both members of the antithesis, ἀνάθημα (offering) and κτῆμα (possession). In the grotto where Dryas first finds Chloe, there are many ἀναθήματα to the nymphs lying about, which previous generations of shepherds have left (1.4); at 1.32, Daphnis and Chloe put funerary ἀναθήματα over Dorcon's grave; at 2.22, in the first use of the word ἀνάθημα in the singular after the prologue, Daphnis reproaches the nymphs for allowing Chloe, who has made them an ἀνάθημα of a flute, a *syrinx*, to be snatched from their very midst by the Methymneans; at 2.31, Daphnis and Chloe hang up the skin of a goat they have just sacrificed to Pan, ποιμενικὸν ἀνάθημα ποιμενικῷ θεῷ ("a rustic *offering* for a rustic god"). Thereafter, the word recurs only in book 4, first where Daphnis offers his pastoral accoutrements (which are there called ποιμενικὰ κτήματα) to Pan, and then where Megacles offers the tokens that had been left with Chloe, by which she had been found again (4.26 and 37). As for κτῆμα, it recurs at 1.1, where the estate on which Daphnis and Chloe live is identified as the κτῆμα of a rich man from Mitylene,[20] whose name, we learn later on, is Dionysophanes; at 1.14, in the middle of Daphnis's declamation against Dorcon, where he lists cheese, bread, and wine as the proper κτήματα of a herdsman; at 2.14, where the Methymneans search for Daphnis, whom they blame for the loss of "not a few κτήματα"; at 3.2, where the Mitylenean army abstains from plundering the κτήματα of the Methymneans; at 4.24, where Dionysophanes counsels Astylus that a brother is worth more than any κτῆμα; and finally at that same passage already mentioned, 4.26, where Daphnis makes an offering to Pan.

Neither of these two words is always used with special emphasis, as the foregoing survey demonstrates; but many of these passages are thematically suggestive, especially that passage in book 4 where "offerings" and "possessions" are brought back together. Daphnis is at the point of transition between the pastoral world and the urban world, and signals that transition by making the κτήματα ("possessions") of the former into ἀναθήματα ("offerings") to the pastoral god. Still, he will never entirely leave the world in which he grew up. The new life that Chloe and he will enter into is neither fully urban nor fully pastoral, but a blending of both. The crisis of book 4 makes the disadvantages of their former estate, in which their destinies are in others' hands, eminently clear; but it is equally clear that Daphnis and Chloe can hardly take their place in urbane Mitylenean society. Neither world is complete in itself, and some sort of mediation is necessary. Someone must intervene to bring Daphnis and Chloe out of their limited pastoral world; and that person, as it turns out, is none other than Gnathon.

It is indeed odd that all the thematic paths that we have followed from the prologue (however tentatively, for the moment) have somehow ended up with this man, who is anything but an admirable or heroic character. He is all jaw (γνάθος); or rather, μαθὼν ἐσθίειν ἄνθρωπος καὶ πίνειν εἰς μέθην καὶ λαγνεύειν μετὰ τὴν μέθην καὶ οὐδὲν ἄλλο ὢν ἢ γνάθος καὶ γαστὴρ καὶ τὰ

28

ὑπὸ γαστέρα ("a man who knew how to eat, and drink himself drunk, and debauch himself after he was drunk, and in fact was nothing other than a jaw, and a belly, and that which lies below the belly" [4.11]). He is, in other words, nothing but appetite, the very fulfillment of Plato's "man of the belly," who lives only to pursue pleasure. Yet it is he who, through his pederastic lust, inadvertently precipitates the anagnorisis of Daphnis, and it is he who rescues Chloe and makes hers possible as well. He is the watcher, too, and the suppliant. This cannot be accidental, and we are compelled to look deeper. Why do all roads lead to this depraved voluptuary?

A fuller answer to that question will necessarily have to wait until we have worked through all four books of the novel proper. For now, we shall have to content ourselves with observing that pleasure, whatever it turns out to be or to mean, is clearly central to this novel. That is made abundantly clear by the diction, κτῆμα τερπνόν. After the prologue, the adjective τερπνός, "pleasant" or "delightful," and the verb τέρπω, "to take delight," occur primarily in two contexts: erotic pleasure, and storytelling. Thus the three remedies prescribed by Philetas are called "lost pleasures" early in book III (3.4), when the advent of winter prevents Daphnis and Chloe from kissing and embracing, and again at 3.9 , where Daphnis consoles himself by kissing and hugging Dryas (!); and then, at 3.17, Lycaenium tells Daphnis that human sexuality has delights not to be found in imitation of the animals. What is even more striking is that some cognate of τερπνός is associated with each of the three aitia in books 1, 2, and 3. Thus Daphnis and Chloe take delight in the wood dove's song (1.23), which prompts Daphnis to tell Chloe the story of Phatta; the listeners take immense delight in hearing Lamon tell the story of Syrinx, and in watching Daphnis and Chloe dance out the parts of Pan and Syrinx; and the singing sailors in book 3 create a "delightful" echo, which again prompts Daphnis to tell Chloe a story.

In addition to this association of delight with μῦθος (mythos), there are two passages in which τέρψις ("delight") is also associated with λόγος (logos), which is, we should remember, a conventional antithesis to μῦθος.[21] At 3.10, the debate between Daphnis and Chloe, which will prove to have a significant role to play in the structure of that book, is called λόγων ὁμιλία τερπνή ("a delightful exchange of words"). But even before that, in a passage pregnant with meaning, Daphnis and Chloe take what proves to be inappropriate delight in Philetas's discourse about the epiphany of Eros: πάνυ ἐτέρφθησαν ὥσπερ μῦθον οὐ λόγον ἀκούσαντες ("they were altogether delighted, as though they had heard a *mythos* rather than a *logos*" [2.7]). *Mythos* and *logos* have been left untranslated here advisedly; for the meaning of these two words is precisely the issue. Philetas has given them a *logos* that they have mistaken for a *mythos*. He has told them a story, and it has pleased them, but they have missed the point. That is why he must go on to give them explicit instructions; but even these are of no avail. From our vantage point as mature and sophisticated readers, we know what Philetas really means by the three remedies he prescribes (kissing, embracing, and lying together naked), but Daphnis and Chloe do not.

Philetas's erotic pedagogy is incomplete, perhaps precisely because his pupils are as yet incapable of telling a *mythos* from a *logos*. Delight is an indispensable part of the telling of stories, but it is not in itself sufficent to make those stories resonate in the lives of their audience. Something else is required, a degree of understanding, a process of education, of παιδεία. Delight itself is notoriously transient; but Longus, in the prologue, promises to embed delight in a κτῆμα, something solid and substantial, which will be for all humanity (πᾶσιν ἀνθρώποις), and which will in fact accomplish all manner of marvelous things. We shall be delighted, but we shall also be instructed, edified, and healed. This is an odd claim for an erotic novel to make, one which we may be forgiven for taking with a grain of salt. But it is too early for us to decide whether or not *Daphnis and Chloe* is capable of doing what it sets out to do. What the prologue accomplishes, if we attend to it, is to prepare us to learn what the next four books have to teach about *mythoi* and *logoi*.

Chapter 3

Book 1:
Erotic *Aporia*

THE MYTH OF PHATTA

One fine summer's day, in the heat of the afternoon, when the
herds are sluggish and there is nothing for Daphnis and Chloe
to do but lie about and amuse themselves, they happen to hear
the mournful call of a dove. Chloe wants to know what the dove
is saying; Daphnis replies by telling her the story of how the
wood dove (ἡ φάττα) came to be a bird: [1]

> ἦν παρθένος, παρθένε, οὕτω καλὴ καὶ ἔνεμε βοῦς πολλὰς
> οὕτως ἐν ὕλῃ· ἦν δὲ ἄρα καὶ ᾠδική, καὶ ἐτέρποντο αἱ βόες αὐτῆς
> τῇ μουσικῇ, καὶ ἔνεμεν οὔτε καλαύροπος πληγῇ οὔτε κέντρου
> προσβολῇ, ἀλλὰ καθίσασα ὑπὸ πίτυν καὶ στεφανωσαμένη πίτυι
> ᾖδε Πᾶνα καὶ τὴν Πίτυν, καὶ αἱ βόες τῇ φωνῇ παρέμενον. παῖς οὐ
> μακρὰν νέμων βοῦς, καὶ αὐτὸς καλὸς καὶ ᾠδικὸς ὡς ἡ παρθένος,
> φιλονεικήσας πρὸς τὴν μελῳδίαν μείζονα ὡς ἀνήρ, ἡδεῖαν ὡς
> παῖς φωνὴν ἀντεπεδείξατο καὶ τῶν βοῶν ὀκτὼ τὰς ἀρίστας ἐς τὴν
> ἰδίαν ἀγέλην θέλξας ἀπεβουκόλησεν. ἄχθεται ἡ παρθένος τῇ
> βλάβῃ τῆς ἀγέλης, τῇ ἥττῃ τῆς ᾠδῆς, καὶ εὔχεται τοῖς θεοῖς
> ὄρνις γενέσθαι πρὶν οἴκαδε ἀφικέσθαι. πείθονται οἱ θεοὶ καὶ
> ποιοῦσι τήνδε τὴν ὄρνιν, ὄρειον ὡς ἡ παρθένος, μουσικὴν ὡς
> ἐκείνη, καὶ ἔτι νῦν ᾄδουσα μηνύει τὴν συμφοράν, ὅτι βοῦς ζητεῖ
> πεπλανημένας.

(Oh maiden, there was once a maiden, beautiful, like you; and
she tended many cattle in the woods, as you [sc. tend sheep]. [2]

Now she was a good singer, and her cows took pleasure in her music. She managed them without striking them with a staff or pricking them with a prod; no, she just sat beneath a pine tree, wreathed with pine, and sang of Pan and Pitys, while her cows stayed close to the sound of her voice.[3] There was a boy herding cattle not far away, who was as beautiful and musical as the maiden was. He took a notion to rival her in song; and he sang in a voice that was louder than hers [since he was a male] but yet sweet [since he was still a boy], and so he lured away eight of her best cows and added them to his own herd. The maiden was very upset at the loss of the cows and at losing the singing contest as well, and she prayed to the gods that she be changed into a bird before she got home. The gods consented and created this bird here, who lives in the mountains, as she did, and is musical, as she was. And even now she is singing a lament for her loss, because she is looking for the cattle that strayed.)[4] (1.27)

This deceptively simple little tale, so straightforwardly told by such a naive teller, contains a great deal of substance not too far below the surface. The first sentence of the story tells us that Chloe and the unnamed maiden (whom we shall call "Phatta" for convenience, since the wood dove is called φάττα in Greek) have a great deal in common.[5] From Daphnis's point of view, this probably means no more than that Phatta and Chloe are both pretty girls who work with animals in the out-of-doors; but from the reader's point of view, there is more to it than that. The story begins with the premise that Chloe and Phatta are much alike and then proceeds to tell of a catastrophe that befalls the latter. The immediate cause of this catastrophe is the intrusion of a male, who is as beautiful as she is and also musical. She cannot compete with him, even on her own terms, and so she asks for and receives the gift of transformation, losing in the process her human identity but retaining her musicality.

What this means for Chloe is not yet clear in detail, but there is something unmistakably ominous about it. A certain eroticism is manifest, though not overt.[6] Phatta sings of Pan's love for Pitys, and then herself falls victim to an intrusive and aggressive male; there are overtones of subliminal rape in all this, as would be obvious enough even without falling back on Freudian analysis. The somewhat ambiguous sexuality of the young cowherd (whom Daphnis quite unconsciously describes in terms most appropriate for an *erômenos*, a *puer delicatus*) only serves to heighten that sense of erotic passion lurking just under the surface. He is beautiful, and his voice is sweet. As it turns out, however, his intentions are reducible to self-aggrandizement, and his impact on Phatta is devastating.

The emphasis on music in this story is striking, especially in the prominence of the "music-hath-charms" theme. It is precisely this, as Deligiorgis and others have pointed out, that links the story thematically with its context.[7] Just before Daphnis tells his story, Chloe has been taking a mid-afternoon nap. A grasshopper, pursued by a swallow, happens to fly into her clothing and at once begins to sing, ὅμοιον ἱκέτῃ χάριν ὁμολογοῦντι τῆς σωτηρίας ("like a suppliant praying in thanksgiving for his salvation" [1.26]). The noise awakens Chloe with a start; Daphnis laughs at her surprise, and then seizes the opportunity to thrust his hand into her tunic to fetch out the grasshopper, which continues to sing. Chloe smiles, takes the grasshopper from him, and puts it back into her tunic.

There are some interesting parallels between this intriguing little vignette (a natural favorite with illustrators) and the Phatta story, which follows it: namely, the connection of singing with salvation, and a certain threat of male sexual aggression, implicit both in the swallow's pursuit of the grasshopper and in Daphnis's temerity. And no sooner is the story told than the implicit becomes all too explicit. Tyrian pirates fall upon the countryside, carry off Daphnis, and steal the cattle of a neighboring herdsman, Dorcon (with whom we shall have more to do somewhat later on), mortally wounding him in the process.[8] With his dying breath, as the pirates make sail with their booty, Dorcon instructs Chloe to play a certain tune upon his shepherd's flute, a tune to which his cattle are trained to respond.[9] She complies, and Dorcon's well-trained cattle immediately start a stampede aboard the pirate ship, swamping it forthwith; all hands go down with the ship, except for Daphnis, who rides to shore on the horns of two of Dorcon's cattle.

The grasshopper incident and the pirate incident, then, mirror each other thematically, while the Phatta story serves as a bridge between them, something like this:

Grasshopper incident (1.26)

    Phatta story (1.27)

Pirate incident (1.28–30)

Thus far Deligiorgis (and, to some extent, Kestner); but the pattern of framing, through the specular reduplication of incidents, does not stop here. At 1.25, right before the grasshopper episode, Daphnis talks to himself as he watches Chloe sleep and complains that all the animals are making so much noise that they will surely awaken her. He ends his soliloquy with a reproach that well illustrates how far from his right mind a herdsman can get, when he is under Eros's spell: ὦ λύκων ἀλωπέκων δειλοτέρων, οἳ τούτους οὐχ ἥρπασαν ("Oh, the wolves are more cowardly than foxes: they haven't grabbed those [noisy goats]"). The wolf is, of course, the traditional archenemy of the herdsman; but the last "wolf" that Daphnis and Chloe met in book 1 was not a wolf at all, but rather Dorcon, who, with less than the best intentions, dressed himself as a wolf in order to prey upon Chloe.[10] When the pirates come, however, this same "wolf" gives up his life in defense of his herd, and, what is more, saves Daphnis from being kidnapped, albeit posthumously. At the funeral which Daphnis and Chloe improvise for Dorcon, his cattle sing a noisy lament, in counterpoint to the goats who would not keep still while Chloe slept. All of this serves, then, to add another layer of specularity to the frame around the Phatta story, expanding it both forward and backward:

Wolves who do not prey upon the flock, and noisy animals (1.25)

    Grasshopper incident (1.26)

        Phatta story (1.27)

    Pirate incident (1.28–30)

A "wolf" who sacrifices himself for his flock, and noisy animals
(1.29–30)

Note how the very arrangement of these images reinforces the
specularity, since the reflected themes recur after the story in
reverse order. This is not simple linear reduplication; rather, a
structural pattern of concentric frames is clearly taking shape,
very similar to what we saw in the prologue. The components of
the frame are thematically connected to the *aition*, primarily by
the sympathetic fallacy, and by the overtones of violence and
death, which lurk none-too-subtly beneath the surface of the
Phatta story. In this idyllic paradise in which our two young
lovers live, all is not as peaceful as it seems.

In striking contrast to the somber overtones in all that we
have seen so far are a pair of specular images that center on the
ever-growing erotic passion that Daphnis and Chloe feel for
each other. Chloe's first flickerings of that particular fire were
aroused by the sight of Daphnis's nude body, as he took a bath; [11]
and ever since then, she has been grasping at every opportunity
to encourage Daphnis to bathe again. At 1.24, such an opportunity comes again, as Daphnis bathes in the river to escape the
heat of the day. ἡ μὲν γὰρ γυμνὸν ὁρῶσα τὸν Δάφνιν ἐπ᾽ ἀθροῦν
ἐνέπιπτε τὸ κάλλος, καὶ ἐτήκετο μηδὲν αὐτοῦ μέρος μέμψασθαι
δυναμένη (For then she observed the beauty of Daphnis on
every limb, and was consumed, unable to find fault with any part
of him). After Daphnis's adventure with the pirates, yet another
opportunity arrives for Chloe to bathe Daphnis, who is a little
the worse for wear. This time, however, she bathes herself, too,
and Daphnis (who has meanwhile fallen in love with Chloe, but
who has not yet seen her undraped form) gets his chance: καὶ
αὐτὴ τότε πρῶτον Δάφνιδος ὁρῶντος ἐλούσατο τὸ σῶμα, λευκὸν
καὶ καθαρὸν ὑπὸ κάλλους καὶ οὐδὲν λουτρῶν ἐς κάλλος δεόμενον
(And then, as Daphnis watched for the very first time, she bathed
her body, white and pure in its beauty, really needing no bath to
be beautiful [1.32]).

It requires no great intuition to see that these two closely parallel incidents are so placed as to expand the frame yet further,
while maintaining its basically specular arrangement, as follows:

A bath with sexual overtones (1.24)

    Wolves out of character and noisy animals (1.25)

        Grasshopper incident (1.26)

           Phatta story (1.27)

        Pirate incident (1.28–30)

    Wolves out of character and noisy animals (1.29–30)

A bath with sexual overtones (1.32)

This last pair, which forms the outer boundary of the frame around the Phatta story, may seem at first blush to have little to do with the themes that govern most of the rest of the frame. There is, however, one important point of contact. The story of Phatta is devoid of any explicit reference to love or sexuality, but the erotic overtones are clear enough, as we saw.[12] Common to all three of the maidens who are the protagonists of the *aitia* is their confrontation with male aggression, to which they respond inappropriately (though they are placed in a position where there are no good choices); and as a result of their failure either to recognize what is happening to them and what can or should be done about it, or to react in an appropriate manner, they are transformed. In the next two *aitia*, we shall see Pan as that male antagonist, and his intentions in both cases are explicitly sexual: that is, he has rape on his mind. This is not true of the boy who lures away eight of Phatta's cattle, but the connection between material aggrandizement and sexual aggression is not, after all, a hard one to understand; and Longus is careful to see that we do not miss the point. For that matter, Pan is incorporated into the story of Phatta by a pointed reference to another story, that of Pitys, which does contain an attempted rape. Phatta's problem, in fact, is that she does not understand the erotic nature of the boy's challenge; and from this failure to understand the nature of Eros, the whole cycle of frame and story gains coherence. As for Daphnis and Chloe, they are aroused as they gaze upon one another's bodies; but they do not know even the name of

Eros, let alone his works, his ἔργα.[13] They are playing a game, then, of which they, like Phatta, know neither the rules nor the stakes.

THE SPEECH CONTEST

The story of Phatta, with its elaborate frame, occupies roughly the second half of book 1. A glance at the content of the first half of book 1 will show that here, too, there are many reduplicated incidents, much like those which were used to frame the Phatta story. This observation raises a perhaps not unreasonable expectation that book 1, like the prologue, will fall into two halves, with a similar framing structure in each half, and that there will be a significant relationship between what stands at the center of each frame.

We might begin by looking at two episodes which quite obviously correspond to each other, and of which passing mention has already been made. At 1.13, Chloe watches Daphnis bathing, and the sight of his nude body brings up strange feelings that she does not understand. At last, driven almost to distraction, she begins to reason with herself, as follows:

νῦν ἐγὼ νοσῶ μέν, τί δὲ ἡ νόσος ἀγνοῶ· ἀλγῶ, καὶ ἕλκος οὐκ ἔστι μοι· λυποῦμαι, καὶ οὐδὲν τῶν προβάτων ἀπόλωλέ μοι· καίομαι, καὶ ἐν σκιᾷ τοσαύτῃ κάθημαι. πόσοι βάτοι με πολλάκις ἤμυξαν, καὶ οὐκ ἀνέκραγον· πόσαι μέλιτται τὰ κέντρα ἐνῆκαν, ἀλλὰ ἔφαγον· τουτὶ δὲ τὸ νύττον μου τὴν καρδίαν πάντων ἐκείνων πικρότερον. καλὸς ὁ Δάφνις, καὶ γὰρ τὰ ἄνθη· καλὸν ἡ σύριγξ αὐτοῦ φθέγγεται, καὶ γὰρ αἱ ἀηδόνες. ἀλλ' ἐκείνων οὐδείς μοι λόγος. εἴθε αὐτοῦ σύριγξ ἐγενόμην ἵν' ἐμπνέῃ μοι, εἴθε αἴξ ἵν' ὑπ' ἐκείνου νέμωμαι. ὦ πονηρὸν ὕδωρ, μόνον Δάφνιν καλὸν ἐποίησας, ἐγὼ δὲ μάτην ἀπελουσάμην. οἴχομαι, Νύμφαι φίλαι, καὶ οὐδὲ ὑμεῖς σῴζετε τὴν παρθένον τὴν παρ' ὑμῖν τραφεῖσαν. τίς ὑμᾶς στεφανώσει μετ' ἐμέ; τίς τοὺς ἀθλίους ἄρνας ἀναθρέψει; τίς τὴν λάλον ἀκρίδα θεραπεύσει, ἣν πολλὰ καμοῦσα ἐθήρασα ἵνα με κατακοιμίζῃ φθεγγομένη πρὸ τοῦ ἄντρου; νῦν δὲ ἐγὼ μὲν ἀγρυπνῶ διὰ Δάφνιν, ἡ δὲ μάτην λαλεῖ.

(Now I am ill, but what the disease is, I don't know. I hurt, and have no wound. I grieve, but I haven't lost any sheep. I burn, but look how shady it is where I'm sitting. How often brambles have scratched me, but I never cried; how often bees have stung me, but I always kept right on eating. But this sting in my heart is more painful than all of those things. Daphnis is beautiful; well, so are the flowers. The music of his flute sounds beautiful; well, so do the nightingales. But I have no interest in those [sc. flowers and nightingales]. I wish I were his flute, so that he would blow into me.[14] I wish I were a nanny goat, so that he would be my goatherd. Oh wicked water, you made only Daphnis beautiful, while I bathed in vain. Dear Nymphs, I pray to you, but you are doing nothing to save the girl who was nursed beside you. Who will put garlands around your heads, after I am gone? Who will raise my poor lambs? Who will take care of the cricket that I worked so hard to catch and take care of, to sing me to sleep in front of the [nymphs'] grotto? Now here I am, I can't sleep because of Daphnis, and she sings in vain.) (1.14)

Not too much later, Daphnis wins a kiss from Chloe, the prize in a speech contest with Dorcon. The kiss has a strange effect on him, not at all unlike that which the sight of his own nude body had on poor Chloe a few days before. He, too, suffers indescribable torments, until at last he, in his turn, begins to talk to himself:

τί ποτέ με τὸ Χλόης ἐργάζεται φίλημα; χείλη μὲν ῥόδων ἁπαλώτερα καὶ στόμα κηρίων γλυκύτερον, τὸ δὲ φίλημα κέντρου μελίττης πικρότερον. πολλάκις ἐφίλησα ἐρίφους, πολλάκις ἐφίλησα σκύλακας ἀρτιγεννήτους καὶ τὸν μόσχον ὃν ὁ Δόρκων ἐχαρίσατο· ἀλλὰ τοῦτο φίλημα καινόν. ἐκπηδᾷ μου τὸ πνεῦμα, ἐξάλλεται ἡ καρδία, τήκεται ἡ ψυχή, καὶ ὅμως πάλιν φιλῆσαι θέλω. ὢ νίκης κακῆς, ὢ νόσου καινῆς, **ἧς οὐδὲ εἰπεῖν οἶδα τὸ ὄνομα** [emphasis added]. ἆρα φαρμάκων ἐγεύσατο Χλόη μέλλουσά με φιλεῖν; πῶς οὖν οὐκ ἀπέθανεν; οἷον ᾄδουσιν αἱ ἀηδόνες, ἡ δὲ ἐμὴ σῦριγξ σιωπᾷ· οἷον σκιρτῶσιν οἱ ἔριφοι, κἀγὼ κάθημαι· οἷον ἀκμάζει τὰ ἄνθη, κἀγὼ στεφάνους οὐ πλέκω, ἀλλὰ τὰ μὲν ἴα καὶ ὁ ὑάκινθος ἀνθεῖ, Δάφνις δὲ μαραίνεται. ἆρά μου καὶ Δόρκων εὐμορφότερος ὀφθήσεται;

(What is Chloe's kiss doing to me? Her lips are more tender than roses, her mouth sweeter than honey, but her kiss is sharper than a bee's stinger.[15] I have often kissed baby kids, and newborn puppies, and the calf that Dorcon gave us as a gift, but this kiss is something new. My breath rushes out, my heart skips a beat, my soul is consumed, and still I want to kiss her again. Oh evil victory! Oh unheard-of disease, *whose name I do not even know how to say* [emphasis added]! Did Chloe put poison in her mouth when she was about to kiss me? Then why didn't she die? Listen to how the birds sing; but my flute is silent. Look at how the baby kids are skipping around; but I just sit here. Look at how the flowers are blooming; but I weave no garlands. No, the violets and the hyacinths bloom, but Daphnis is wasting away. Will even Dorcon come to be handsomer to look at than I am?) (1.18)

The parallels between these two soliloquies are manifest. Both speeches are delivered in analogous circumstances, and much of their vocabulary and imagery is parallel, as a perusal of both passages will surely convince even the most skeptical reader. The rhetorical disposition of the two speeches is also much the same: both speakers begin by expressing their bewilderment over their condition; reflect that their previous interactions with animals have not prepared them for what is happening now; wonder why they are each so much in the other's power; express an apparently paradoxical wish to be near the other; blame the external circumstances; and end by complaining that they are wasting away. Everything about these two speeches serves to connect them closely together.

The theme of erotic ignorance emerges from a comparison of these two speeches with particular force, in light of what we learned from the story of the wood dove. Daphnis and Chloe are in the grips of one of the most powerful forces in human life; but the particular circumstances of their background (or so we are told) prevent them from knowing even what to call their affliction, let alone what it is or what to do about it. The only real explanation that Longus offers for this incredible naiveté is in reference to Chloe: ὅ τι μὲν οὖν ἔπασχεν οὐκ ᾔδει,[16] νέα κόρη καὶ ἐν ἀγροικίᾳ τεθραμμένη καὶ οὐδὲ ἄλλου λέγοντος ἀκούσασα τὸ ἔρωτος ὄνομα ("What she was experiencing she did not know, since she was a young girl, raised in the country, and had never heard anybody else speak the name of Eros" [1.13]). There is a certain irony here, of course. Children who are raised in the country, around stock animals, usually learn "the facts of life" from direct observation, rather sooner than their contemporaries in the city. There is, to be sure, more to human sexuality than procreation, which may indeed be Longus's point; but for him to assert that, *precisely because she is a shepherdess*, Chloe knows nothing about Eros, is more than slightly absurd. Why does Daphnis know nothing about Eros, when Dorcon, his would-be rival, who is also a herdsman and not much older than Daphnis, knows both "the name and the works of Eros" (1.15)? [17]

To say that this whole situation is absurd does not mean that Longus is guilty of some literary transgression. On the contrary, two sly allusions in and around Daphnis's soliloquy invite the reader to recognize and appreciate the depth of the absurdity. Just before the soliloquy, we are told that Daphnis will not eat or drink, and his face has become χλωρότερον . . . πόας θερινῆς ("greener than the grass of spring" [1.17]). This may remind some readers, surely not accidentally, of a well-known fragment of Sappho: χλωρότερα δὲ ποίας/ ἔμμι ("I am greener than the grass"). [18] An even more obvious allusion than this, however, can be heard in Daphnis's soliloquy itself, where the phrase Δάφνις δὲ μαραίνεται ("Daphnis is wasting away") recalls the lovesick Daphnis who is the subject of Theocritus's first idyll. Both of these allusions, to Sappho and to Theocritus, seem to connect Daphnis with the whole tradition of erotic poetry and thus render his incredible naiveté (and Chloe's) all the more ridiculous. [19] The lover whose passion is like a disease is a familiar enough figure in erotic poetry, ancient and modern, lyric and bucolic. Both Daphnis and Chloe are very clearly associated with such figures by these allusions, then, but with a significant difference. The lovesick poet, or the lovesick shepherd of the pastoral, usually knows well enough what is wrong with him. [20]

Why, one wonders, has Longus given us protagonists who are so incredibly ignorant of what we are wont to call "the facts of life"? It may be for nothing more than comic effect, of course;

but then again, there may be more to it than that. If there is so very much that Daphnis and Chloe do not understand, an educative process is clearly called for, else the joke will start to wear thin. In the next book, in fact, an erotic *paideia* will begin to take shape, an education which will prove to be the engine driving *Daphnis and Chloe* to its conclusion. We shall meet two teachers before it is all over, and hear all manner of pedagogical language. That which we have been calling erotic ignorance, then, is in reality erotic *aporia,* that lostness, that insufficiency of resources with which, Plato constantly reminds us, genuine and deep learning must begin. It is all but impossible to teach anything of value to students who think they already know what is needful.

Immediately after Chloe's soliloquy, Dorcon, who has become enamoured of her, begins to pay her court, although she and Daphnis are far too naive to realize the nature of his attentions. At last he contrives to enter into a speech contest with Daphnis; the prize is to be a kiss from Chloe, who will also be the judge. The speeches, then, are to be directed to her, to give her reason to award the prize to one or the other on their respective merits. Daphnis, of course, wins the contest and gets the prize; Dorcon, disappointed ("Curses, foiled again!" we can almost hear him say), goes off to lay another plot, while Daphnis reacts to that kiss in the way we have already seen. Dorcon's machinations, then, serve as the immediate frame for the speech contest, while the lovers' soliloquies form another layer of framing, as follows:

Chloe's soliloquy (1.14)

    Dorcon's machinations (1.15)

        The speech contest (1.16)

    Dorcon's further machinations (1.17)

Daphnis's soliloquy (1.18)

The apparent formation of a frame here, very much like the one we discovered around the story of Phatta, seems to suggest that this speech contest needs a closer look, which in fact it does.

A careful reading of both speeches will show that the whole scene is informed by many of the same thematic preoccupations that we found in the Phatta story.

"ἐγώ, παρθένε, μείζων εἰμὶ Δάφνιδος, καὶ ἐγὼ μὲν βουκόλος, ὁ δὲ αἰπόλος· τοσοῦτον οὖν ἐγὼ κρείττων ὅσον αἰγῶν βόες· καὶ λευκός εἰμι ὡς γάλα καὶ πυρρὸς ὡς θέρος μέλλον ἀμᾶσθαι, καί με ἔθρεψε μήτηρ, οὐ θηρίον. οὗτος δέ ἐστι μικρὸς καὶ ἀγένειος ὡς γυνὴ καὶ μέλας ὡς λύκος· νέμει δὲ τράγους, ὀδωδὼς ἀπ' αὐτῶν δεινόν, καὶ ἔστι πένης ὡς μηδὲ κύνα τρέφειν. εἰ δέ, ὡς λέγουσι, καὶ αἲξ αὐτῷ γάλα δέδωκεν, οὐδὲν ἐρίφων διαφέρει." ταῦτα καὶ τοιαῦτα ὁ Δόρκων καὶ μετὰ ταῦτα ὁ Δάφνις· "ἐμὲ αἲξ ἀνέθρεψεν ὥσπερ τὸν Δία, νέμω δὲ τράγους τῶν τούτου βοῶν μείζονας, ὄζω οὐδὲν ἀπ' αὐτῶν, ὅτι μηδὲ ὁ Πάν, καίτοιγε ὢν τὸ πλέον τράγος. ἀρκεῖ δέ μοι τυρὸς καὶ ἄρτος ὀβελίας καὶ οἶνος λευκός, ὅσα ἀγροίκων πολουσίων κτήματα. ἀγένειός εἰμι, καὶ γὰρ ὁ Διόνυσος· μέλας, καὶ γὰρ ὁ ὑάκινθος· ἀλλὰ κρείττων καὶ ὁ Διόνυσος Σατύρων καὶ ὁ ὑάκινθος κρίνων. οὗτος δὲ καὶ πυρρὸς ὡς ἀλώπηξ καὶ προγένειος ὡς τράγος καὶ λευκὸς ὡς ἐξ ἄστεος γυνή· κἂν δέῃ σε φιλεῖν, ἐμοῦ μὲν φιλήσεις τὸ στόμα, τούτου δὲ τὰς ἐπὶ τοῦ γενείου τρίχας. μέμνησο δέ, ὦ παρθένε, ὅτι καὶ σὲ ποίμνιον ἔθρεψεν, ἀλλὰ εἰ καλή."

("Oh maiden, I am larger than Daphnis, and I am a cowherd, while he is a mere goatherd; and so I am as much better than he is, as cows are better than goats.[21] My skin is as white as milk, and I am as blond as grain about to be harvested; and a human mother raised me, not an animal. This fellow here is as small and beardless as a woman, and as dark as a wolf. He reeks of the goats he herds, and he is so poor he can't even keep a dog properly fed. If, as they say, a nanny goat gave him milk, he is not at all different from a kid.")

Dorcon spoke all these things, and other things along the same line; afterward, Daphnis spoke as follows:

"A goat nursed me, like the one who nursed Zeus. The goats I herd are better than his cows. I don't reek of goat, any more than Pan does, and he is more than half goat. I am content with cheese, and plain bread, and white wine, all of which are the treasures of wealthy countryfolk. I am beardless, and so is Dionysus; I am dark, and so is the hyacinth. But Dionysus is greater than the satyrs, and the hyacinth greater than the lilies. This fellow here is blond, like a fox; bearded, like a goat; and white, like a woman from the city. When it comes time for you to kiss one of us, it will be my mouth you kiss, but you will be kissing the hair around his mouth. And remember, oh maiden, that a sheep nursed you, but you are beautiful.") (1.16)

Daphnis' *refutatio* consists largely in converting the liabilities that Dorcon has urged against him into assets; he responds to every point that Dorcon makes, though he does not handle the issues in the same order in which Dorcon raised them.[22] Most readers will have already noted (even in the translation, where they are inevitably somewhat attenuated) the parallels in structure and language between these speeches (especially Daphnis's) and the lovers' soliloquies; what may be less immediately apparent, though of hardly less significance, is that these speeches prefigure certain of the themes we have already seen in the Phatta story. That both Dorcon and the unnamed boy of the Phatta story are cowherds cannot really be a casual coincidence. The threat which Dorcon is posing to Daphnis is really quite analogous to that which confronts Phatta. In each case, a cowherd of no small natural endowment is out to aggrandize himself by appropriating something that belongs to another; and in each case, the method is seduction. Dorcon is out to charm Chloe away from Daphnis, just as the boy charmed eight cows away from Phatta.

This is not to say, however, that the relationship between Dorcon and the young cowherd of the Phatta story is one of simple equivalence. The equation is more complex than that, primarily because Daphnis must be figured into it, with surprising results. Dorcon is obviously proud of his masculinity, to which he contrasts the apparent femininity of Daphnis; and the outward indication of that masculinity is his beard.[23] The boy of the Phatta story, however, is beardless, unlike Dorcon and like Daphnis. It is precisely because his voice is loud (by virtue of his masculinity) but also as sweet as a woman's (by virtue of his tender age) that the boy succeeds in "enchanting" Phatta's cattle. From this perspective, the young cowherd has as much in common with Daphnis as with Dorcon. What is happening here is that Daphnis is being presented with two models of masculinity in which aggression toward females is assumed but the means of expressing that aggression are much in contrast. The boy assimilates and exploits his latent femininity, while Dorcon is the paradigm of the male as brute; hence his "wolfishness." At the same time, Daphnis himself is at least potentially yet another model of masculinity, distinguished from the two cowherds by his relative lack of aggression. He is about to become an erotic male, however, and as such he will have to comes to terms with that innate masculine aggressiveness.

There is a sexual dimension to all this that should be mentioned now, though the full significance of what Longus seems to be implying here will not be clear until book 4. In Greek society, at least until the advent of Christianity, a boy was a socially acceptable sex object for a grown man and reached the apex of his desirability precisely when he was on the threshhold of manhood, in the early stages of puberty. Both the cowherd and Daphnis have certain qualities in common with women, of which beardlessness is the most obvious; they could easily be *pueri delicati*, that is, catamites. They are male, but not yet men, and this puts them in an ambiguous position vis-à-vis both the female and the mature male. All three of the males in book 1 vaunt their innate superiority to the female, explicitly in the speeches, implicitly in the story of Phatta; but in both cases, the two males with female attributes are finally triumphant.[24] In Daphnis's case, however, his erotic naiveté vitiates his triumph. He wins the contest with Dorcon, but he does not know what the stakes really are, and in fact the fruits of his victory take a quite unexpected shape; ὦ νίκης κακῆς ("Oh evil victory!"), he is finally driven to exclaim. It is too early yet to say how all this will finally be resolved, but we may begin to see where it is going.

To this point, then, another complex frame has developed around a passage of some thematic consequence. Our experience with the layer upon layer of framing around the *aition* of Phatta, as well as the abbreviated form of this structure we encountered in the prologue, suggests that we might expect to find further layers of framing around the speech contest, also. When the incidents that come immediately before and after the lovers' soliloquies are juxtaposed, it is not too difficult to see that here, too, there are several layers of framing, still arranged on the specular model, rather as follows:

The first ten chapters of book 1 are consumed with setting the stage for the main action of the novel. We learn how first Daphnis and then Chloe (for reasons as yet unknown) are exposed in the country shortly after their birth. Apparently, to judge from the tokens (γνωρίσματα) found with them, they are not of peasant stock. They are each found and suckled by animals, picked up by shepherds, and then named and raised by the two families as though they were natural children. When they reach the ages of fifteen and thirteen, respectively, their adoptive fathers are commanded in parallel and simultaneous dreams to send their foster children into the fields to tend their flocks, with the result that Daphnis and Chloe become companions and friends. In chapter 10, then, we are given a sketch of how they pass their days.[25] All this leads, finally, to the incident with which the story of Daphnis and Chloe really begins in earnest, in chapter 11. A she-wolf, who has hungry young to feed, has been ravaging the flocks in the vicinity of the fields where Daphnis and Chloe pass their days together. The local shepherds pockmark the countryside with pit traps, in an ultimately futile effort to catch her. One day, Daphnis pursues one of his male goats who has injured another in a fight; in his fury he runs without looking and falls into one of these traps. Chloe enlists the aid of a nearby cowherd (the first appearance of Dorcon) and pulls Daphnis out of the pit. He is terribly soiled, and Chloe takes him to a nearby spring to bathe him; we have already seen what happens to her when she gets an eyeful of him in the bath.

It will be recalled that Dorcon's machinations to get his hands on Chloe made up the immediate frame around the speech contest. The next trick that Dorcon tries, after his effort to discredit Daphnis in Chloe's eyes, is to induce her adoptive father, Dryas, to give him Chloe as his bride; but Dryas, who suspects (based on the tokens and the clothing that he found with Chloe when she was a baby) that his foundling daughter was born for higher things, spurns Dorcon's gifts. The frustrated Dorcon then hits upon a strategem for falling upon Chloe and raping her. He covers himself with the skin of a wolf, and sneaks up upon her while Daphnis is momentarily occupied elsewhere. Unfortunately for his designs, however, the dogs catch his scent, and fall upon him; he is saved from being torn limb from limb only when he calls out to Daphnis and Chloe, who call off the dogs. Thus he is discovered. So ignorant are Daphnis and Chloe of Eros, however, that they fail to understand what Dorcon intended and laugh at what they take to be a harmless prank.

The two incidents just described (Daphnis falling into the wolf trap, and Dorcon trying to rape Chloe) have more than a little in common, even on the most superficial narrative level. To begin with, both have a great deal to do with wolves. The first of these is a real wolf, who can almost be forgiven for her predation, because it is natural; she succeeds in her efforts to provide for her young and evades the traps set for her. The second "wolf" is no wolf at all but a human in the guise of a wolf, whose motives no decent person will condone, and who is betrayed and almost destroyed. There is an antithesis here, then, between a "natural" wolf and an "artificial" one, and between a she-wolf and a human male; and it might be tempting to read into the success of the former and the failure of the latter some evaluative statement here about Nature and Artifice, φύσις and τέχνη, or male and female. But that would be premature, at this point; the issue will recur. We shall see how the image of the wolf also recurs, in book 3, by which time it will be easier to understand what Longus is trying to establish by playing these two wolves off against each other.[26] The rapacious appetite of the wolf, which is both natural and destructive, stands for a part of human nature with which we must all deal, in one way or another; but our appetitive nature cannot be merely suppressed or denied. The whole problem awaits resolution.

This is by no means the end of the parallels between the two incidents at hand. On both occasions, someone falls into a trap of sorts and must be rescued. Chloe is instrumental in effecting both rescues, that of Daphnis in the first instance, and of Dorcon in the second. We have already seen how Daphnis and Dorcon represent two competing models of masculinity; here we see how both seem to rely upon the woman. We can also see how a certain lack of understanding and foresight led each of these young men into their respective traps. It is not merely that Daphnis failed to look where he was going. He flew into a rage because two of his male goats had been fighting, and in the heat of his anger he chased the victor, wanting to punish him. For us readers, who are always presumed to know that which Daphnis and Chloe do not—that is, the name and the works of Eros—it is not very hard to deduce why these billygoats were fighting, especially if we keep in mind that this is all happening in the springtime. Daphnis's rage, which has all but fatal consequences, comes from his failure to understand why male goats fight each other, and how necessary it is that they do so. As for Dorcon, he thought, wrongly, that he could assume the outward appearance of a wolf without having to accept the consequences of being a wolf. He, like Daphnis, almost pays with his life for his mistake. Clearly, then, it is not enough to know, as Dorcon does, both the name and the works of Eros. We cannot yet know what *is* enough, but then, we still have three more books to read. For now, suffice it to note that the themes of the wolf, the trap, and the rescue identify yet another pair of specular images, expanding this frame outward still further.

The outer limits of the frame around the speech contest are fairly easy to identify. In chapters 9 and 10, as has already been remarked, Longus describes the season of the year (which is spring) and the pastimes enjoyed by Daphnis and Chloe. All the incidents that follow come close upon one another, until the spring is gone, and the summer follows, at chapter 23. Here, we are treated again to a word picture of the season, its effects upon Daphnis and Chloe, and their pastimes, slightly different now because of summer's greater heat. This leads, then, right into the beginning of the frame around the Phatta story.

SUMMARY

This may be a good time to summarize what has been seen so far, before we go on to look at the rest of *Daphnis and Chloe*. In book 1, Longus uses an elaborate scheme of paired incidents to create specular frames, both of which serve to highlight two passages of considerable thematic importance: first, a speech contest between Daphnis and Dorcon, in which competing models of masculinity are expounded and evaluated; and second, an apparently digressive narrative, the *aition* of Phatta, which explores the consequences of erotic naiveté and male aggression. We have seen how each frame consists of members that support and develop the themes in the highlighted passages, and how each of these two cycles are thematically interconnected, although a final resolution of what this all means will naturally have to wait until we have followed these themes in their development through the rest of the novel. The result (to bring it all together) is something like this:

Spring and its occupations (1.9–10)

   A wolf, a trap, a rescue (1.11–12)

      Chloe's soliloquy (1.14)

         Dorcon's machinations (1.15)

            The speech contest (1.16)

         Dorcon's further machinations (1.17)

      Daphnis's soliloquy (1.18)

   A wolf, a trap, a rescue (1.20)

Summer and its occupations (1.23)

A bath with sexual overtones (1.24)

   Wolves out of character, and noisy animals (1.25)

      The grasshopper (1.26)

         The story of Phatta (1.27)

      The pirates (1.28–30)

   Wolves out of character, and noisy animals (1.29–30)

A bath with sexual overtones (1.32)

Although this diagram serves its proper function as a graphic representation of the specular arrangement of redoubled themes to form frames, it is, of course, somewhat out of scale. We should not be misled into imposing a symmetry that is not really there. In the case of "Dorcon's machinations," for example, one sentence is reflected in an entire chapter; and the grasshopper episode is one chapter against three. Literature, after all, is not engineering. Perfect bilateral symmetry may be of considerable utility in building a bridge or a triumphal arch, but as an aesthetic principle it leaves something to be desired. Another disclaimer, rather along the same lines: the structural model given here is not, either in intent or execution, all-inclusive. Not every single incident in *Daphnis and Chloe* has a specular reflection, and not even all the reflections are specular or part of a narrative frame. Thus, for example, the "exposure and discovery" scenes in the first chapters are redoubled, to be sure, but they are not arranged in quite the same way as are, for example, the lovers' soliloquies. The framing is there, beyond any reasonable doubt; but Longus does not belabor it to the point of making it tiresome.

Each frame derives its coherence from the recurrence of themes and incidents that are so arranged as to mirror each other in a chiastic order, so that we end up where we began; for this reason, it would not be inaccurate to call each frame a "cycle." There is a certain tension here, of course: by using the term "cycle" instead of "frame," we give up some of the imagery of painting. If, however, we use the term "frame" instead of "cycle," we may be in danger of forgetting that there is a movement in time here. Despite all of Longus's play in the prologue with the idea that he is painting a novel, or telling a painting, this is a narrative after all, and it moves through time, both from the teller's perspective and the reader's. Neither term, then, could be used without giving up certain connotations that may well prove to be central to what *Daphnis and Chloe* is all about. The term "cycle" has one advantage, however, in that it provides a useful and congruent term, "pivot," for that which is highlighted by each frame. As we move into the first cycle in book 1, it is precisely at the speech contest that we turn and begin to work our way back out. English provides no handy term for "that-which-is-framed"; thus, to avoid the constant repetition of awkward locutions, we will henceforward speak of "cycles" organized around "pivots."

This leaves one element for which a convenient term is needed: the pairs of specular images which go together to form the cycles. The most descriptive available term for these pairs, which fits into the same semantic field as "cycle," is "ring." If one were to arrange the incidents of the novel along a time line and then draw a figure to connect those elements that reflect or re-duplicate each other, the result would be a series of concentric circles, or rings. The use of the term "ring" will also help to pre-serve a spatial dimension lost when "cycle" is adopted in place of "frame." To some readers, of course, the ring as a unit of struc-ture is indicative of what is usually called "ring composition." Since no two critics who talk about "ring composition" seem to mean exactly the same thing by it, we need not feel compelled to accept a great deal of unnecessary baggage along with the term "ring," which we are using here in a simple descriptive sense. "A foolish consistency," as Emerson put it, "is the hobgoblin of little minds."

Equipped with these definitions, then, we may now proceed to consider the structure of book 2. For there is every reason to suppose that the structural pattern developed in such detail for the prologue and book 1 will continue on through book 2, and, for that matter, through book 3 as well. Several significant clues point in that direction. First and most obviously, each of the next two books in question contains an *aition* with patent similarities to the story of Phatta; and second, there are many incidents in these later books that seem to mirror each other in the same way that, for example, the lovers' soliloquies do in book 1. It is not really necessary, in fact, to proceed quite so inductively through the next two chapters as we have done so far. For book 1, the diagram was developed piece by piece, primarily because it was necessary to do two things at once: both to demonstrate that the two cycles existed, and to show how they worked. But to main-tain this procedure now would be continually to reinvent the wheel. In the next two chapters, then, for the sake of convenience, the procedure will be reversed: a diagram will first be adduced for each book and then explicated in detail. There are surprises in these two books, to be sure; but the development takes place along lines that are already becoming clear.

Chapter 4

Book 2:
Learning the Name of Eros

We know before we begin that we will find an *aition* in book 2, and we may note at the outset that it is placed within its book very nearly where the *aition* of Phatta is found in book 1: that is, roughly 80 percent of the way through the book. There are also paired speeches in book 2, very similar in outline to the speech contest of book 1: that is, we find a speech in which Daphnis is attacked, answered by a second speech in which he defends himself and counterattacks. This second exchange of speeches is placed in a position within its book analogous to that occupied by the speech contest between Daphnis and Dorcon in book 1: that is, somewhere between one-third and one-quarter of the way into the book. If we assume, not unreasonably, that the exchange of speeches and the *aition* are the two pivots of the two cycles in book 2, it is possible to construct a diagram for book 2, along these lines:

Fall and its pursuits (2.1–2)

A. Philetas's revelations (2.3–7)

    B. Daphnis's (and Chloe's) lack of confidence (2.9–11)

        C. The Methymnean hunters (2.12–14)

Pivot: The "trial" of Daphnis (2.15–17)

        C′. The Methymnean army (2.19–21)

     B′. Daphnis's lack of confidence (2.21–22)

A′. The nymphs' revelations (2.23)

a. The fidelity of Pan (2.28)

    b. Reunion (2.30)

        c. An offering to Pan (2.31)

           d. Lamon and Dryas dance (2.32)

               e. Garrulous old men (2.32)

                   f. Philetas asked to play (2.33)

                       g. Tityrus's mission (2.33)

Pivot: The *aition* of Syrinx (2.34)

                       g′. Tityrus's return (2.35)

                   f′. Philetas's playing (2.35)

               e′. A silly old man (2.36)

            d′. The dance of Daphnis and Chloe (2.37)

        c′. An offering to Daphnis (2.37)

    b′. Reunion (2.38)

a′. The fidelity of Daphnis (2.39)

THE FIRST CYCLE

Book 2 begins with a description of the autumn and its pursuits, which serves to link together the two cycles of book 1 with the beginning of book 2. The first two chapters of book 2 serve as a sort of prologue, then, to the beginning of the first ring (A), in which old Philetas, who serves as *praeceptor amoris*, tells Daphnis and Chloe about an epiphany he has seen in his garden. At long last, Daphnis and Chloe learn what to call this strange affliction they are both enduring: that is, they learn the name of Eros. Philetas, in addition to this, tells them that they are under the special protection of Eros. Then, pressed by the two young lovers, he gives them a three-part prescription for the relief of their erotic discomfiture: kissing, embracing, and lying together naked.

Philetas's instructions are manifestly incomplete. Daphnis and Chloe immediately try out the first two remedies, but to no avail. Innate scruples, apparently, prevent them from going on immediately to the third remedy, so that they soon find themselves no better off than they were before. The protection of Eros seems to be of no use (B). Later on, when Chloe has been kidnapped by the Methymneans' punitive expedition, Daphnis has no faith in the benevolence of the divine world, and even goes so far as to upbraid the nymphs for allowing Chloe to be taken from under their very noses (B'). The ring B−B' is informed, then, by human diffidence about the efficacy of the divine.

The nymphs respond to Daphnis's reproaches at B', not by punishing him for offending their numinosity, but by revealing to him, in a dream, that Pan, a god to whom he and Chloe have thus far failed to pay any particular attention, will intervene to save Chloe. At the end of their speech, the nymphs remind Daphnis that Eros will take care of the two lovers: τὰ δὲ ἄλλα μελήσει περὶ ὑμῶν Ἔρωτι ("Everything else about you will be Eros's concern" [2.2]).

The involvement of divinity (specifically, of Eros) in the lives and loves of Daphnis and Chloe has been hinted at all along, but becomes manifest here in book 2.[1] The instruction that the two lovers get from Philetas at A is the first step in their progress from erotic naiveté to erotic fulfillment; thus it is answered by Daphnis's dream vision of the nymphs at A', which contains not only a reminder and reassurance of the providential power and benevolence of Eros, as Philetas had explained it to them, but also an additional piece of instruction. Daphnis and Chloe, as country folk, are bound to know the name and attributes of Pan (to whom, indeed, Daphnis alludes in telling Chloe the story of Phatta), but they have never paid him any particular attention. Nevertheless, as the nymphs tell Daphnis, it is Pan who will redeem Eros's pledge and rescue Chloe. Thereafter, Daphnis and

Chloe are admonished to include Pan in all their offerings and libations, an injunction they faithfully observe for the rest of their lives.

It has been said of Pan in *Daphnis and Chloe* that he is nothing but a δαίμων, a divinity of lower rank, who is entrusted through-out the novel with carrying out the will of Eros.[2] There is, to be sure, a real connection between Pan and Eros, as this ring (among others) reveals; and it is clear enough that Pan's rescue of Chloe is part of Eros's designs for (or on) her. But the rela-tionship between these two divinities is more complex than that of employer and employee, or client and agent. Pan is not merely the rustic Eros. θεὸς ὁ Πὰν ἐρωτικός ἐστι, Chloe will soon say, "Pan is an erotic god"; but she will at once add, καὶ ἄπιστος ("and untrustworthy" [2.39.2]).[3] To say that Pan is an "erotic" god is a double-edged statement, to say the least. It is motivated, in context, by the story of Pan and Syrinx, in which Pan has acted the role, not of divine agent, but of oversexed male. He will sometimes do the work of Eros, to be sure, but what he really seems to be is some sort of mediator between Eros, the divine personification of love, and mortal lovers. He is tied to both worlds, the human and the divine, in that Daphnis has already identified himself with Pan once (in the speech contest in book 1), while ring A–A' highlights his divine connections with Eros. Since Pan is part animal (goat from the waist down) and part god, his very person is an allegory of the contradictions and paradoxes of love, which is sometimes divine and sometimes bes-tial. Pan thus represents (in a properly etymological sense of the word "re-present") a problem that Daphnis (and Chloe, too) will have to overcome.

The most immediate threat that Daphnis must face, however, comes from a different direction entirely. The idyllic world in which these characters live has already been invaded once, by the Tyrian pirates; at 2.12, it is invaded again, this time by a group of rich young men from Methymna, who come to seek the pleasures of a fall hunting trip in the country. The Methymnean hunters, arrogant and careless as only rich young men can be, wreak havoc with the hapless villagers along the coast. When their hunting trip is suddenly ended by the disaster that meets them at the hands (or teeth, rather) of Daphnis's goats, no reader is likely to feel much sympathy. There is good reason to pause, however, before writing off the Methymneans as mere villains, foils for the rustic virtue of Daphnis. With characteristic irony, Longus has gone to some lengths to connect these dissolute youths with himself, and even with us, the readers. It was, after all, while *hunting* in Lesbos that the authorial persona came upon the painting to which all of what we are now reading is avowedly a response. And there is more. The language that Longus uses at 2.12 to describe the beauties of the countryside, which have attracted the Methymneans to come on this hunting trip of theirs, is remarkably like that of the first few sentences of the prologue. More than the obvious repetition of the word ἄλσος, "grove," there is also a shared emphasis on the aesthetic rivalry between nature (ἡ φύσις) and human skill (ἡ τέχνη), a theme which will surface again at a crucial moment.[4] The recurrence of this particular theme in the midst of this cycle reminds us of the prologue; what is more, it serves to put the Methymneans into a position analogous to that assumed by the author at the outset of the novel. The young men from Methymna, like Longus himself, are hunters from elsewhere, who intrude upon the countryside, drawn by its charms. Like most of Longus's readers, too, they are of the city, not herdsmen like Daphnis or Philetas. Their depredations result from their failure to perceive that the country is a world coordinate with their own.

This ironic identification of the Methymneans with Longus himself, on the one hand, and with the novel's readers, on the other, leads directly to an important observation: to wit, that it is precisely in those areas wherein the Methymneans are most like the author and his public that they are most unlike Daphnis. Hunting, in antiquity, was the pastime of the rich; Daphnis is very poor, and is (or is thought to be, at any rate) a slave. The Methymneans are from the city, but Daphnis is a goatherd and does not even live within that part of Lesbos controlled by Methymna. All of this gives considerable point to the speeches exchanged during the "trial" of Daphnis in book 2, which forms (as did the speech contest in book 1) the pivot of the first cycle. In book 1, Daphnis was set off against Dorcon, a young herdsman superficially rather like himself but in essence a kind of opposite. Here, then, Daphnis is set off against an entire group of young men, who are even more clearly his opposites.

There are many points of contact between the speech contest in book 1 and the "trial" scene in book 2. Some of these are obvious, others less so. Each exchange of speeches pits Daphnis against an opponent who is his opposite, in certain ways, but to whom he is inextricably linked in other ways. In both speech contests, Daphnis's victory results from his ability to convert his liabilities, as urged against him by his opponents, into assets. The cleverness with which he does so belies the naiveté otherwise predicated of him, for he can meet, match, and defeat opponents who are much better endowed for the challenge at hand than he is (or ought to be). What this suggests is that there is more to Daphnis than meets the eye. We already know that Daphnis, even though he himself does not yet know it, was born to a wealthy family from the city, which means that he has much more in common with the Methymnean youths than any of them realize. Thus he is ironically identified with the very people to whom he is apparently contrasted, in much the same way as he was simultaneously identified with and contrasted to Dorcon in book 2.[5] They are, in certain respects, εἴρονες of each other.

Each of Daphnis's victories is attended by unforeseen negative consequences. Chloe's kiss, the prize of victory in book 1, seemed to him to be more like a bite than a kiss, so sharp and painful were its effects. So, too, Daphnis's victory in book 2 has unforeseen evil consequences. On the simplest narrative level, the speciousness of Daphnis's rhetorical victory is revealed by the closing of ring C–C', when the Methymnean expedition comes to avenge the rough handling that their youth have received. Daphnis, whose cleverness has twice snatched (rhetorical) victory from the jaws of defeat, is helpless to respond to the capture of Chloe. In book 1, also, Daphnis's defeated opponent attempted force. Dorcon was thwarted by his own stupidity, in that he failed to foresee the consequences of disguising himself as a wolf, though Daphnis's own ignorance kept him from recognizing what was really happening. In book 2, however, the Methymnean army accomplishes, at least partially, what Dorcon failed to do; as for

Daphnis, he knows what has happened well enough, even though he can do nothing.

And that is what tells us how the pivot of the first cycle in book 2 marks an advance from its analogue in book 1. Daphnis did not know what was really at stake in the speech contest with Dorcon; but when he comes up against the Methymneans, even this naive young goatherd knows that the stakes have suddenly become very high. Competing for a kiss from Chloe is one thing; fighting for one's liberty is another. In book 1, then, Daphnis fights for Chloe against Dorcon, who is an ironic reflection of himself; he wins, almost in spite of himself, and suffers the consequences of a victory won in complete ignorance of its terms. In book 2, he fights for himself against the Methymneans, who are also perverse reflections of his own identity, as yet unrecognized, and again suffers serious consequences as a perverse result of his rhetorical victory.

THE SECOND CYCLE

When we turn to the pivot of the second cycle of book 2, the *aition* of Syrinx, we can see that here, too, the stakes have been raised. This story of a maiden transformed into a musical plant is closely parallel in structure to that of Phatta. A young maiden, threatened by a male antagonist, is transformed by the mercy of the gods into a phenomenon of nature, one which produces a pleasing sound. Both stories are told in narrative contexts that make them seem incidental or digressive; but so much trouble is taken in both cases to identify the respective heroines with Chloe that no perspicacious reader is likely to be misled.[6] Despite these similarities, however, there are some significant differences between the two stories, differences which can hardly be without interpretive significance. The dove sings of its own accord, for one thing, while the reed must first be fashioned into a musical instrument, and then played. Thus both maidens escape their predicaments by becoming a musical part of nature, but with this great difference, that Phatta still moves and breathes, while Syrinx is fixed to the earth. She is living but not animate until she is first killed (by being cut off at the roots) and then filled with another's breath.

There is a further important difference between the two *aitia* on the erotic level. Phatta's transformation took place as a result of her inability to cope with the loss of her cattle, while Syrinx faces, at the critical moment, the prospect of rape. Thus the implicit erotic connotations of the Phatta story have now become explicit and denotational. This movement from the implicit to the explicit, taken together with the movement from the dove to the reed, reveals what the thematic relationship between book 1 and book 2 really is. At issue is the female response to male aggression, and the consequences of different responses to different forms of that aggression. The more patently erotic the male's intentions, the less satisfactory the options available to the female. Thus Phatta, confronted with the subliminally erotic aggression of the neighbor boy, must choose between transformation and a continuation of her grief and chagrin. As a consequence of her choice, she loses her human identity (though she continues to express her grief through the mournfulness of her song), but she is wild and free and need no longer have anything to do with the source of her misery. Syrinx, confronted and entrapped by Pan, must either be transformed or raped. She ceases to be even so much as animate, and in fact becomes an attribute of the very god who caused all this to happen, much as the laurel tree became the attribute of Apollo.[7]

All of this naturally calls further attention to the name and nature of Syrinx's male antagonist, Pan, the paradox of whose nature informs the outer ring of both the first and the second cycle here in book 2. The great paradox of ring a–a' lies in a passage already mentioned: to wit, Chloe's characterization of Pan as ἄπιστος, "untrustworthy." Near the end of book 2, Daphnis, who has already furthered his ongoing identification with Pan by dancing the role of Pan in a mimetic dance, is compelled to swear an oath of perpetual fidelity, precisely because of that identification. The paradox lies in the fact that, as an agent of divine Providence in the life of Chloe, Pan has been anything but "untrustworthy"; on the contrary, he has decisively intervened to save her (a), even though neither she nor Daphnis had ever previously paid him any particular attention. Only in the story of Syrinx, which Daphnis and Chloe have just heard, is the charge of untrustworthiness possibly justified. But that is enough, in Chloe's mind, and she demands assurance (a′). Daphnis will, after a fashion, break this oath: he will learn from another woman (a former prostitute from the city) the works of Eros, as he and Chloe learned the name of Eros from Philetas. Does this mean that he, too, is "untrustworthy"? He is a male who plays the flute with consummate artistry; he is a goatherd; and he is in love. Could it be that the only thing protecting Chloe from an onslaught like that which fell upon Syrinx is Daphnis's ignorance?

Rings c–c′ through g–g′ are in a manner all related, in that all the chapters from 31 through 37 are consumed in the great celebration of Chloe's rescue, which is Pan's act of salvation. The celebration begins with the offering of a goat to Pan (c), centers on the telling of a story in which Pan figures prominently, and ends with the transmission of a flute, a σύριγξ, from Philetas, the erotic pedagogue, to Daphnis (c′), who stands in for Pan with what may now seem to be monotonous regularity. That Daphnis's inheritance of Philetas's flute is manifestly a sign of the transmission of potency from the old to the young should be pellucid to all but the most obdurate.[8] This gives a certain point, then, to rings e–e′ and f–f′, where the interplay between the old and the young is the primary theme: ring e–e′ plays old men bragging about their youth (e) off against the wild Dionysiac dance (e′) of old Dryas (who behaves here in a manner reminiscent of Cadmus and Tiresias in Euripides' *Bacchae*). The construction of ring f–f′ is patent in the promise and its fulfillment, a pattern of framing that will recur around the pivot of the second cycle in book 3. Philetas is asked by Daphnis and Chloe to play his flute (f), and then complies (f′), after young Tityrus has run home to fetch his father's instrument; it is while Tityrus is away that Lamon tells the story of Syrinx.

Taken as a whole, then, book 2 clearly proceeds along the lines set out by book 1. The fact that Daphnis and Chloe now know the name of Eros and experience his benevolence resolves part of the great problem posed by both cycles of book 1, the problem of erotic ἀπορία. They remain, however, profoundly ignorant of the works of Eros, his ἔργα. What is more, Daphnis proves in book 2 to be capable of defending himself, to a limited degree, though he is still quite incapable of defending Chloe. And he has become ever more closely associated with Pan, the erotic antagonist of Syrinx; the implication seems to be that he poses a threat to Chloe, however unaware he himself may be of what that threat entails. Chloe's extraction of an oath, at the end of book 2, shows that she has at least a dim vision of what lies ahead. Daphnis does not.

Chapter 5

Book 3:
Learning the Works of Eros

Book 3, at first glance, may well seem to lack an obvious counterpart to the speech contest in book 1 or the trial scene in book 2.
But it does have an *aition*, and a closer examination will show
that there is also something at the pivot of the first cycle analogous
to the paired speeches in the first two books. And the analogy itself, once it is grasped, will help to clarify our view of the nature
and function of what we have been calling "the first cycle."

The structural blueprint of book 3 looks something like this:

A. The abortive war between Methymna and Mitylene (3.1−2)

  B. Winter, and its effects on Daphnis and Chloe (3.4−8)

    C. A sacrifice to Dionysus (3.10)

      D. Nape and Dryas cook dinner (3.10)

Pivot: Daphnis and Chloe argue (3.10)

      D'. Nape calls Daphnis and Chloe to eat (3.11)

    C'. The worship of Dionysus (3.11)

  B'. Spring, and its effects on Daphnis and Chloe (3.12−13)

A'. An abortive attempt to make love (3.14)

  a. Lycaenium teaches Daphnis the works of Eros (3.16–18)

    b. Lycaenium advises Daphnis not to do this with Chloe (3.19)

      c. Daphnis decides to follow her advice (3.20)

        d. A ship sails by, bound for Mitylene (3.21)

          e. Echoes (3.21–22)

            f. Chloe offers a reward (3.22)

Pivot: The story of Echo (3.23)

            f'. Chloe pays the reward (3.23)

          e'. Echoes (3.23–24)

        d'. Suitors come for Chloe (3.25)

      c'. Dryas stalls the suitors (3.25)

    b'. Myrtale tells Daphnis why he cannot have Chloe (3.26)

  a'. Daphnis wins a bride-to-be (3.27–34)

THE FIRST CYCLE

Book 3 begins with a most curious episode. The Mityleneans, apprised of the Methymnean raid that resulted in the capture (and rescue) of Chloe, dispatch a punitive expedition. Their army, marching overland because the winter storms have made the sea dangerous, almost catches Methymna unawares; but the Methymneans, who have since learned the truth about the depradations for which their young men are responsible, send out a herald to offer terms. They promise, in return for the peaceful withdrawal of the Mitylenean army, to return the remaining spoils of their expedition against the shepherds, so that the two cities can again live in peaceful commerce on land and sea. The Mitylenean general dispatches messengers to Mitylene and requests further orders, which are not long delayed: the terms offered by Methymna are accepted, and the army returns home without having fired a shot (so to speak).

This whole episode seems manifestly intrusive in its narrative context. The pastoral frame of reference is momentarily broken, and Longus's diction and style, like the content, approach that of "serious" historiography. Anyone with an ear for Greek style and more than a nodding acquaintance with Greek historical literature should be able to detect Longus's subtle and elusive play with the style and diction of Thucydides. The aesthetic effect of this intrusive piece of quasi-serious history is striking and unusual. It is rather as though a chamber orchestra has been playing Vivaldi, when suddenly the cellos begin to play a few bars of Beethoven at his most serious, only to drop it after a few bars and go back to playing Vivaldi. The effect is at least in part humorous, but there is clearly something ominous about it, too. For some reason, yet to be revealed, Longus has seen fit to remind us, just here, of a wider world, full of violence and danger on a far larger scale than anything Daphnis and Chloe are likely to encounter on their isolated farm.

With this as prologue, in which there is an incidental reference to the fact that winter has come, the text moves directly into a description of winter, the season of death. There have been some scholars, intent on proving or disproving the thesis that Longus was well acquainted with Lesbos, who have drawn attention to the fact that winters on Lesbos are not (and were not in antiquity) as severe as the winter described here in book 3.[1] Whether or not this is true, it is quite irrelevant in this context. Longus must paint a harsh winter, because the thematic development of the text demands it here. Those who have followed the course of books 1 and 2 will understand that. Daphnis and Chloe began in complete ignorance of the name and works of Eros. They have had to learn who Eros is; and along the way, they have been taught (or shown) his power, including something of the dangers that lurk in the sexual nature of human beings. They have yet to learn the works of Eros, however; and they have not yet really dealt with death, or at least have not recognized it as the precise antithesis of Eros. Winter must come, then, so that they may learn how love survives death.

As winter (B) is the season of death, so spring (B') is the promise and fulfillment of resurgent life. Daphnis and Chloe may now resume their life together in the fields, which has been interrupted by winter. The obvious correspondence of these seasonal images produces, then, a well-defined ring, however trite it may seem. Characteristically, though, Longus pushes matters just a little further. Both winter and spring bring their own discomforts to the lovers: winter separates them, confining them indoors, while spring subjects them to newly regenerated passions they still do not know how to assuage. In both cases, it is Daphnis who takes the first steps to overcome the difficulties posed by the seasons. This seizure of the initiative by Daphnis cannot be accepted, by Chloe or by the attentive reader, without a certain ambivalence, in view of what has so far been done with and by assertive males. This ambivalence is made all the deeper here by the fact that Daphnis's particular strategm for reuniting himself with Chloe in mid-winter is a hunting trip. The resonance of "Daphnis the Hunter" need hardly be belabored now. A similar ambivalence, then, may be felt at B', where Daphnis suggests to Chloe that they do something about their feelings. Chloe is full of doubts and reservations, which Daphnis overbears. To say that Daphnis bids fair to be a rapist, like Pan, would be going too far; but there is a shadow over both these scenes, all the same.

However pellucid the ring formed by the seasons and their effects, it is not the outermost ring of this cycle. When we juxtapose what comes just before the description of winter (i.e., the abortive war between Methymna and Mitylene) against what comes just after the description of spring (Daphnis's futile attempts to mate with Chloe), the results are both illuminating and surprising. Balanced against a brief digression into the world outside this self-contained pastoral world (A) is an episode (A') with which, at first glance, it seems to have little in common. Daphnis and Chloe see their animals mating and are filled with erotic passion. They decide to attempt Philetas's third remedy; but Daphnis intimates that there may be something beyond merely lying together γυμνὸς γυμνῇ. He suggests that he do to her what the rams are doing to the ewes, and the billy goats to the nanny goats. He and Chloe exchange observations about the techniques involved, and then proceed to try it out—and fail. At last Daphnis sits upon the ground and weeps, bewailing the fact that he is καὶ κρίων ἀμαθέστερος εἰς τὰ ἔρωτος ἔργα ("more un-learned even than billy goats in the works of Eros" [3.14.5]).

The tendency to use love and war as metaphors for each other is not a modern invention. As early as Homer, Ares and Aphrodite were lovers, and a later mythic tradition made them husband and wife. To trace the persistence of this theme from Homer's time to the second century A.D. would be both digressive and otiose just here; those who may be inclined to doubt are invited to look at Lucretius's treatment of sex in book IV of his *De Rerum Natura,* and (perhaps even more apposite) at the love scenes between Lucius and Fotis in Apuleius's *Metamorphoses.*[2] This is all part of the ambivalence of sex, which involves love and pleasure and ecstasy and union, all inextricably commingled with blood and pain and aggression and penetration. Later on in book 3, Daphnis will begin to learn all this and must deal with it; for now, ring A–A' serves to raise the issue, all in the context, as we have seen, of winter and death.

Ring A–A' also serves to point up an important contrast between war and love, in addition to that paradoxical analogy. Both the war and Daphnis's attempt to make love to Chloe are not brought to their logical conclusions. The war ends without violence, as Daphnis's efforts end without intercourse. In the first instance, however, the result of things not coming to fruition is peace and a return to a pleasant status quo; but Daphnis and Chloe experience anything but peace from their failure, while the status quo is, unbeknownst to them, about to change dramatically. And the proximate cause of the change is that someone has seen them trying to mate.

Before we follow this trail any further, we need to finish our examination of the first cycle. The obvious parallel between the sacrifice to Dionysus described at 3.10 (B) and the libations and hymns mentioned at 3.11 (B') narrows the rings in upon the pivot, while the preparation of the meal on the one hand (C), and the eating of it on the other (C'), bring us to this short but remarkable conversation between Daphnis and Chloe:

ἦν δὲ αὐτοῖς καὶ φιλημάτων ἀπόλαυσις συνεχὴς καὶ λόγων
ὁμιλία τερπνή. "διὰ σὲ ἦλθον, Χλόη." "οἶδα, Δάφνι." "διὰ σὲ
ἀπολλύω τοὺς ἀθλίους κοψίχους." "τίς οὖν σοι γένωμαι;" "μέ-
μνησό μου." "μνημονεύω νὴ τὰς Νύμφας ἃς ὤμοσά ποτε εἰσελ-
θοῦσα εἰς ἐκεῖνο τὸ ἄντρον εἰς ὃ ἥξομεν εὐθὺς ἡνίκα ἂν ἡ χιὼν
τακῇ." "ἀλλὰ πολλή ἐστι, Χλόη, καὶ δέδοικα μὴ ἐγὼ πρὸ ταύτης
τακῶ." "θάρρει, Δάφνι· θερμός ἐστιν ὁ ἥλιος." "εἰ γὰρ οὕτω γέ-
νοιτο, Χλόη, θερμός ὡς τὸ καῖον πῦρ τὴν καρδίαν τὴν εμήν."
"παίζεις ἀπατῶν με." "οὐ μὰ τὰς αἶγας, ἃς σύ με ἐκέλευες
ὀμνύειν."

(There came a time when they stopped kissing for a while, and
had a pleasant exchange of words.

"I came on your account, Chloe."

"I know, Daphnis."

"I'm killing these poor thrushes on your account."

"Who am I to you?"

"Remember me."

"I do remember, by the nymphs—I swore by them once, near
that grotto, where we will go right away, as soon as winter fades."

"But there is a lot of winter, Chloe, and I am afraid that I will
fade before it does."

"Be brave, Daphnis. The sun is hot."

"I wish it were as hot, Chloe, as the fire that is burning my
heart."

"You're teasing me."

"I am not, by those same goats you ordered me to swear by.")

(3.10)

This is a remarkable passage, on several scores. *Daphnis and
Chloe* is by no means devoid of dialogue, but nowhere else in the
entire novel does that dialogue approach so nearly to the give-
and-take of real conversation. At the same time, the whole passage is extremely artful; its casualness belies the subtlety of its
undertones, which any reader attuned to Longus's style and
preoccupations will quickly perceive. It is, in fact, very close in
form to what in a drama would be called *stichomythia* (i.e., στει-
χομνθία).[3] For that matter, there is also a particular term that
one might apply to the pivots of the first cycles in books 1 and 2,

THE WORKS OF EROS

each of which is a rather patent example of declamation, a rhetorical exercise. Understanding the relationship between these things, and the significance of that relationship, requires a brief excursus.

One of the salient features of the practice of rhetoric in late antiquity was the declamation, which is a speech, delivered to the general public by a professional orator or a noted teacher of rhetoric, typically on the same sorts of topics that were usually assigned to students in the schools of rhetoric. Thus the origin of the declamations is to be found in the schools, where rhetoric was always the primary subject. Over the centuries, the schoolmasters had developed a fairly large library, so to speak, of standard hypothetical scenarios in which speeches might be delivered. Some of these (called *controversiae* by the Romans) were fictive legal cases; others (the *suasoriae*) were based on historical or mythical situations, wherein some well-known character or group of characters was faced with an important decision. In the schools, then, the master would require a student to assume the character of some person involved in the fictitious situation and then to speak on one side or the other (often on both) of the matter at issue; the student's efforts would then be compared, for good or ill, to the efforts of other students, of previous orators and teachers, and not infrequently of the master himself. It is from the last of these, as it seems, that the practice of declamation arose. The master's demonstrations of his own skill in handling the stock topics for the edification of his pupils were gradually extended into public forum, and so rhetoric gradually became a spectator sport. The preserved orations of the major figures of the Second Sophistic, such as Aelius Aristides and Herodes Atticus, are for the most part the texts of just such declamations as these.[4]

Antiquity generally recognized three distinct species of oratory: forensic, deliberative, and epideictic. These were to be essentially distinguished from each other by their concern with the past, the future, and the present, respectively. Accordingly, there were various kinds of declamations that one might go to hear. Forensic oratory, which accounted for most declamations, was based on the *controversiae*, and so speeches of this sort were typically cast as fictive courtroom oratory, of prosecution or defense. Deliberative oratory, on the other hand, was involved with *suasoriae*, which often involved a mise-en-scène in a legislative body, council, or assembly of some sort; the contest between Ajax and Odysseus for the arms of Achilles was always a favorite. The most common form of epideictic declamation (to round out the catalog) was the panegyric, such as Aelius Aristides' oration, *To Rome*. There were, however, other epideictic forms, such as the ecphrasis, in which the orator would lavish all his rhetorical skill on the description of a work of art, or sometimes a building, a garden, or a lovely locale. The trick was to paint a mental picture, with words, that would create in the mind of the listener as nearly as possible the same effect as would the sight of the object itself. (This last form may prove to be of particular interest to us, since, as we have already seen, Longus plays with the notion that all of *Daphnis and Chloe* is an ecphrasis, in a riddling and paradoxical way.)

It is perhaps not too difficult to see how the speech contest in book 1 and the trial scene in book 2 can be called "declamations." We could easily go further and say that the speech contest in book 1 represents deliberative oratory, while the trial scene in book 2 is clearly forensic. But what about this odd conversation between Daphnis and Chloe in book 3?

A certain element of competition was always part of the "game" (in Greek, ἄγων [*agôn*]) of the declamation, as all the sporting metaphors used so far have clearly implied. Sometimes the competition was merely implicit: the public would turn out to hear a certain orator speak on a certain subject on a certain day and would naturally afterward compare his treatment of the subject to orations they might have heard before on the same subject, to the enhancement or detriment of the orator's reputation. At other times, however, the competition might be more direct, and two orators might appear to argue contrary positions on the same subject, or (perhaps more often) a rhetorician would appear, more or less uninvited, to "heckle" a rival's declamation.[5] There was often an element of challenge, too, in that the audience would occasionally be invited to propose a topic (ὑπόθεσις [*hypothesis*]), which the orator would then undertake to address extempore. There is some resemblance here to modern competitive debate, though the analogy is fairly weak and cannot be pushed too far. And it is to this especially agonistic declamation that the "debate" between Daphnis and Chloe seems to refer. That the latter is a declamation of sorts is even suggested by the phrase that Longus uses to describe it: λόγων ὁμιλία ("an exchange of words/arguments/speeches"), a phrase which, in another context, we might justifiably render "debate."

This tips Longus's hand. What he is placing at the pivot of the first cycle in each book is an exercise in formal rhetoric, of a kind both fashionable and familiar in his day: that is, a declamation. A taste for rhetoric pervades the whole novel, of course, so that displays of rhetorical artistry and point, in the broader sense of "rhetoric," are by no means confined to these particular passages. The descriptions of nature and of the seasons, the lovers's soliloquies, the lessons of Philetas, Daphnis's lament over the loss of Chloe—passages like these, too, are essential to what we might call the "pallette" of the professional rhetorician. Still, there is something unique about the three declamations thus far set apart by the structure. All three are carefully set up: as soon as Dorcon proposes a speech contest, the second-century reader knows exactly where we are.[6] Similarly, the convention of the mock trial would be familiar to anyone who spent a good deal of time going to declamations. Even the *stichomythia* bears a distinct resemblance to a species of rhetorical exercise that one might well have heard in the theatre, when competing declaimers would attempt to refute one another.[7]

The mention of theatre here is not accidental. The rhetoricians of Longus's day gave their declamations in theatres, and they sometimes collusively reenacted real-life situations in order to provide a matrix for their displays of verbal pyrotechnics. Conversely, the classical drama was always given to rhetoric. Euripides laid himself open to the barbs of Aristophanes precisely because of what the latter perceived as overblown and sensationalizing rhetoric, though this does not mean that Sophocles, or even Aeschylus, was ever immune to the Athenian predilection for sophistry. The Latin tragedies of Seneca, written a century or so before *Daphnis and Chloe*, are so very rhetorical that it has been conventional to suggest that they were written to be de-claimed rather than performed.[8] Each of these "declamation" scenes, then, has something of the theatre about it; but whether it is the theatre of the rhetorician or of the playwright seems im-possible to determine, at least for the moment.

In books 1 and 2, then, the pivot of the first cycle has been a declamation, in which Daphnis has been pitted against a male antagonist. In book 3, that antagonist, who before turned out to be an ironic reflection of Daphnis himself, is missing; but the analogous role of interlocutor is played by Chloe. She strikes the keynote at once: "οἶδα," she says, "I know." She knows why Daphnis has come; but she does not know "who she is to him." There is an untranslatable play here upon a fairly common fig-ure of speech in Greek. The interrogative pronoun with the dative is often used to say something like "What does that matter to me?" as when, in the story of the wedding at Cana in the Gos-pel of John, Jesus says to Mary, τί τοῦτο ἐμοὶ καὶ σοί, γυναί; ("What concern is this [sc. the fact that the bridegroom has run out of wine] of mine, or yours, woman?"). On one level, Chloe is asking Daphnis why she matters so much to him: "Am I really that important to you?" At the same time, the question τίς οὖν σοι γένωμαι means literally "Who am I, then, to you?" Even more literally, "Who have I become to you?" Significantly, Daphnis does not answer this pregnant question. Finally, Chloe knows that spring will come, that the sun's heat will bring life back; but she does not know if Daphnis is serious or not. Her statement, translated literally, means "You are playing with me, while in the process of deceiving me." This reminds us that Eros is a playful little boy who is incredibly dangerous. (It may also remind us that a novelist is also a deceiver and a player.)

Daphnis's side of this debate reveals more than meets the eye. He refers explicitly, and strikingly, to his destruction of little birds. Chloe, who has already been compared (by Daphnis) to a bird (that is, to Phatta), has reason to feel just a little alarmed by this. Challenged by Chloe's "Who am I to you?" he evades the issue and asks her, in a distinct non sequitur, to remember him. Chloe's reply recalls the oaths these lovers exchanged at the end of book 2; and this, in turn, seems to elicit Daphnis's fear that he will "fade"—manifestly, "die"—before the winter ends. Even the sun's heat brings no comfort, for Daphnis, in the dead of winter, is on fire, being consumed. By now, despite what appears to be an adamant refusal to follow a logical train of thought, Daphnis's underlying preoccupation is clear. He feels death all around him. That is why he has taken the initiative to seek Chloe out in this specious bird hunt; and that is also why, the next spring, he is the one who feels most keenly the urgency of erotic longing.

THE SECOND CYCLE

Chloe, of course, is not the least prepared to help Daphnis resolve the problem of erotic urgency posed by the first cycle. It is, rather, an "experienced" woman, from the city, who will take him in hand and show him τὴν τέως ζητουμένην ὁδὸν ("the till-now-sought-for road" [3.18]). The whole scene between Daphnis and Lycaenium is one of the most intriguing incidents, and Lycaenium herself one of the most intriguing characters, in all of *Daphnis and Chloe.* Their encounter obviously requires close and careful scrutiny.

Daphnis's sexual encounter with Lycaenium breaks several "rules" at once. To begin with, at least from the standpoint of bourgeois morality, Daphnis has broken his oath to Chloe. He never tells her of Lycaenium, as she never told him of the kiss she gave to the dying Dorcon in book 1. How innocent are these children, really? Then, too, Longus has transgressed that important convention of the Greek novel, the obligatory chastity (or at least mutual sexual fidelity) of hero and heroine.[9] As for Daphnis himself, he ambiguously seems both to know and not to know that his dalliance with Lycaenium is tantamount to infidelity. We who read *Daphnis and Chloe,* on the other hand, are under no illusions. This whole episode, in fact, is unmistakeably part of that fun that Longus consistently has with the conventions of the ancient novel, a topic which will be taken up in a later chapter.

Much has been written about the character of Lycaenium.[10] Her very name is an elaborate polysemous joke. The suffix "-ium" (-ion in Greek) is grammatically neuter, not feminine; the use of

a neuter form for a woman's name, in Greek or Latin, very often
means that the person so-named is a prostitute.[11] There is, in addition, evidence that variations on "she-wolf" names were much
affected among prostitutes in Graeco-Roman antiquity.[12] This
confirms any suspicions which might be aroused by the fact that
Lycaenium is from the city and is erotically experienced: she is a
former prostitute who has married and left "the life" behind.

This last point brings out another level of irony in this character. In book 1, the image of the wolf was pervasive, and ambiguous: the real wolf (λύκαινα, *lykaina*), whose depredations could
be forgiven, was played off against a human masquerading as a
wolf, Dorcon, who was not so easily forgiven. Here, in book 3,
we have a human "she-wolf," who seems to be something like
both of the "wolves" in book 1. She is erotic and predatory; but
she performs what certainly seems to be an essential service. She
completes that part of the lesson which Philetas left untaught:
that is, the ἔργα of Eros. In that sense, then, it would be safe
enough to say that she is doing nature's work. But this inoffen-
sive and easy inference has tempted more than one scholar to go
further, to see her as a mystagogue, one charged with teaching
initiates the mysteries into which they seek induction.[13] Lycaenium certainly tempts that conclusion when she propositions
Daphnis with such words as these: ἐρᾷς . . . , Δάφνι, Χλόης, καὶ
τοῦτο ἔμαθον ἐγὼ νύκτωρ παρὰ τῶν Νυμφῶν δι' ὀνείρατος, αἵ
μοι καὶ τὰ χθιζά σου διηγήσαντο δάκρυα καὶ ἐκέλευσάν σε
σῶσαι διδαξαμένην τὰ ἔρωτος ἔργα ("'You are in love . . . with
Chloe, Daphnis; I learned this at night from the nymphs, in a
dream; they told me of yesterday's tears, and they ordered me to
save you by teaching you the works of Eros'" [3.17]).

This is all very well and sounds very mystical and profound,
except for one thing: Lycaenium is lying.[14] In chapter 15, Longus
tells us, in unambiguous terms, how Lycaenium has seen Daphnis
in the fields and lusted after him. She has surreptitiously observed his futile attempts to consummate his passion for Chloe
and has recognized this as her opportunity to get what she
wants. There has been no dream. Insofar as she is a mystagogue
of Eros, then, she plays the role for her own reasons, which are

anything but disinterested. Thus when she has finished her lesson, she enjoins Daphnis always to remember that she, not Chloe, first made a man of him (3.19).

Whether or not Lycaenium is properly seen as a mystagogue of Eros, she is certainly his pedagogue. This naturally invites a comparison with Philetas. Philetas, who is old and male and rustic, teaches Daphnis and Chloe the first thing that they must know to become lovers: the name and function of Eros. Lycaenium teaches Daphnis, and only Daphnis, the rest of the lesson. The language she uses indicates clearly the inadequacy, both of the old man's erotic pedagogy, and of Daphnis's clumsy attempts to learn directly from nature: τὰ δέ [sc., τὰ ἔρωτος ἔργα] ἐστιν οὐ φίλημα καὶ περιβολὴ καὶ οἷα δρῶσι κριοὶ καὶ τράγοι ("These [that is, the works of Eros] are not [just] kissing and hugging and such things as the rams and the billy goats do" [3.17]).[15] Lycaenium, who is young, female, and urban, will make it possible for Daphnis to do what Philetas could only hint at, all too obscurely. So much for any facile conclusion that in *Daphnis and Chloe* the city comes off second best in any comparison with the country.

But there is more at issue here than the city mouse and the country mouse; another brief excursus seems to be in order. One of the chief battlegrounds in the ongoing war between philosophy and rhetoric in antiquity was the education of the young. Both the sophist and the philosopher were teachers; the former promised eloquence to his pupils, the latter wisdom. It is in this light that we should probably understand the parallel "careers" of these two teachers in *Daphnis and Chloe*, Philetas and Lycaenium. Philetas tells Daphnis and Chloe a story, but it does them little good: they are delighted, ὥσπερ μῦθον οὐ λόγον ἀκούσαντες ("as though they had heard a *mythos* and not a *logos*"), but not instructed, or at least not enough to derive any practical benefit from the teaching.[16] Enlightenment does not come until Lycaenium teaches Daphnis what Philetas's words really mean. "['Ί]θι," she says to him, "παραδίδου μοι τερπνὸν σαυτὸν μαθητήν· ἐγὼ δὲ χαριζομένη ταῖς Νύμφαις ἐκεῖνα διδάξω" ("'Come on, give me your sweet self as my student: I will teach you these things, as a favor to the nymphs'" [3.17]). Then, when the lesson is over, we hear more of this "pedagogical" language: τελεσθείσης δὲ τῆς ἐρωτικῆς **παιδαγωγίας** ὁ μὲν Δάφνις ἔτι ποιμενικὴν γνώμην ἔχων ὥρμητο τρέχειν ἐπὶ τὴν Χλόην καὶ ὅσα **πεπαίδευτο** δρᾶν αὐτίκα ("After he had had his erotic *lesson*, Daphnis, since he still had the mind-set of a herdsman, set out to run to Chloe and do at once the things he had just been *taught*" [3.19]).[17] He has yet more to learn, however; and indeed, so protracted is the whole process by which Daphnis and Chloe learn about Eros that the reader may well be reminded of Plato's admonition (in the *Republic*) that the student who wishes to learn philosophy must go by τὴν μακροτέραν ὁδόν, "the longer way."[18] So it is that neither Philetas, the speaker of words, nor Lycaenium, the doer of deeds, is entirely successful as a teacher. It is not that Philetas is merely a sophist who fails, and even less that Lycaenium is a philosopher. *Daphnis and Chloe* as a whole cannot be reduced to a simple allegory of the war between philosophy and rhetoric. What does seem to be at issue is a certain rivalry between two schemes of education: one founded on discourse (λόγος), which is represented by Philetas, and which, though it starts the lovers on their way to fulfillment, cannot guide them all the way there; the other, a "practical" education (the ἔργα), which is represented by Lycaenium, and which, though it shows Daphnis the "till-now-sought-for road," also stops short of complete success.

Does this imply that there is another teacher, someone who will take Daphnis and Chloe all the way to the full knowledge of Eros? If the Platonic analogy may again be invoked, we must answer yes. The third teacher will be the philosopher, who, in the *Republic*, follows after the teachers of music and gymnastics, to complete what they have left undone. No such character appears in the course of Longus's story, of course; but the fact remains (if we may look ahead for just a moment) that Chloe finally does learn the lesson. This is made abundantly clear by the last sentence of *Daphnis and Chloe*:

Δάφνις δὲ καὶ Χλόη γυμνοὶ συγκατακλιθέντες περιέβαλλον ἀλλήλους καὶ κατεφίλουν ἀγρυπνήσαντες τῆς νυκτὸς ὅσον οὐδὲ γλαῦκες· καὶ ἔδρασέ τι Δάφνις ὧν αὐτὸν ἐπαίδευσε Λυκαίνιον,

καὶ τότε Χλόη πρῶτον ἔμαθεν ὅτι τὰ ἐπὶ τῆς ὕλης γινόμενα ἦν
ποιμένων παίγνια.

(Daphnis and Chloe lay down together naked, and embraced and
kissed each other, staying awake all night even more than owls;
and Daphnis did some of what Lycaenium had taught him, and
then Chloe first learned that all those goings-on in the woods
were shepherds' games.) (4.40)

In this last sentence, Lycaenium is mentioned by name, and
Philetas is clearly invoked by language that recalls his "three
remedies." What brings their respective lessons to fulfillment is
not, however, any shadowy third teacher but rather the working
out of the plot, for which, it will be recalled, the Greek word is,
literally, "myth"; and all this is the work, not of any one character, but of the author.[19] For λόγος (logos) has two possible an-
tonyms: ἔργον (ergon, "work" or "fact") and μῦθος (mythos). With
the meaning of the latter term we have already had some deal-
ings and will have yet more.

In book 2, the instruction that Philetas gave to Daphnis and Chloe
was structurally balanced by the dream vision of the nymphs, in
which Daphnis learned how Eros would make manifest his providential protection of Chloe. In book 3, the instruction given by
Lycaenium (a) is also balanced by an episode that begins with
Daphnis's having a dream vision of the nymphs, who again promise salvation (a'). Here, the nymphs tell Daphnis how to become
a husband.[20] He must find a dead dolphin, rotting on the shore.
So odd is this that we are tempted to take it as a symbol of something, which, of course, it is. The dolphin was always associated
with Dionysus; that is why this particular narrative detail has
always been, for those who want to read Daphnis and Chloe as a
Dionysiac allegory, grist for the mill. As was the case with the
mystagogy of Lycaenium, however, there is a fly in the ointment.
The dolphin in question is not a miraculous messenger from on
high but a real dolphin, all too corporeal, who has swallowed a
bag of money from that ship lost by the Methymneans in book 2;
it is not merely dead but putrid, so much so that Daphnis can
hardly stand to approach it. Dionysus's totemic animal could

hardly appear in a more unsavory light; and the whole thing seems more and more to be an elaborate joke, much like the rapacity (and mendacity) of Lycaenium. Anyone who wants to take all this in dead earnest will have to swallow very hard.

The final episode in book 3 closes the ring very neatly. Daphnis and Chloe, in high spirits because they have just been formally betrothed, are frolicking in the fields when Daphnis spots an apple still clinging to its branch after the others have fallen off or been harvested: καὶ ἓν μῆλον ἐπέκειτο ἐν αὐτοῖς ἄκροις ἀκρότα-τον, μέγα καὶ καλὸν, καὶ τῶν πολλῶν τὴν εὐωδίαν ἐνίκα μόνον ("And one apple remained, the highest in the very heights [of the tree], big and beautiful and alone, unique among all the others in the sweetness of its smell" [3.33]). Many have seen in Longus's diction here an echo of a famous fragment from the poems of Sappho: οἷον τὸ γλυκύμαλον ἐρεύθεται ἄκρῳ ἐπ' ὕσδῳ, / ἄκρον ἐπ' ἀκροτάτῳ, λελάθοντο δὲ μαλοδρόπηες· / οὐ μὰν ἐκλελάθοντ', ἀλλ' οὐκ ἐδύναντ' ἐπίκεσθαι. (As when the sweet apple grows red upon a high branch, / High among the highest, and the apple pickers missed it— / No, they didn't miss it, they couldn't reach it).[21]

What the fragment from Sappho means is not difficult to grasp. The first word, οἷον, clearly indicates that our fragment is a simile. That it is a simile for a virgin seems almost as clear, especially since the information available about the fragment suggests that it comes from an *epithalamium*, a wedding song, composed to be sung at the entrance to the bridal chamber. Daphnis's boldness in climbing the tree to fetch the apple, Chloe's reluctance for him to do so, her anger at his persistence, and the words he uses to placate her with the gift of the apple, all point to Longus's conscious appropriation of the referent of Sappho's simile along with its language. Daphnis is on the very threshold, at last, of manhood. And the two of them are on the threshold of marriage. As we shall see, this involves a certain risk for the still-virginal Chloe, whose fate is more and more in Daphnis's hands.

The two episodes (a–a') in which Daphnis becomes a man/ husband, ανήρ, are followed and preceded, in the usual specular arrangement, by episodes in which he receives advice (or something like advice) from women (b–b'). Lycaenium tells Daphnis that Chloe, because she is a virgin, will bleed and cry out the first time he does with her what he has just done with Lycaenium. Later on, Myrtale (his adoptive mother) explains to Daphnis that he is far too poor to be an acceptable suitor for Chloe's hand. Both of these women, then, tell Daphnis something he would rather not hear, something that will keep him from achieving his most immediate object. He is momentarily checked in his progress toward erotic fulfillment, though rather clearly more so by what Lycaenium says. What Myrtale says is only a temporary problem, which divine providence solves at once.

Herein lies an important distinction, which leads into the next ring. Lycaenium has no intention of preventing Daphnis from making love to Chloe; she only means to warn him that it will not be quite the same. It is Daphnis who decides that the blood and the pain are not acceptable prices to pay, so that he abstains from making sexual advances to Chloe until after they are married (c). Thus the obstacle presented by Lycaenium's warning is internal and personal. On the other hand, the obstacle to the marriage, as explained by Myrtale, is social and external. It has nothing to do with an exercise of will. Thus Daphnis's decision not to make love to Chloe is not answered by any decision he makes, but rather by a decision that Dryas makes (c'), to stall the importunate suitors. In the process, Chloe's predicament, the predicament of every marriageable woman in ancient Greek society, is made clear: her fate, the course of her life, will always be decided by men, first by her father, and then by her husband.

The pivot of the second cycle is, of course, the *aition* of Echo. The rings which immediately surround this pivot are fairly elaborate, and some of them are very subtle and intricate. At 3.21, a ship sails by, and Longus is at pains to tell us that it is laden with fish for the tables of the rich in Mitylene; the detail is ominous, in that we have already seen what happens when rich men from the city arrive by sea.[22] The implicit threat posed to the penniless Daphnis by those who have more money than he (d) soon becomes explicit, when suitors for Chloe's hand begin to approach Dryas (d'). This crisis, in which Lycaenium's lesson is of no use, will have the greatest import for the further development of the plot, as we shall soon see.

As Daphnis and Chloe watch the ship going by, they hear first the sailors singing and then the echo of their song bouncing off the cliffs. Chloe (whose naiveté in this passage is almost beyond belief) does not know what an echo is (e), but Daphnis does; he is in possession of knowledge beyond that of Chloe, and in other matters besides the etiology of echoes. Chloe promises him ten kisses as a reward for enlightening her (f); when he has done so, she is delighted to pay (f').[23] Then Daphnis plays his flute, and Chloe hears the echo of his music (e') with the new understanding given her by the story she has just heard.

The story that Daphnis tells here is not at all the familiar story of Echo, the nymph enamoured of Narcissus. The latter makes no appearance in this story at all; and Echo, rather than pining away until she is nothing but a voice, is instead ripped to shreds by shepherds, who are temporarily maddened by a spurned and vindictive Pan. The scattered pieces of her body retain their voice, and speak reflected words. What is truly appalling about all this is that the links between Echo and Chloe are so manifold and so obvious. At the pivot of the first cycle, in fact, Longus has already likened her to an echo: τοιαῦτα ἀντιφωνήσασα πρὸς τὸν Δάφνιν ἡ Χλόη καθάπερ ἠχώ ("Chloe, having answered Daphnis in this way like an echo" [3.11]).[24] Like Echo, too, Chloe is a virgin, while the blood of Echo's dismemberment can hardly fail to remind us of Lycaenium's warning. This whole awful story, then, brings to a climax the theme of death with which book 3 began. Life implies death; sex is a metaphor for renewed life, the answer to death, and yet, with painful irony, involves blood and pain. Life, death, and sex are all inextricably interwoven.

It would be a mistake, however, to assume that all the overtones of the Echo story are ominous. Many have noted (and exploited) the resemblance between the story Daphnis tells here and certain well-known myths about death and dismemberment. The most obvious parallel is the story of Orpheus, the mythical archetype of all musicians, who spurns the company of women after his unsuccessful attempt to rescue Eurydice from the underworld. He is set upon by Maenads, who rip him to pieces in the usual way; but his head floats down the river, still singing. (Significantly, one minor tradition has it that this singing head

floated out to sea and came ashore on Lesbos.) Often syncreti-
cally fused with the Orpheus myth is the dismemberment of
Zagreus-Dionysus, who is torn apart by the Titans and reassembled by Zeus (or Hermes, at the latter's command); in some
versions, Zagreus is a mortal, apotheosized by his death and resurrection into the god Dionysus. Both of these tales of dismemberment were central cult myths for the mysteries, as can be
easily imagined.

Naturally enough, these manifest parallels, which it would be
both useless and unnecessary to deny, have provided considerable ammunition for those scholars who argue that all of *Daphnis
and Chloe* is an allegory of the mysteries. What we have already
seen, however, may suggest that, for Longus, the mystery cults
subserve other aims, which are specifically literary. Throughout
book 3, the text has been concerned with life, death, and sex,
and this provides a thematic matrix into which the imagery
of the mysteries fits very well. Thus the evocation of death-and-
resurrection myths in the story of Echo serves to remind us that
death implies life as much as life implies death. This can be
taken in a religious sense, of course; but we have already seen
how consistently Longus resists taking divine imagery too seriously, as in the matters of Lycaenium's motives and the rotten
dolphin. To read *Daphnis and Chloe* as a relentless religious allegory, therefore, is ultimately as perverse as to avert one's eyes
from the patently religious imagery that intrudes itself upon our
attention throughout the entire novel.

The story of Echo is the last of the digressive *aitia* and the climax of a sequence. Chloe has thus far been clearly and unambiguously identified with all three female protagonists. Let us
now briefly review how these *aitia* have progressed:

Phatta was a mortal girl, confronted with male aggression in a
very sublimated form: an anonymous boy, who is undoubtedly
male, and yet, like all boys, has something of female sexuality
about him. Daphnis and Dorcon were both parallel to him, showing that one aspect of Daphnis's nature might pose a threat to
Chloe. Because of her unbearable grief, Phatta asked for transformation and became a musical bird: no longer human but free
and animate nonetheless.

Syrinx was a mortal girl who consorted with nymphs. Her male antagonist was Pan, who had rape on his mind and who, again, was somehow to be connected with Daphnis. She was transformed as an alternative to rape, and became a "musical" plant: still alive, but rooted in the ground, until plucked and filled with another's breath.

Echo is mortal, but born of a nymph mother, and raised among the divine and semidivine. She is again confronted by Pan, but it is not rape this time. Pan is jealous of her musical ability, for one thing; for another, he is apparently disappointed sexually, but this is enigmatically stated, so that we cannot be sure what precisely has happened.[25] She is transformed, not as a merciful alternative to a death from grief, or to rape, but only after she has been violently dismembered.[26] Mother Earth preserves her voice, out of love and respect for the nymphs; there is, however, an undertone of resurrection.

Thus Chloe, through these stories, is confronted with the central mysteries of life. What this all means for her, and for Daphnis, will be revealed in book 4.

Chapter 6

Book 4:
Man and Wife

The final book of *Daphnis and Chloe* seems in various ways to depart from the narrative pattern, and to some extent even from
the tone and ambience, of the rest of the novel.[1] To begin with,
in all the excitement of the denouement, no one seems to have
the time to tell anyone else a story. It would seem, then, that
there is no *aition* in book 4. Only slightly less troublesome is
the apparent absence of something obviously analogous to the
speech contest in book 1, the trial scene in book 2, or the "debate" in book 3; in other words, a quick glance at book 4 fails to
turn up an obvious declamation, which might serve as a pivot for
a presumed "first cycle." Still, there are some obvious reduplica-
tions in book 4, which suggests that we may find specular images
here, too; and where there are specular images, so far, there
have been rings. But working them out, in the face of these difficulties, will require a return to something like the inductive
method we used to explicate the structure of book 1.

MYTH

The two anagnorisis scenes of Daphnis and Chloe are clearly
parallel to each other. On one level, these scenes in book 4 serve
to balance the corresponding scenes in book 1, in which Daphnis
and Chloe are in turn exposed, nurtured by animals, and discov-

ered by the shepherds who become their adoptive fathers. We saw that these "finding" scenes at the very beginning of the novel seem to be outside of (or prior to) the overall structural scheme of the first book, and in fact they do not work themselves out in that distinctive chiastic or specular manner which prevails throughout most of the rest of *Daphnis and Chloe*. First a series of things happens to the infant Daphnis, A–B–C, and then the same things happen to Chloe, A'–B'–C'. If the parallel anagnorisis scenes in book 4 are carefully examined, however, it quickly becomes apparent that they are constructed rather differently from the exposure scenes in book 1. One of the salient features of a specular image is that it reflects its original accurately, but in reverse (A–B–C, C'–B'–A'), which has, in fact, been true of the specular images with which we have dealt so far. This is not true of the exposure and discovery scenes in book 1, where the finding of the infant Chloe is merely a doublet of the similar scene that preceeds it. By contrast, Longus seems to have gone to such trouble to make Chloe's anagnorisis scene a specular image of Daphnis's that a certain amount of strain becomes apparent.

At a moment of crisis, when Daphnis is about to be awarded as a plaything to the pederast Gnathon, Lamon steps forward and announces that Daphnis was not born a slave. Challenged to produce evidence of this remarkable assertion, he goes home and fetches back the tokens that he found with the infant Daphnis. The master, Dionysophanes, immediately recognizes these tokens and calls to his wife. She, too, knows them at once, and says aloud what they both have instantly realized: φίλε ἄνερ, ἡμέτερόν ἐστι τὸ παιδίον· σὸς υἱός ἐστι Δάφνις, καὶ πατρῷας ἔνεμεν αἶγας ("Dear husband, the child is ours: Daphnis is your son, and he has been herding his father's goats" [4.21]).[2] Astylus (Dionysophanes' other son) then runs to fetch the boy now known to be his brother; he gives Daphnis some of his own rich clothes to wear, brings him back before the crowd, and presents him to their common father. Dionysophanes then proceeds to tell those assembled how and why he came to expose the child, and why he is now, after being restored to good fortune, more than pleased to have him back. As a token of his transition from shepherd and slave to master and heir, Daphnis dedicates the accoutrements of his pastoral life, his *pastoralia,* (τὰ ποιμενικὰ κτήματα [4.26]) to Dionysus.

Meanwhile, Chloe, who has fled the scene in despair, is kidnapped by Lampis but almost immediately rescued by none other than Gnathon, who is anxious to redeem himself in the eyes of his would-be catamite turned master. The next day (as it remains painfully unclear what is to become of the proposed marriage between Daphnis and Chloe), Dryas appears with the tokens that he, in his turn, found with Chloe, and then suggests to the group (not unreasonably) that Chloe, too, must be of noble birth.[3] This time, no one present recognizes the tokens, but it is abundantly clear that Chloe is no more the daughter of Dryas than Daphnis is the son of Lamon. The decision is made that all should return to Mitylene together, where the mystery of Chloe's birth will be unraveled. Before they leave, Chloe, like Daphnis, dedicates her pastoral accoutrements, this time to the nymphs. After they arrive in Mitylene, Dionysophanes (following instructions he received in a dream) invites all the noble families of the city to a great banquet at his house. While Chloe herself waits in an antechamber, Dionysophanes commands a servant to circulate among the crowd with Chloe's recognition tokens. One of the wealthiest men of Mitylene, Megacles, cries out at once that they are his, and proceeds to tell the assembled crowd how he was forced by hard times to expose a daughter, whom he now, in his prosperity, wants back. Chloe is then brought out, richly dressed, and presented to him.

Thus the anagnorisis of Chloe is a specular image, not merely a reiteration, of that of Daphnis. The result is something like this:

A. Daphnis is acknowledged to be Dionysophanes' son and is then brought before his father, richly dressed for the first time (4.20–23)

   B. Dionysophanes tells the story of Daphnis's exposure (4.24)

      C. Daphnis dedicates his *pastoralia* (4.26)

      C'. Chloe dedicates her *pastoralia* (4.32)

   B'. Megacles tells the story of her exposure (4.35)

A′. Chloe is brought before her father richly dressed and is acknowledged as his daughter (4.36)

This pattern has worked itself out so many times by now that its operation here could only with difficulty be denied. Conversely, recognizing that all this shows every sign of being the second cycle of book 4 leads directly to two important inferences: first, that somewhere between the two "dedication" scenes we shall find something analogous to the *aitia* that have lain at the pivot of the second cycle in each of the first three books; and second, that there is likely to be a first cycle, too, in book 4.[4] We shall deal with both of these inferences, then, beginning with the first.

At 4.27, Longus shifts the scene away from the spontaneous celebration that follows the anagnorisis of Daphnis, and moves the focus to Chloe: Ἐν ᾧ δὲ Δάφνις ἐν θυσίαις ἦν,[5] τάδε γίνεται περὶ τὴν Χλόην ("While Daphnis was involved in his sacrifices, this is what was going on with Chloe"). This kind of "meanwhile" is a stock in trade for the other ancient novelists; the fact that the hero and heroine of most Greek novels are separated for much of the novel makes such narrative strategies inevitable, if sometimes infelicitous. Longus, on the contrary, though he does indeed separate his protagonists from time to time, indulges in "Meanwhile, back at the ranch" only here.[6] To those scholars who have seen *Daphnis and Chloe* as a kind of hybrid, a conventional "love romance" grafted onto the tradition of pastoral poetry, this particular passage is easily explained (away) as a seam or joint between the two members of which they imagine the whole novel to consist. That is not an especially helpful way of reading *Daphnis and Chloe*, however, and the results of the present reading suggest that a more important transition is being marked here than a seam between Theocritus and Chariton. Rather, the diction here serves to detach the incidents about to enfold and make them into a kind of miniature, enclosed within the larger context of book 4. And these incidents are precisely περὶ τὴν Χλόην, literally, "about Chloe."

What happens to her is this: Lampis, a brutish cowherd with a certain resemblance to the late Dorcon, sees in all the excitement surrounding Daphnis's anagnorisis an opportunity to have his

way with Chloe and kidnaps her. The deed is witnessed and re-
ported, ultimately, to Daphnis; but he is paralyzed by fear and
shame, and so responds to the situation by sitting in the garden
and lamenting to himself the untoward consequences of his newfound identity. He is overheard by none other than Gnathon,
who promptly runs to Lampis's hut and rescues Chloe from the
villain's clutches. He then brings her back and presents her to
Daphnis, with the request that Daphnis, in effect, show his grati-
tude by forgetting that unfortunate episode in which Gnathon
had attempted to seduce Daphnis. The latter is pleased to comply,
and embraces his beloved Chloe. There still remains, however,
the ticklish problem of the marriage; but this is solved by Dryas,
who proceeds at once to show Chloe's *gnorismata* to Dionysophanes and Cleariste, with the results that we have already seen.

It does not require an excess of imagination to see several interesting parallels between this episode and the *aitia* of Phatta,
Syrinx, and Echo. All the basic elements are present. There is a
beautiful young maiden who has been successively and unambiguously identified with each of the three others; there is a male
antagonist who is a cowherd like Phatta's antagonist and intends
rape like Pan; there is a confrontation between them, and a cry
for help; and, at the last, the maiden emerges from that confrontation in some other guise: she is not what she was before.
What this means, in short, is that the pivot of the second cycle in
book 4 is what amounts to the *aition* of Chloe.

This has been prepared for, of course, and not only through
the identification of Chloe with Phatta, Syrinx, and Echo. In
book 2, after Chloe has been kidnapped by the Methymnean expedition, its general, Bryaxis, is visited by a dream vision of Pan,
in which the latter upbraids the former for laying hands on
Chloe, παρθένον ἐξ ἧς Ἔρως μῦθον ποιῆσαι θέλει ("a girl of
whom Eros wants to make a myth" [2.27]). Now an *aition* is, after
all, a species of myth; and, lest we miss the point, Longus is careful to use the word "myth" in or around each of the *aitia* in
books 1, 2, and 3.[7] That book 4, then, contains the *aition*, or
"myth," of Chloe should come as no real surprise. What is surprising, on the other hand, is that the role of the teller, which is
played by Daphnis in books 1 and 3, and by Lamon in book 2, is
played in book 4 by someone entirely outside of the novel's fic-

tive world: that is, by Longus himself. Longus has been preparing us all along, it seems, to witness the birth of a myth, one which emerges, not from a timeless tradition, but from the pen of this author. This, as we shall see, is something of profound importance.

Chloe's *aition*, then, is the culmination of the whole process of development that started with Phatta in book 1, and has proceeded through the stories of Syrinx and Echo. In each case, a female protagonist is confronted by a male antagonist who wants something she has. Thus confronted with male sexual aggression, the woman must choose between accepting the loss or being transformed, becoming something other than a παρθένος, a maiden. For Phatta, Syrinx, and Echo, the latter alternative involves the loss of human status; but for Chloe, there is another way. She can choose to be possessed by Daphnis, a male who has been progressively educated in his role as sexual aggressor and has even had a turn at being a sexual object himself. By this choice she is able to be both human and a possession: that is, a wife. As such, she finds a modus vivendi with male sexuality, one which is appropriate to her nature and to her situation. Her finding of such a way out is thus the thematic end toward which the structure of the whole novel has been tending. This is what renders *Daphnis and Chloe* capable of being both an offering to the divine world and a delight for the human, as was promised in the prologue: namely, that it is a myth, a story that builds a bridge between the human and the divine.

To this point, then, we have followed the cycle that frames the myth of Chloe inward to its pivot. We have not yet reached, however, the outermost ring. The anagnorisis of Daphnis was precipitated, as we saw, by the efforts of the pederast Gnathon to obtain Daphnis as his plaything. This begins with Gnathon's effort to seduce Daphnis, who spurns his overtures with contempt and finally throws him on the ground. Gnathon, determined to have his way, solicits his master, Astylus, to have Daphnis brought to the city to serve in the household, thus putting him at Gnathon's disposal. Astylus consents, but Lamon intervenes by revealing that Daphnis is of higher birth than anyone had suspected, with the consequences we have already seen.

The language used by Daphnis in reply to Gnathon's homosexual proposition clearly evokes the language of that important scene in book 3, where Daphnis and Chloe try to consummate their passion by imitating the sheep and the goats. The parallel is obvious when the key sentences from each passage are juxtaposed:

τῆς δὲ [sc. Χλόης] πυνθανομένης τί πλέον ἐστι φιλήματος καὶ περιβολῆς καὶ αὐτῆς κατακλίσεως καὶ τί ἔγνωκε δρᾶσαι γυμνὸς γυμνῇ συγκατακλινείς, "τοῦτο," εἶπεν, "ὃ οἱ κριοὶ ποιοῦσι τὰς ὄις καὶ οἱ τράγοι τὰς αἶγας."

(When she [that is, Chloe] asked what more there was than kissing and embracing and that whole business of lying together, and what he knew of that a nude man might do lying next to a nude woman, he answered, "The same thing that the rams do to the ewes, and the billy goats to the nanny goats.") (3.14)

τοῦ δὲ (sc. Δάφνιδος) βραδέως νοήσαντος καὶ λέγοντος ὡς αἶγας μὲν βαίνειν τράγους καλόν, τράγον δὲ οὐπώποτέ τις εἶδε βαίνοντα τράγον οὐδὲ κριὸν ἀντὶ τῶν ὄιων κριὸν οὐδὲ ἀλεκτρυόνας ἀντὶ τῶν ἀλεκτορίδων τοὺς ἀλεκτρυόνας, οἷός τε ἦν ὁ Γνάθων βιάζεσθαι τὰς χεῖρας προσφέρων.

(Daphnis finally understood and said that it was fine for billy goats to mount nanny goats but that no one had ever seen a billy goat mount another billy goat, or a ram mount a ram instead of ewes, or roosters mount roosters instead of hens. Gnathon, then, was ready to force the issue, and laid hands on him.) (4.12)

One might already suspect that the intended sexual transaction between Gnathon and Daphnis might be an ironic image, an εἴρων, of the proposed marriage between Daphnis and Chloe, even if nothing more were said. But in fact there are further reasons to connect them. Both Gnathon's attempted acquisition of Daphnis and the latter's marriage with Chloe involve the regularization of sexual relations, wherein one partner becomes the exclusive sexual property of the other.[8] Daphnis is a party to both of these "arrangements"; but his role in each situation is obviously reversed. However naive and innocent he appears to be, Daphnis is the pursuer of Chloe, as Pan is the pursuer of Syrinx. Conversely, he is the quarry of Gnathon, and is placed, at the very crisis of the novel, precisely in the role usually played by

Chloe. There is, then, no small irony in the use of his encounter with Gnathon as a specular image, albeit a perverted one, of his marriage with Chloe. This irony is further compounded by the fact that marriage and its perverse image together constitute the outer ring of the very cycle which frames the myth of Chloe.[9] And all this may serve to explain why it must be Lampis, not Daphnis, who plays the "Pan" role in what we have come to recognize as the *aition* of Chloe: the whole point of Daphnis's erotic education has been to teach him *not* to play that role.

We are now prepared to understand how it happens that in chapter 2 we could follow the lexical threads of the nouns ἱκέτης and θεατής from the prologue to this absurd figure of Gnathon. He is a character we are prepared to detest and abominate, embodying as he does everything that is perverted about sexuality. Yet he turns out to be necessary, after all, precisely because he also embodies everything that is the precise inverse of Daphnis himself. He is ugly, urban, depraved, while Daphnis is beautiful, pastoral, and innocent; but we have seen that the latter's innocence ultimately proves to be an obstacle to his growth, so that he must lose at least some of it before he can become a man. Thus his world, his κόσμος, must learn how to incorporate that for which Gnathon stands, in order to control it. Marriage does not operate by suppressing sexuality but rather by disciplining it, as Gnathon is finally disciplined and thereby redeemed.

ECPHRASIS

The explication of the second cycle of book 4, now at least provisionally complete, leads directly to that second inference mentioned at the beginning of this chapter, that the presence of a "myth" at the pivot of an elaborate cycle of specular images implies the presence of a preceeding "declamation" cycle. By process of elimination, then, we seem to be virtually compelled by all this to view the first ten chapters of book 4 as the first cycle of that book. The results generated by such a hypothesis turn out to be neither repugnant nor contrived. The outer limits of this cycle are not overly difficult to pick out, after all. Book 4 begins with the arrival of a messenger, heralding the imminent arrival of the master, Dionysophanes; at 4.10, Astylus arrives, a few days ahead of his father. These two arrivals, then, which set the stage for the denouement of the novel, constitute the outer ring for the first cycle. As we move inward from here, we find, just within this outer ring, the beautiful garden that Lamon tends for his master.[10] More particularly, at 4.1, Lamon begins his feverish preparations for Dionysophanes' arrival, concentrating his efforts on the garden. At 4.7, however, Chloe's disappointed suitor and soon-to-be abductor, Lampis, despoils the garden, throwing Lamon into great despair. His efforts to impress the master (described at 4.4–6) will be in vain; the beauty of the garden, which is rendered in loving detail at 4.2–3, is spoiled.

What emerges from all of this is a cycle something like this:

A. The coming of Dionysophanes is announced (4.1)

    B. Preparations begin (4.1)

        C. The beauty of the garden (4.2–3)

        C'. The beautification of the garden (4.4–6)

    B'. Despoliation and despair (4.7–9)

A'. The arrival of Dionysophanes is heralded (4.10)

What lies in the center of this cycle? The answer comes from a consideration of the themes that connect the description of the garden (C) with the description of Lamon's effort to get it (and the whole farm) ready for the master's inspection (C'). The garden represents an attempt to improve upon the beauty of nature; the plants and trees are beautiful but require the gardener's hand (always concealed) to reveal their beauty to the eye. There are two desired effects: to make the artful appear natural and to make the natural appear artful. This causes two principles that are usually distinct, φύσις, "nature," and τέχνη, "skill," to be conflated and harmonized into the creation of something more beautiful than either alone could achieve. This is made clear by the very language Longus uses here, which is characteristically both playful and evocative:

τέτμητο καὶ διακέκριτο πάντα, καὶ στέλεχος στελέχους ἀφειστή-
κει· ἐν μετεώρῳ δὲ οἱ κλάδοι συνέπιπτον ἀλλήλοις καὶ ἐπήλλατ-
τον τὰς κόμας· ἐδόκει μέντοι καὶ ἡ τούτων φύσις εἶναι τέχνης.
ἦσαν καὶ ἀνθῶν πρασιαί, ὧν τὰ μὲν ἔφερεν ἡ γῆ, τὰ δὲ ἐποίει
τέχνη· ῥοδωνιαὶ καὶ ὑάκινθοι καὶ κρίνα χειρὸς ἔργα, ἰωνιὰς καὶ
ναρκίσσους καὶ ἀναγαλλίδας ἔφερεν ἡ γῆ.
(Everything was cut and trimmed, and root was separated from
root; overhead, the branches ran together and were entangled [lit.,
"intermixed their hair"]. Their natural growth, in sum, seemed to
be the result of artifice [lit., "their nature seemed to be from art"].
There were also beds of flowers, of which the earth produced
some, and others craft made: [11] the roses and hyacinths and lilies
were the works of a [human] hand, while earth brought forth the
violets, narcissuses, and pimpernels.) (4.2)

Both the work of human hands and the fruits of the earth itself can be destroyed, of course (B′), by that same human hand
which is capable of making them beautiful (B). All the flowers
just mentioned are mentioned again, by name, when Lamon la-
ments for his garden, with one significant exception: the lily,
which was then, as it is now, associated with spring and resurrection.[12] Even Dionysus, whose altar sits in the very midst of the
despoiled garden, has not saved the flowers, and Lamon fully
expects to share the fate of the mythical Marsyas, hanged from a
pine tree. All his work, the labor of years, has vanished in an in-
stant. As we have already seen, however, the arrival of Dionysophanes (whose name, let us observe, means "manifestation
of Dionysus") will bring about results far different from those
Lamon anticipates. Thus the peacefulness of the garden belies
the violence that will visit it (B), while the fear and panic that beset Lamon and his family belie the entirely unexpected good fortune that will result from the master's visit (B′).

In the midst of all this, in the midst of the garden, in the midst
of the work of preparation, in the midst of the destruction, by
which it is not touched, but to which it seems apparently indifferent, lies the altar of Dionysus.

ἵνα τοῦ παραδείσου τὸ μεσαίτατον ἐπὶ μῆκος καὶ εὖρος ἦν, νεὼς
Διονύσου καὶ βωμὸς ἦν· περιεῖχε τὸν μὲν βωμὸν κιττός, τὸν νεὼν

δὲ κλήματα. εἶχε δὲ καὶ ἔνδοθεν ὁ νεὼς Διονυσιακὰς γραφάς·
Σεμέλην τίκτουσαν, Ἀριάδνην καθεύδουσαν, Λυκοῦργον δεδεμέ-
νον, Πενθέα διαιρούμενον· ἦσαν καὶ Ἰνδοὶ νικώμενοι καὶ Τυρ-
ρηνοὶ μεταμορφούμενοι· πανταχοῦ Σάτυροι πατοῦντες, πανταχοῦ
Βάκχαι χορεύουσαι. οὐδὲ ὁ Πὰν ἠμέλητο, ἐκαθέζετο δὲ καὶ αὐτὸς
συρίζων ἐπὶ πέτρας ὅμοιον ἐνδιδόντι κοινὸν μέλος καὶ τοῖς πα-
τοῦσι καὶ ταῖς χορευούσαις.

(At the very center of the garden, from both its length and its
breadth, there was a shrine of Dionysus, and an altar. Ivy embraced the altar, while vines wound round the shrine. On the
inside, the shrine had Dionysiac paintings: Semele giving birth,
Ariadne sleeping, Lycurgus bound, and Pentheus being dismembered. On it were also the defeat of the Indians and the transformation of the Tyrrhenians; and everywhere were Satyrs prancing
about, and Bacchants dancing. Nor was Pan neglected: he was sitting on the rocks, piping, as though making a common melody
for the prancing [Satyrs] and the dancing [Bacchants]).

In books 1, 2, and 3, the first cycle framed what we came to
recognize as declamations: respectively, a speech contest, a mock
trial, and a debate. Here we add yet another rhetorical genre,
the ecphrasis, from the stock in trade of the rhetorician. This in
itself, that it is an ecphrasis, should be enough to call our attention to the shrine of Dionysus, even if the structural analysis of
book 4 had not led us to it. In order fully to understand the implications of all this, however, we shall need to broaden our
scope for a moment.

There is an unmistakable Dionysiac coloration to much of
Daphnis and Chloe. Those who believe that Longus was intent
upon writing an allegory of the mysteries have noted all of
the various passages where this coloration becomes most manifest: the festival of Dionysus at the beginning of book 2; the
mid-winter Dionysiac celebrations in book 3; the providential
dolphin; the altar of Dionysus; and the name of the master,
Daphnis's true father, Dionysophanes.[13] We have already seen,
however, that Longus often seems to undermine the seriousness
of this symbolism. The providential dolphin, for example, is
dead, rotten, and stinking; and as for Dionysophanes, he is any-

thing but godlike. He may be a manifestation of Dionysus, but he is also a very conventional character, drawn in large measure after the model of the paterfamilias characters of the New Comedy: benign, but altogether conventional in his moral standards and not particularly perceptive.[14] Neither the stinking dolphin nor this semi-comical "manifestation of Dionysus" fits terribly well with an allegorical (and thus, *ex hypothesi*, deadly earnest) reading of *Daphnis and Chloe*.

The altar, on the other hand, is not handled in an overtly humorous way. All the myths alluded to are of the greatest cultic and mythic significance for the worship of Dionysus. Underlying them, also, are many of the primary themes of the novel, though much depends here upon the reader's knowing each story to which allusion is made, from beginning to end. Thus the first picture is Semele giving birth to Dionysus, a scene which certainly seems innocent enough on its face; but those who know the story will recall that Semele did not give birth to Dionysus in anything like the ordinary way. She was tricked by Hera, jealous as always of her husband's paramours, into demanding of Zeus that he manifest himself to her in all his divine splendor. He was forced to comply, because he had sworn in advance to Semele that he would grant any request that she might make, in order to prove his love (and his identity). Semele was at once incinerated by the brilliance of the revealed godhead of the king of the gods. Zeus snatched the fetus of his unborn son from her burning body and implanted it in his own thigh, where it grew to term and was born as the god Dionysus. No ordinary childbirth, this, but an awful story of human frailty betrayed by divine jealousy; and Dionysus is a motherless god.

The next figure is Ariadne, sleeping. This is the mortal woman beloved of Dionysus; he found her, asleep, on the island of Naxos, where she had been marooned by Theseus. The latter was, of course, returning home from his successful encounter with the Minotaur, an adventure in which he owed his survival to Ariadne, the daughter of Minos; she had fallen in love with this young Athenian and had betrayed her father. There were differing explanations in antiquity as to why Theseus left Ariadne on Naxos. According to the best-known version, Theseus really wanted nothing to do with a foreign woman who had betrayed her own father for a stranger, even though that stranger was himself, and decided to lure her onto the island and leave her as she napped on the beach.[15] There she was found by the always-itinerant Dionysus, who pitied her, fell in love with her beauty, and made her his consort. In another version, however, Theseus had no intention of abandoning Ariadne, except that Dionysus came along and stole her: who can resist an amorous god?[16] But whatever version Longus means to evoke, this "sleeping Ariadne" has either just been abandoned or is about to be raped or both.

The stories of Lycurgus and Pentheus both belong to a cycle of myths surrounding the advent of Dionysus and his worship in Greece. Both of these men were kings who resisted the introduction of Bacchic rites into their kingdoms, and both were ruthlessly destroyed. In neither case did the god raise his own hand; each of the recalcitrant kings was destroyed by a madness that the god induced, in his victim or in others. Readers of Euripides' *Bacchae* know the story of Pentheus, dismembered by (among others) his own temporarily maddened mother. Lycurgus was a king of Thrace, who cut off his own legs in a fit of temporary insanity, because he mistook them for vines; later, he was dismembered by his own subjects, who had been told that they would never taste wine again while Lycurgus lived.[17] Neither of these are pretty stories; the story of Pentheus was, in fact, rather well suited to be the last tragedy performed in Athens before the victorious Spartans temporarily suspended the Greater Dionysia after the Peloponnesian War. The *Bacchae* is also the only tragedy in which Dionysus, the god of tragedy, plays a major role; that, and the frequent prominent repetition in the play of forms of the verb $\theta\varepsilon\acute{\alpha}o\mu\alpha\iota$, "see," from which the word "theatre" itself is derived, might lead one to suspect that the *Bacchae* is, on at least one level, a self-conscious reflection on the nature of tragedy. That brings us close, in a way that we shall shortly see, to what Longus is doing in this whole ecphrasis.

Dionysus's mythical conquest of India, and his transformation of certain Tyrrhenian pirates into dolphins, are also two of the same sort of myth, in which Dionysus takes awful revenge upon a group of people who dishonor his godhead. We have seen pirates before, of course: in book 1, Daphnis, along with Dorcon's cattle, is seized by just such pirates.[18] But the pirates that Daphnis meets become, not dolphins, but rather the first pirates in surviving literature ever to be drowned by stampeding cattle. Piracy must have been a dangerous life indeed. More to the point, the peculiar fate that befalls these pirates signals that all is not as it seems. When an ordinary seafarer can die a cowherd's death, or be transformed into a dolphin, something in the usual scheme of things seems to have gone awry.

The ancient reader would at once have recognized the ubiquitous satyrs and bacchants depicted on the altar, as will any modern reader who is at all familiar with Greek art. Satyrs, like nymphs, are semidivine beings; they resemble Pan in being half human and half goat and are the very symbols of lechery. They are invariably depicted with erect phallus, usually in amorous pursuit of nubile bacchants. Pan, in other words, is sitting on the rocks and providing background music for scenes of pursuit and rape not at all unlike those in the *aitia* of which he himself has been the central character so many times.

By this point, the conclusion toward which all this has been tending should be clear. Women betrayed and endangered by lustful males; males, in turn, undone by their resistance to the ineluctable, which results from their ignorance of what is really at stake; transformations, pursuits, rapes, and gods who make music through it all—here, in a nutshell, are the themes with which all our "pivots," both the declamations and the myths, have been involved. The ecphrasis of the shrine of Dionysus, which reminds the reader of the quasi-ecphrastic nature of the novel itself, is also a thematic recapitulation of everything that has happened up until this point. Thus the pivot of the first cycle, on the one hand, anticipates the *aition* of Chloe; but also, and significantly, it looks backward, to the prologue. For the shrine of Dionysus is not, of course, the first ecphrasis we have seen in *Daphnis and Chloe*. We can hardly fail to recall how, in the prologue, Longus teasingly casts the whole of his novel as an extended ecphrasis. Thus it is not surprising to find that the diction Longus uses in the ecphrasis of Dionysus's shrine, and especially of the paintings, the γραφαί, is highly redolent of the prologue. Analogues to two of the images on the painting which ostensibly inspired Longus to write *Daphnis and Chloe* are also found on the paintings in Dionysus's temple: the women giving birth and the pirates. The two ecphrases are linked together, then, by images of women doing something that only women can do and of violent men who live by theft and pillage. This can hardly be casual or accidental, when so much else that happens in *Daphnis and Chloe* revolves around the meaning of masculinity and femininity; but only the content of the first cycle in book 4, itself developed through the whole course of *Daphnis and Chloe*, makes it possible for the reader to begin to understand what is really meant by the words of the prologue. And even this suggests an answer to the enigma of how *Daphnis and Chloe* can be as much a picture as a story: for the eye moves back and forth across a picture, grasping the essential relationships between the parts only by referring back, again and again, to what it has already seen.

It should be clear, at this point, how book 4 fits into the economy of *Daphnis and Chloe* as a whole. On the one hand, the themes developed in the first three books are brought to a kind of fruition in book 4, as the marriage of Daphnis and Chloe somehow completes the dialectic of male and female; on the other hand, book 4, far more than the intervening books, brings back to the reader's mind the hints and suggestions of the prologue. The theme of ecphrasis is brought together with declamation in a surprising way, just as the theme of "etiology" is brought together with the larger theme of storytelling. Thus what is really remarkable, finally, about the two cycles of book 4 is that both of them really constitute the text alluding to itself. The point may not be easy, but it is essential. The first cycle contains an ecphrasis that reminds us of how, in a certain way, we have been reading a picture all along. The "myth" of Chloe, on the other hand, is not really a "myth" at all, at least not in the ancient sense. It is not a traditional tale but rather a story that has been concocted. What is more, the very way in which Longus goes about setting up the construction of his private "myth" makes us, his readers, privy to the plot. Thus the text draws attention to itself precisely as a text, deliberately breaking, in the process, any illusion of reality. So this is not history, either. It is not a "true" story at all but rather the product of someone's imagination. Ironically, however, it can do what it does only because it is fiction and not history. No preexistent story, no matter how "plasmatic" its treatment, could teach us exactly what *Daphnis and Chloe* teaches us, any more than a treatise or diatribe on whaling could replace *Moby Dick*. We who have grown up in a world where the novel has long been the dominant form of narrative literature may be far too complacent about all this.

The analysis of the narrative architecture of *Daphnis and Chloe* is now complete. What we have before us is a piece of self-aware and self-reflecting fiction, which describes itself as an erotic history, and in which the dominant themes identified by the structure are rhetoric and myth. The latter terms in particular, and a certain dialectic between them, seem to be the dynamo which makes the whole thing work. Clearly, then, the time has come to grapple with the meaning of myth and rhetoric.

Chapter 7

The Dialectic of
Myth and Rhetoric

THE SECOND SOPHISTIC

Longus wrote, according to the best evidence, sometime in the last quarter of the second century A.D. or the first quarter of the third.[1] That date places him squarely within the Second Sophistic, which, among other things, constituted a revolution of sorts in the teaching and practice of rhetoric.[2] This may well account for certain facets of Longus's style, which shows at many points a certain proclivity toward rhetorical display, as several previous scholars have noted.[3] It may also account for the thematic importance of rhetoric in *Daphnis and Chloe*, as revealed by the structure of the novel. But a really satisfactory understanding of the issues involved here will require an excursus of sorts on the subject of the Second Sophistic, and of rhetoric generally.

The chronological boundaries of the Second Sophistic, like those of almost any literary or intellectual movement, are indistinct. Flavius Philostratus, a second-generation member of the Second Sophistic, and its primary ancient chronicler, gave the movement its name. His *Lives of the Sophists* (conventionally *Vitae Sophistarum*, for the Greek Βιοὶ τῶν σοφιστῶν) dates the genesis of the Second Sophistic all the way back to Aeschines, in the fourth century B.C.; but Philostratus's account jumps immediately from there to the end of the Flavian dynasty, late in the first century of our era, when one Nicetes, a Greek rhetorician, came to Rome and began to give declamations.[4] We know little of this Nicetes, however, and his very existence is open to question. For all practical purposes, the history of the Second Sophistic really begins in earnest with Dion of Prusa, who gave declamations in Rome after the death of the emperor Domitian in A.D. 96, a decade or so after the shadowy Nicetes. At the other end of its lifespan, the Second Sophistic (which depended from the beginning, not merely on the tolerance, but on the active support of the Roman emperors) ended with that fifty-year period of military anarchy which ensued after the death of Alexander Severus in A.D. 234. The end was hardly an abrupt one: already when Philostratus wrote, in the first decades of the third century (under Caracalla), the movement was clearly past its prime. Its high tide came in the reigns of the "five good emperors": Nerva, Trajan, Hadrian, Antoninus Pius, and Marcus Aurelius, collectively known as the Antonines, whose years in power correspond fairly closely with what we call the second century A.D.

An incautious reader may have gotten the impression from what has just been said that there is no reason to question whether such a thing as Philostratus's "Second Sophistic" ever existed, or, if it did exist, exactly what it was. But that is not the case: as eminent an authority as Ulrich von Wilamowitz-Moellendorff, in a review of André Boulanger's edition of Aelius Aristides, remarked that "[v]on der schlechthin unbrauchbaren Erfindung des Philostratos, der zweite Sophistik, hat er [sc. Boulanger] sich nicht losgemacht" ("He [sc. Boulanger] has not freed himself from the utterly useless invention of Philostratus, the Second Sophistic").[5] And even if Wilamowitz's extreme skepticism is rejected (as it is by most modern scholars) there really is no fundamental consensus as to what the term "Second Sophistic" means. A very broad, even elastic definition is implied by the breadth of the discussions anthologized in *Approaches to the Second Sophistic*. For these scholars, the term "Second Sophistic" seems to encompass the whole literary-intellectual culture of the Graeco-Roman world, from the beginning of the Flavian dynasty to the end of the Severan. Albin Lesky, on the other hand, has a somewhat more specific, ever-so-slightly narrower definition; for him, the term "Second Sophistic" really denotes a certain Hellenizing movement, a kind of renaissance, which arose during the period in question as the Greeks struggled to reclaim a heritage that seemed in some danger of being lost.

Whatever its possible cultural or pyschological or historical implications, however, the starting point for any discussion of the Second Sophistic must be rhetoric: that is, the practice and teaching of Greek rhetoric during the second and third centuries A.D. For although there are things to be said in favor of those broader definitions of the Second Sophistic, it is very specifically to rhetoric that, as readers of *Daphnis and Chloe*, we must now turn our attention, and not merely because there is something "rhetorical" about Longus's prose style. Rhetoric, in the strictest sense of the word, is incorporated into the very plot of *Daphnis and Chloe*, as we have just learned.

It is important to bear in mind here just what the issues were that exercized the rhetoricians of this period. In the nineteenth century, the Second Sophistic was usually interpreted in terms of the much older competition between Attic and Asianic oratory, as though it represented, in fact, the victory of one of these over the other.[6] It was Eduard Norden who pointed out (in 1898) that both Attic and Asianic rhetoric had influential adherents in the Second Sophistic, and that, in the surviving speeches of any given rhetorician, the contrast between the two styles is likely to function more as a dialectic than as a dichotomy.[7] But there is a more important battle going on during the Second Sophistic than a squabble between the Attic and the Asianic styles, a battle implicit in the very name "Second Sophistic." Philostratus coined the term because it seemed to him that his times had seen the rise of a new generation of sophists, who were both more skilled and more important than their immediate predecessors. What is more interesting yet, however, is that he clearly conceives of the Second Sophistic as a recrudescence of the ancient war between rhetoric and philosophy. Throughout his *Lives of the Sophists*, Philostratus attempts to distinguish between ῥήτορες, mere "rhetoricians," and σοφισταί, "sophists," on the presumption that the latter term is somehow intermediate between the former and φιλόσοφοι, "philosophers," properly so called. Here is what he says to justify this distinction: Σοφιστὰς δὲ οἱ παλαιοὶ ἐπ-

ωνόμαζον οὐ μόνον τῶν ῥητόρων τοὺς ὑπερφωνοῦντάς τε καὶ
λαμπρούς, ἀλλὰ καὶ τῶν φιλοσόφων τοὺς ξὺν εὐροίᾳ ἑρμηνεύον-
τας. ("The ancients called 'sophists' not only those of the rhetoricians who were exceptionally eloquent and brilliant, but also
those philosophers who discoursed with good style.")[8]

Philostratus probably makes too much of these distinctions,
and the intellectual claims he makes for the rhetoricians of the
Second Sophistic may well be exaggerated; but to dismiss the
work of the Second Sophistic as mere rhetoric, on the grounds
that a preoccupation with rhetoric naturally precludes real intellectual substance, begs the question.[9]

Not to say, of course, that a certain disdain for the rhetoric of
late antiquity is hard to understand. To modern tastes, there
seems to be something almost inescapably silly, or perhaps decadent and corrupt, about the declamations of the Second Sophistic, especially when one remembers that the topics debated with
such skill and (sometimes) passion were seldom matters of contemporary controversy. The declamations mostly dealt with subjects from the remote past, from myth and poetry, or Greek history. But that absence of "topicality" is, of course, precisely the
point. The schools of both Greece and Rome had originally
stressed rhetoric for the most practical of reasons: in both so-
cieties, eloquence was a path to power, and not infrequently the
only path. Roman boys of aristocratic lineage learned rhetoric
because someday they would be taking their places in the Senate,
and a degree of eloquence would help them to become the mov-
ers and shakers there. Or at least that was the idea in Republican
times. After Augustus, however, what the Senate said meant less
and less as the years went by. Eloquence might be spent in *adu-
latio*, in flattery, but earth-shaking decisions were made elsewhere. Still, however, with characteristic tenacity, the schools
clung to their curriculum and produced generations of orators
who had little or nothing of importance to do with the fruits of
their rhetorical education.[10] It is precisely when rhetoric becomes
politically superfluous that it can become a spectator sport. Eloquence can no longer be measured by its effectiveness in the real
world; instead, it comes to be measured by its own internal yard-
stick, as any sport ultimately is. In the case of rhetoric, that yard-

stick is primarily a stylistic one; hence the older perception that the only real issue in the Second Sophistic was style.

The very word "rhetoric" is seldom used in our day without some sort of pejorative connotation. Perhaps that is because of the horrible examples of Hitler and Mussolini, who rose to power on the strength of their oratory; or perhaps it is because the art of verbal persuasion seems to have become the province of used-car salesmen, television evangelists, and demagogues, so that one finds it hard nowadays to say the word "rhetoric" outside of phrases like "mere rhetoric," "empty rhetoric," or "dangerous rhetoric." But then, *nihil sub sole novum;* for allusion has already been made here to a certain "war" between philosophy and rhetoric in antiquity. So what is rhetoric, really, and why does it seem to attract to itself such uncomplimentary epithets, then and now?

Rhetoric has been variously defined, and its relationship to philosophy variously understood. It is Plato, as so often, who was the first to articulate for us, clearly and profoundly, the fundamental issues at stake in the war between philosophy and rhetoric. A full and detailed discussion of Plato's attitudes toward rhetoric would naturally exceed any reasonable bounds for a book on Longus;[11] but a brief survey may suffice here, at least to get the issues on the table.

PHILOSOPHY AND RHETORIC

There are two Platonic dialogues that deal directly, primarily, and explicitly with rhetoric: the *Gorgias* and the *Phaedrus*. In the *Gorgias*, Socrates seems to be arguing that rhetoric is nothing more than the craft or skill (τέχνη) of lying persuasively; but in the *Phaedrus*, his attitude appears to be both more subtle and more generous.[12] Rhetoric, as it appears in the three speeches of the *Phaedrus*, is something that can certainly be mendacious; but it can also be put to the service of truth. In fact, the fundamental teaching of the *Phaedrus* may well be just this, that the capacity to lie is a necessary and ineluctable concomitant to the capacity to tell the truth. This perception of Plato's seems to be worked out concretely, after a fashion, in the *Apology*, a dialogue that is itself an oration. In his exordium Socrates disclaims any eloquence on his own part, while directly connecting the persuasiveness of his accusers with their mendacity. Only if "eloquent" (δεινὸς λέγειν) means "speaking the truth" will he consent to be called an orator of sorts, but even so he is not an orator like Meletus or Anytus. This said, however, the speech which Socrates then proceeds to deliver is a textbook example of the rhetorical art, even on the pragmatic level of disposition. This disjunction between Socrates' disclaimer of eloquence and the manifest eloquence of his speech seems to imply, again, that there are two kinds of rhetoric, good and evil, which are somehow utterly different, but utterly inextricable: one cannot learn the one without acquiring the tools for the other.

Something like this is the starting point for Aristotle's *Rhetoric*. Rhetoric is a discipline (an ἐπιστήμη), which can be systematically studied to good effect. Like dialectic, to which it serves as "counterpoint" (ἀντίστροφος), it is a discipline naturally implicit in (or propaideutic to) all others.[13] That is why it can be either good or evil: it has no subject of its own, but rather teaches us how to be persuasive in any argument, good or bad, important or trivial. At the same time, rhetoric is distinguished from dialectic precisely on the grounds that dialectic aims at certain knowledge of the truth of things (μάθημα), while rhetoric is limited to the probable (πίστις). This is, in fact, the very definition of rhetoric for Aristotle: finding the means of persuasion (πίστεις). There is such a thing as rhetorical truth, then, but it is truth of a different (and implicitly lower) order than philosophical truth. If one assumes that ideas (or thoughts, or categories) exist without necessary reference to, or dependence on, any particular articulation thereof in words, then rhetoric is not the realm of truth and ought to be, at best, ancillary to philosophy. Rhetoric does not teach us anything that is absolutely true but only the techniques by which we may persuade others of our own opinions about the truth. These techniques can be used just as easily to prove false opinions as true ones; hence the fear and suspicion with which philosophy, or at least metaphysical philosophy, has always tended to view rhetoric.

The validity of this line of argument has always seemed quite self-evident to some, who conclude from all this that truth is the property or province of philosophy, and not of rhetoric. There are, however, some serious problems with the underlying premises.[14] If thought exists independently of language, then of what does it consist? That is the rock upon which any number of metaphysical vessels have foundered, and all efforts to evade the problem by devising some transcendent means of communicating truth have thus far failed. Rhetoric may indeed provide the tools with which true opinions can be undermined. But it is also preeminently the science of speaking well (Quintilian's *ars bene loquendi*), and without speech there is no way of approaching the truth, either to attack it or to understand it. In the absence of some infallible (in both the active and passive sense) "metalanguage," we are left with words as not only the vehicle but the tenor of thought itself. Sloppy or murky language cannot really coexist with clear and lucid thinking, as any teacher of college undergraduates well knows; if, then, one is going to teach students how to think clearly, one had better begin by teaching them how to express themselves clearly.

The quarrel between philosophy and rhetoric was never resolved in antiquity, and it has broken out afresh over and over again in the intellectual history of the West.[15] Philostratus's efforts to distinguish the σοφιστής from the ῥήτωρ, on the one hand, and the φιλόσοφος, on the other, however unconvincing or even futile they may seem, reflect his desire to reach some sort of resolution, a via media. Clearly, if language is the only possible medium of thought, or the only medium by which thought can be communicated, then those whose thought and teaching is devoted to language ought to be considered philosophers. Just as clearly, however, some people are capable of speech without content, of saying nothing and saying it very well, of "making the worse appear the better cause." The difficulty lies always in distinguishing the first group from the second. Philostratus, for his part, attempts to solve the problem inductively: he simply selects, of all the declaimers and teachers of the previous generation, those who seemed to him to have been rather more serious than others. This is hardly a satisfactory approach, but an alternative does not at once present itself. The war between philosophy and rhetoric remained unresolved in antiquity and remains so to the present day.

PHILOSOPHY, POETRY, AND MYTH

It was, of course, not only with rhetoric that ancient philosophy had to contend, in order to claim the truth as its sole province. Even better known than the war between rhetoric and philosophy is that between the latter and poetry. The locus classicus for this war is, of course, Plato's *Republic*, where Socrates adverts to παλαιὰ μέν τις διαφορὰ φιλοσοφίᾳ τε καὶ ποιητικῇ ("a certain ancient contention between philosophy and poetry").[16] One of the most interesting things about what Socrates says here is that he calls this contention παλαιά ("ancient"). The examples he adduces to testify to the antiquity of the struggle are all "unphilosophical" or "antiphilosophical" phrases and passages from the poets.[17] This does not mean, however, that the contention to date had been one-sided, with only the poets striking blows. It is possibly true that Socrates' attack on poetry qua mimesis in the *Republic* is a novel one, but it is certainly not the case that no philosophers before Socrates (or Plato) made concerted attacks on traditional poetry; even those philosophers who themselves wrote in verse had long since begun the assault. Early Greek philosophy began precisely when such thinkers as Anaxagoras set the poetic, mythical view of the world, inherited from Homer and Hesiod, on the margins, and tried to look at the fundamental cosmological and cosmogonical problems from a rational and critical perspective, rather than a mythical one. Discursive reason (λόγος) is separated out from narrative (μῦθος) and hereafter goes its own way.[18]

It was inevitable, of course, that the quarrel, which began with cosmology, would escalate into a moral conflict.[19] Once that same critical reason was brought to bear on moral questions, the authority of the poets in these matters, too, was bound to be questioned. A famous fragment of Xenophanes states the moral problem very plainly: πάντα θεοῖς ἀνέθηκαν Ὅμηρός θ' Ἡσίοδός

τε / ὅσσα παρ᾽ ἀνθρώποισιν ὀνείδεα καὶ ψόγος ἐστιν, / κλέπτειν
μοιχεύειν τε καὶ ἀλλήλους ἀπατεύειν. ("Homer and Hesiod attributed to the gods / all things that are shameful and a disgrace
among humans, / stealing, fornicating, and deceiving one another.")[20] This, of course, is precisely the point of attack used by
Socrates when he first proposes to expel the poets from the ideal
state. Homer presents exempla of behavior and attitudes that no
well-ordered state can possibly tolerate.

The bone of contention, then, is one of content and not of
technique. It is not because their speech is metrical that the poets
are philosophy's antagonists; Xenophanes and Parmenides had
demonstrated that meter (like rhetorical technique) could be put
to the service of philosophy. The real problem is that the poets
tell deleterious stories in a captivating manner. Such stories are
antithetical to the moral truth of philosophy, *whether or not they
are literally true*. This even the poets could hardly deny; one
thinks at once of Hesiod's encounter with the Muses at the beginning of the *Theogony*:

> ἴδμεν ψεύδεα πολλὰ λέγειν ἐτύμοισιν ὁμοῖα,
> ἴδμεν δ᾽, εὖτ᾽ ἐθέλωμεν, ἀληθέα γηρύσασθαι.
> ("We [sc. the Muses] know how to tell many falsehoods
>   that are like what is real:
> but we also know how to proclaim the truth,
>   when we want to.")[21]

Of course, the Muses never really tell Hesiod (nor does he tell
us) how to distinguish the one kind of story from the other.
What we hear, whether true or false, are the myths. This brings
us back, full circle, to Ionian cosmology and the beginnings of
the "ancient contention." The fundamental issue, then, is revealed to be myth, or, perhaps more specifically, the mythical
model of truth. Not all poets, after all, are to be expelled from
Socrates' ideal state but only the writers of tragedies and Homeric epics, which is to say the writers of myths.

But what, then, is a myth? Any teacher who has ever taught a
class on myth, or any student who has read much on the subject,
knows how many and various are the answers to that simple but
vital question. Definitions range from such deliberately broad

ones as G. S. Kirk's "traditional tale" to the obscurities of struc-
turalist or semiotic definitions, according to which myth is a metalanguage or a system of signs and codes or a species of human
communication in which fundamental social relationships and
tensions are expressed and mediated through the interplay of
characters and events.[22] It is not even clear within whose academic province the study of myth properly belongs. Is mythology a division of anthropology? of literature? of pyschology? of
religion? of the classics? Of all of them, it seems, and yet of none
entirely. Fortunately, however, there is no compelling reason to
settle these issues here and now. Kirk's definition of "myth" is,
after all, more a definition than an explanation or interpretation, and a definition is what we are after now. A definition, in
the strict sense, should circumscribe the thing to be defined, setting it apart from all other things. It does not require that we
explain how something works, or even what it does. A myth,
then, is a traditional tale. It is traditional in that it is attested, ancient, and anonymous. It is a tale because it tells what somebody
once did. What the poet does, then, is not to create a myth but to
retell it.

In this respect, the derivation of the English word "poet"
from ποιήτης, which is in turn formed from the base of the verb
ποιέω, "to make," can be somewhat misleading. When we discover that the craftsmen of ancient Greece used this very same
verb to proclaim their manufacture of a particular piece of work
(ΝΙΚΟΜΗΔΗΣ ΕΠΟΙΗΣΕ), there is likely to be a great temptation, on the part of modern students, to overstate the poet's role
as "maker," that is, as creator or demiurge of a self-contained
universe. But we are conditioned in this by a certain vision of
poets and poetry, a vision which we owe primarily to the roman-
tics and which would be distinctly anachronistic if applied to ancient Greece. The potter, after all, does not "make" his clay;
rather, he takes the clay and *makes it into* something. And even
the shape into which he forms this clay is not of his own devising; at his hands, the lump of clay becomes an amphora, an
oenochoe, or what-have-you. His contribution, then, is to make
this particular lump of clay into a vessel of this particular shape.
The exercise of his private will is therefore restricted to the

choice of which clay, which shape. In this respect, the analogy to ancient Greek poetry is rather exact. Homer "made" the *Iliad*, but he did not "make" Achilles; nor did Aeschylus, Sophocles, or Euripides "make" Orestes, regardless of which one of them wrote about him first. All three of them made Orestes into a tragedy, in one way or another.

This brings up another issue. Students in mythology courses are wont to ask, when told that there are multiple versions of a given myth, which one is the right one. The impulse to ask that question is a natural one, but the answer must always be the same: there really is no one "right" version. The myth qua story exists independently of whatever words are used to tell it on any one occasion, just as the historical datum is what it is, no matter what one chooses to say about it. That is why Aeschylus, Sophocles, and Euripides can all tell the myth of Orestes' matricide but in very different ways, to very different ends. We need not decide which of them is "telling the truth" about Orestes. Each version tells "a" truth, which is not necessarily "the" truth about Orestes but is nonetheless a particular truth about the human condition. Worrying over "the" truth about Orestes only gets in the way of learning whatever truth is implicit in the myth. It is not for nothing that the Latin word *versio* means "turning." We have something (the myth per se) in our hands. We turn it one way, and describe what we see; then we turn it another way, and describe again. Another turning, another version. And the whole of the object is not described by any one version, not even by the sum of all versions. There is always a side turned away.

That is at least part of the reason why myth and fiction, far from being comfortable bedfellows, are distinctly antagonistic to each other in the ancient context. At the risk of belaboring the point, let us repeat: a myth, as usually understood, is produced by centuries of tradition, not by a single intellect at one point in time. There is always a source, someone from whom the teller learned the myth, upon whose authority the teller relies, as Lamon, in *Daphnis and Chloe*, relies upon the veracity and authority of the Sicilian shepherd in his own retelling of the myth of Syrinx. The ancient writer who handles myths is thus constrained to keep within certain limits in elaborating them; however broad the poetic license granted to someone like Sophocles, for example, he is not free to alter the broad outlines of the received story of Oedipus, who must kill Laius, solve the riddle of the Sphinx, become tyrant of Thebes, marry Jocasta, learn the truth, blind himself, and so on. This relative lack of artistic freedom was not a great problem in the fifth century B.C., when the old myths still resonated; but by Longus's day, some six centuries later, they were inevitably growing old, perhaps ossifying. The world was not as it had been, but the old myths clung on, protected in the postclassical world by the sanctity of the classical tradition. To the modern reader, the obvious solution to the resulting artistic impasse is to dispense with the constant retelling of traditional myths, and write fiction; but this is only obvious because the leap from myth to fiction is so far behind us now that we have forgotten how dangerous it was.

This said, we ought to pause for a moment and acknowledge that there was, after all, one legitimate place in the ancient world for stories that were not verified by tradition or testimony: namely, comedy. Beginning with Aristophanes, the comic poets were clearly allowed to invent their own plots and to people them with invented characters. In a sense, then, there is some ancient, classical precedent for the idea of fiction. It may be germane to point out, however, that the scope of even this comic fiction was quite restricted. The Old Comedy of Aristophanes, to begin with, was always highly topical and presented its audience with some real contemporary persons—Cleon and Socrates and Euripides and many others—in every play, all mixed in with fictional characters like Strepsiades. The New Comedy, on the other hand, gives us fictional characters, but with a striking lack of originality. Many of Menander's characters repeat themselves from one play to the next, with only a change of name; and certain favorite plot devices recur again and again. By the time we get to the Roman comic playwrights, we are back to "retelling." Terence's defensiveness about accusations of *contaminatio* tells us volumes.

It is probably fairly easy for most readers to see what is so unsatisfactory for the philosopher about the mythical approach to truth. The truth of myth, which is the truth of traditional poetry, is always a partial truth, a glimpse of the truth, and not the truth in and of itself. Oddly enough, though, Plato himself makes frequent recourse to myths in his dialogues: one thinks of the myth of Er, for example, which follows immediately upon the second attack on poetry in book 10 of the *Republic*, or the myth of the charioteer in the *Phaedrus*. Why, one might reasonably ask, does Plato, the apparent archenemy of the poets, fall back on myth in this seemingly paradoxical way? The answer would seem to be that he recognized the necessity of some vehicle for such truths as could not be approached or captured by discursive reason. What distinguishes Plato's myths, however, from the "traditional tales" of epic and tragedy is that Plato seems to have invented them: that is, they are not traditional. There is no small irony, then, in Socrates' invocation of the Muses in his telling of the myth of Er. The philosopher appears in the guise of a new Homer, usurping the poet's position as the special favorite of the Muses. And he does so precisely by breaking with the past, by replacing the old myths that are continually retold with new ones, of which he, the philosopher, is actually the demiurge.[23]

If Plato had actually succeeded in claiming myth for philosophy, the history of later Greek literature would almost certainly have been very different. But in fact philosophy never came to terms with myth, nor myth with philosophy. No one ever again wrote "philosophical" myths in quite the same way as Plato had; certainly Aristotle did not, and most subsequent philosophers, ancient and modern, have tended to write more like Aristotle than like Plato. In the centuries that followed, then, the poets reclaimed myth. The Hellenistic poets and scholars were responsible for a great recension, not only of the Homeric poems, but of the traditional myths in general. The effect of the process of recension was, however, probably unexpected and unintended. The corpus of Greek myth still possessed a certain dynamism in Plato's day, without which Plato's struggle with Homer over the ownership of myth (which is to say, of a large part of the realm of truth) would make little sense.[24] By the time of Callimachus, however, the myths had become artifacts. At just this stage, and not before, it is possible to speak properly of "mythology"; myth has become an object of study, a monument from the past, utterly impressive and utterly dead. By the second century of the present era, the old myths had lost all vitality. Like clay that has been worked and reworked over and over again, they had lost their plasticity. It is not that they ceased to be of importance; on the contrary, classical Greek literature without them is as inconceivable in the second century A.D. as in the second century B.C. But they had outlived their usefulness, because they no longer resonated in the lives of those who heard them retold.

MYTH AND RHETORIC

At this point, the reader may recall that rather similar things were said about the rhetoric of the Second Sophistic, that it had somehow outlived the circumstances in which and through which it had come into being. This similarity is not merely casual or coincidental. Rhetoric and myth in ancient Greek literature have a complex relationship with each other, one which goes beyond the apparently incidental fact that both somehow occasionally came to blows with philosophy. Both present models of truth that are in fundamental conflict with that of metaphysical philosophy. By the second century A.D., again, both seem to have fallen into decadence, still exerting influence, even to the extent of choking off innovation, but fundamentally out of touch with the world from which and in which they were each created.

None of this should be taken to mean, however, that rhetoric and myth are comfortable bedfellows. On the contrary, there is a fundamental disharmony between them, which may in fact run deeper than the conflict between either of them and philosophy; for their respective models of truth are essentially incongruent. To put the conflict in the simplest terms, a myth consists of a story without necessary reference to the actual words used to re-tell it on any particular occasion, while rhetoric consists of words without necessary reference to a story. The myth is prior to, and independent of, the particularities of the occasion upon which it is retold, while rhetoric might properly be called the science of the occasion: how to say just the right thing at just the right moment. Or again, rhetoric is a means by which any subject can be handled, while a myth is a "subject" that can be expressed by a variety of means.

Now it is clear, of course, that myth and rhetoric each provides a certain amount of material for the other, and in that sense one might view them as complementary. The rhetoricians were fond of mythical exampla, and many of the topics for declamations were drawn from mythical situations; for that matter, "narration" ("narratio," διήγησις) was one of the components of rhetorical disposition. Myth, on the other hand, is no stranger to rhetoric. Certainly Greek poetry, from its Homeric roots on down, was always conscious of rhetoric; it is of no small significance that the first "act" of the *Iliad* is Chryses' speech to the Achaean army. If the Greek poet is a sculptor and the myth is his stone, then rhetoric is one of his chisels. The conflict between myth and rhetoric is, in fact, more of a dialectic than a repugnance: each would be sterile without the other. There is something almost Heraclitean about this, a παλίντροπος ἁρμονίη ("back-turning harmony"), which consists of exactly countervailing pulls in opposite directions and which achieves concrete form in the two symbols of Apollo, the bow and the lyre.[25]

Could it be, in fact, that the dialectic of myth and rhetoric is the "back-turning harmony" of Greek literature, from Homer on down to the Christian era? Could it be that the two wars between poetry and philosophy on the one hand, and between rhetoric and philosophy on the other, are simply incidental to the dialectic of myth and rhetoric, which is both older and deeper?

These questions are too broad, and probably too ambitious, to be answered simply. To some extent, the rest of this book will consist of a certain groping toward some answers, which will necessarily remain incomplete and imperfect. For the moment, however, the very asking of such questions serves to throw into perhaps sharper relief the possible significance of the novel, and perhaps especially of *Daphnis and Chloe*, in the history of ancient Greek literature. Insofar as the dialectic between myth and rhetoric had reached a kind of impasse in late antiquity, the rise of prose fiction had the potential of providing a way out; for fiction, by its very nature, mediates between myth and rhetoric. The root of the contention between myth and rhetoric is the nature of truth, after all; and the central problem for the ancient Greek novel, as we shall see, is the problem of verification, of how to tell the truth by telling a story that is not true. Myth is the retelling of traditional tales, rhetoric is a display of individual virtuosity in the use of words, and fiction is the display of individual virtuosity in the creation of a story.

These reflections have led us to a kind of program for the next chapters. It seems that *Daphnis and Chloe*, as an erotic history preoccupied with myth and rhetoric, is deeply engaged in a conversation of sorts with much of the previous history of Greek literature and thought—that is, with tradition. What we must now do, then, is to examine, in the light of what we now know, precisely how that conversation with tradition takes place, and on what levels.

PART II

Encountering the Tradition

Chapter 8

The Ancient Greek Novel

NOVELS AND ROMANCES

In the central hallway of the St. Louis International Airport, high above all the hustle and bustle, the coming and going, the to-ing and fro-ing of a busy metropolitan airport, and surrounded by a thousand manifestations of the latest modern technology, there hangs from the ceiling a most incongruous object: a full-size replica of the "Spirit of St. Louis," the funny little airplane in which Charles Lindbergh made the first solo flight across the Atlantic. Few passersby venture more than a moment's glance at this monument to progress; but perhaps the present writer is not the only traveler who has stopped to look and been struck by the incongruity of this piece of tin, in this place. Outside, the 747s thunder off the runway at speeds unthinkable in 1927, in a quotidian routine that, in its very ordinariness, could hardly contrast more with the raw physical courage and endurance that Lindbergh demanded of himself and his machine. One wonders how it can be that these two objects, a 747 and the "Spirit of St. Louis," are both designated by the same noun, "airplane." And yet they are, and not without reason, after all: a more or less straight line of development and progress in aeronautical engineering connects them.

To some modern readers, perhaps most, it may well seem that the prose fiction of antiquity is to the modern novel precisely what the "Spirit of St. Louis" is to the latest jumbo jets. Some may find the ancient novels irrelevant to contemporary concerns, literary or otherwise, and pass on, like passengers hurrying to board their flights without a thought for those who have paid so high a price for the convenience and safety of travelers. Others may pause to wonder and marvel at the march of progress, like those who see in the very fragility of an old airplane a sign of how far we have come, since the days when one man earned the adulation of the world for doing what tens of thousands now do every day, without comment or incident. For such as these, the ancient novels are museum pieces, literary curiosities, monuments to progress, no more and no less; but still, such texts as these would seem to be uncertain claimants, at best, to the title of "novel," precisely because we take the novel to be a living, breathing genre.[1] Such a reader would no more think of reading an ancient Greek novel for pleasure or enlightenment than he or she would think of flying from New York to Paris in the "Spirit of St. Louis." And this in itself may be enough to explain why the ancient Greek novels, as a group, though they have had both detractors and defenders, have had but few serious readers;[2] for it is hard to read any text that one is predisposed to see as a relic or an antique with anything more than antiquarian curiosity.

The difficulty with all this, of course, is that the analogy between ancient Greek novels and antique airplanes is neither very exact nor very helpful. Literature, after all, is not engineering, which is to say that its history is not controlled by a cumulative process of continual improvement upon past advances. Any approach to literary history that is based on an implicit faith in inexorable progress, as though everything written in the past were written to prepare the way for the future (namely, ourselves), is rightly suspect. That is the characteristic hubris of modernity, an arrogance which not only effectively obscures our understanding of the past, literary and otherwise, but also just as effectively prevents us from understanding ourselves in the context of the present.[3] Intellectual humility is not a vice to which we are much given these days, but without it we will make little or no progress in reaching any such understanding—or (to return to the matter at hand, and put an end to the homily) in achieving the rather more modest goal of understanding *Daphnis and Chloe*.

The prejudices of modernity being what they are, anyone who sets out to discuss something called "the ancient Greek novel" is all but compelled to begin by acknowledging the great difficulties implicit in the terms themselves. The very phrase "ancient Greek novel" seems to be a hopeless anachronism, at best, and perhaps something worse, a ridiculous oxymoron, in that the collocation of "ancient" and "novel" flies in the face of some very widely accepted notions of what a novel is, and, for that matter, of what ancient Greek literature is. University curricula in modern literature are usually based on the assumption that the novel, however one chooses to define or explain it, is a peculiarly modern phenomenon, unlike almost any other literary form; for their part, most classics departments are often content to leave modern literature's claim of exclusive domain over prose fiction mostly unchallenged.

What makes this whole situation even more intractable is that the meaning of the operative term, "novel," is itself not entirely clear. For even without that problematic qualifier "ancient Greek," the definition of "novel" is perhaps as controversial a topic as even the most contentious of critics could wish for. The problem is intricately entangled with some serious issues in modern literary theory. Most readers educated in the Anglo-American tradition have been taught that the novel, properly so called, was invented during the eighteenth century, in England. There are still those who will defend this Anglocentric position, but the chorus of dissenters is growing.[4] Some of these would-be revisionists argue that the French invented the novel a century or more before Daniel Defoe, Samuel Richardson, and Henry Fielding; others, that the first novels were written in Spain at some still earlier date, *Don Quixote* being an obvious candidate for "the first novel." Recalcitrant Anglocentrists are wont to reply, however, that the French or Spanish works advanced by the dissidents are not really novels at all but rather "romances," which are (presumably) horses of a different color. The romance may be admitted as a predecessor of the novel, perhaps even as a sort of protonovel, still surviving on the periphery of the genre; but a romance is not the same thing as a novel.

It does not even simplify things much to note, as some will do, that not every major European language has separate names for the "novel" and the "romance." Both genres are called "roman" (that is, "romance") in French, and the Germans have rather uncharacteristically borrowed both the word itself and its referent. As for the English word "novel," it is derived from the Italian "novella," which means not "novel" but "short story," or that which even in English is sometimes called "novella." One could take this to mean that this whole controversy about "novels" and "romances" in English is a logomachy; but then, the converse might also be true, that the Continental usage blurs a meaningful distinction between two types of literary composition, which are similar in form but quite different in both intent and execution. Even if it be conceded, however, that "novel" and "romance" are not merely synonyms and that there are, in fact, two genres with two distinct natures, sorting out the relationship between them is still not easy. For one thing, it is not at all clear whether "novel" and "romance" are mutually exclusive categories, or whether the one term properly designates a certain species of the genus designated by the other term.

Hardly less troublesome is the almost complete semantic reversal within the last century in the evaluative connotations of the two terms, especially as opposed to each other. Nathaniel Hawthorne averred, in the preface to *The House of the Seven Gables,* that the romance was a far less restricted form than the novel and thus a far more suitable vehicle for serious literature than the more pedestrian novel; but nowadays, at least in ordinary English usage, novels are respectable and serious, while what the popular bookstores sell under the rubric "romance" is subliterary trash. When we add to this already complicated picture the medieval genre exemplified by the *Roman de la rose* and the like, and the problem of its relationship (or lack of relationship) to later prose fiction, in France or Spain or anywhere else, the difficulties are even further compounded.[5]

These are treacherous waters, indeed, and must be approached with caution. But this thorny issue of nomenclature, however interminable and frustrating the discussion may seem, is not without consequences for what lies ahead. The problem is that many readers are used to calling such texts as *Daphnis and Chloe* "ancient romances" rather than "ancient novels"; and the terms are simply not interchangeable. It must be conceded that "ancient romance" is indeed more traditional, and perhaps still more common, than "ancient novel"; but its use seems to beg some important questions.[6] In popular parlance, at least, regardless of the currently fashionable usage among experts, the word "novel" is clearly a generic term, while the word "romance" is used to identify a particular type of novel. To call any ancient work of extended prose fiction a "romance" is thus to anticipate a verdict we are not yet prepared to render, especially since it remains so very unclear exactly what type of novel a "romance" would be. Furthermore, the use of any term like "the ancient romance" may well tempt the incautious into associating the ancient genre at issue with the medieval romance, with which such works as *Daphnis and Chloe* actually have little or nothing in common.[7]

Perhaps the best way out of this apparent impasse is simply to posit a working definition. Let "novel," for the present purposes, designate *an extended prose narrative, in which the characters and the plot are mostly or entirely invented, imagined, or contrived by the author.* This is not only a definition cast in terms that Aristotle would have understood and approved, consisting as it does of two parts, a genus (extended prose narrative) and a difference (invented or contrived); but it is also one which brings into useful prominence the "newness" implicit in the "nov-" stem itself. That the words "novel" and "new" are actually cognates is not merely coincidental and will turn out to be rather important for our purposes here.[8] The novelist, unlike any other narrative artist in antiquity, is not retelling a story he received from some other source but telling a story never told before, and hence "new," or "novel." There is good reason, then, to call the texts which we are about to consider "novels," in the broadest possible sense, though we must do so with two explicit provisions: first, that they will not necessarily fit anyone's a priori prescriptions for the modern genre usually called "novel," whatever one conceives that to be; and second, that the ancient novelists themselves could not possibly have understood what the novel would someday come to be, and many of them would surely not have wanted to call attention to the "novelty" of their texts.

There are some seven or eight extant complete texts in ancient pagan literature that might properly be called "novels," according to this working definition. That dubious eighth is Petronius's *Satyricon*. There are two others in Latin: the well-known *Golden Ass* (or *Metamorphoses*) of Apuleius, and the anonymous *Life of Apollonius of Tyre*, which is fairly well known to students of the medieval romance, but not otherwise. In Greek, there are none nearly as well known as either the *Satyricon* or the *Golden Ass*. Five are extant, and more or less complete: *Chaereas and Callirhoe*, by one Chariton of Aphrodisias; *Anthia and Habrocomes*, by an author known only under the nom de plume Xenophon Ephesius; *Leucippe and Clitophon*, by Achilles Tatius; *Daphnis and Chloe;* and *Theagenes and Charicleia*, by Heliodorus.[9] Most of these are also known by other titles.[10] They are listed here in what is probably chronological order and span a period from the last quarter of the first century A.D. to perhaps 350 A.D., though the latter date may be too late for Heliodorus by as much as a century. It is with these texts, then, that the balance of this chapter will be concerned.[11]

At most major universities, the most diligent of searchers would be hard put to it to discover more than a handful of scholars, perhaps even in the classics department, who have ever heard of any of the Greek novels just mentioned, though most will have heard of Petronius and Apuleius. This is by no means a purely modern phenomenon; indeed, the ancients themselves did not even have a name for what we have just agreed to call the "novel." The literary establishment of later classical antiquity took little notice of the texts in question; such grammarians as even deigned to take notice of them consigned them to the backwaters of such other, older genres as history, or sometimes (interestingly enough) drama. This failure to give the nascent novel a home of its own is not hard to explain. On the one hand, the texts in question, precisely because they are prose fiction, depart significantly from the "classical" canons of literary composition, which provided no basis for a nice distinction between fiction and lying. Hence there is something disreputable about the whole project of writing fictional stories in prose, ab initio.[12] On the other hand, taken as a whole, the corpus of the ancient Greek novel is not an overwhelmingly impressive or distinguished one, in terms of literary quality. The ancient critics may well be forgiven for apparently regarding the novel as a literary experiment which failed to bear fruit. This is not to say that their judgment was or is correct but only that it is not hard to understand.

Succeeding centuries, however, have sometimes been rather kinder. The Byzantines produced any number of novels patterned on the ancient ones; indeed, it is to one of these Byzantine novelists, Nicetas Eugenianus, that we owe our earliest notice of *Daphnis and Chloe*.[13] Naturally, the ancient Greek novels were quite forgotten in the Latin West during the Middle Ages;[14] but when the Renaissance rediscovered the language and culture of ancient Greece, the Greek novels found some new and appreciative readers. Alonso López de Pinciano, a sixteenth-century Spanish scholar, named Homer, Vergil, and Heliodorus as the three canonical epic poets of antiquity without a blush.[15] Longus, too, found admirers in the sixteenth century, though not, for the most part, among classicists: *Daphnis and Chloe* was first committed to print, not in an editio princeps of the Greek text, but in a very popular French translation by Jacques Amyot, which is still a monument of French literature in its own right. Texts and translations continued to be published in respectable numbers well into the nineteenth century, as witness Goethe's oft-quoted enthusiasm.[16]

Still, it may seem odd, at first, to speak of a "tradition" of the ancient Greek novel. Though the genre may have been several centuries old by Longus's time, it was certainly not a "classical" genre, as the Greeks might have thought of "classical," and hence seems to be deficient precisely in terms of tradition. But one can speak of a certain history of the Greek novel prior to Longus; and at least the literary sense of the word "tradition" really requires no more than that there be predecessors who worked in the same genre. For that matter, enough evidence exists (in the form of extant texts, references to and synopses of yet others, papyrus scraps, reasonable conjectures, and the like) to make it possible for us at least to outline the shape of that tradition.

THE "RECIPE"

It is not at all uncommon for theories about the origins of the ancient novel (Greek and Roman) to assign *Daphnis and Chloe*, implicitly or explicitly, to a niche all its own: usually, "the pastoral romance," as though it were, so to speak, a tangent in the development of the genre, if not almost as sui generis as Petronius's *Satyricon.*[17] It seems to stick out like the proverbial sore thumb from among its fellows, even if we are careful to avoid overemphasizing the similarity of most of these texts to one another.[18] But there are reasons why it is such a temptation to overstate the esssential sameness of the ancient Greek novels, and reasons, too, why this temptation increases exponentially if *Daphnis and Chloe* is set aside. By the time most readers have read one or two of these books, reading another one (again, *Daphnis and Chloe* excepted) can be rather like watching a Western, at the movies or on television, if one grew up with the genre. It becomes possible to predict with fair accuracy, at any given moment, what is likely to happen next. When one cowboy says, "It's quiet out here," the other cowboy will say, "Yeah, too quiet," and the Indians will shortly appear. In the same way, then, an assiduous reader of ancient Greek novels, given a passage where the hero and heroine are on board a ship, knows with some confidence that there are pirates just over the horizon. Not that surprises are impossible; many changes can surely be rung on the familiar themes. Still, if a movie were to be set in the Old West, but no horses or cows or Indians or gunslingers or sheriffs should appear, then by that very omission the movie would not be a Western, at least in the usual sense. In that same way, a long work of prose fiction from ancient Greece that did not concern itself with the trials and tribulations of two young lovers would not in any useful sense be a part of this genre.

The question, then, becomes this: If *Daphnis and Chloe* seems not to be compounded of the same ingredients as the other four ancient Greek novels, should it then be regarded as somehow essentially separate from them, as not really participating in the same tradition? The easy answer is clearly yes; but the matter is important enough to deserve second thoughts. This question of Longus's assumed position vis-à-vis the tradition of the ancient Greek novel can hardly be answered satisfactorily, in fact, without some data a little more substantial than an initial impression. In particular, it stands to reason that we really ought to have some sense of what the "ingredients" in question actually are.

What follows is not intended to be an exhaustive list of all the recurrent themes in the ancient Greek novels and may exhibit exclusions or inclusions that one reader or another will quarrel with; but then, this book is not a comprehensive history of the genre. For the same reason, no judgments will be made here as to the relative importance of these themes or their possible bearing on the much-disputed origins of the novel.[19] And while we may remark at the outset that many of these themes are not original with or unique to the ancient Greek novels, and that many in particular seem to have originated in the Middle Comedy, this is not really the time or the place to make anything of that. I shall focus my attention here on those "ingredients" which Chariton, Xenophon Ephesius, Achilles Tatius, and Heliodorus have in common, and exclude whatever does not find at least some play in every one of them. For the sake of the argument, then, I shall temporarily set *Daphnis and Chloe* aside and see if it is possible to extract from the remaining four texts a certain set of themes that seem to be more or less constitutive of the tradition.[20]

It may be necessary at this point to clarify the precise relationship between the words "tradition" and "theme." Part of the difficulty here is that the latter term is notoriously vague and can be applied to quite disparate phenomena, ranging from the very general (the tenor or substance of an entire work) to the very particular (a recurrent image, or incident, or even a trope). What any of this has to do with "tradition," or how a given set of themes may be called "constitutive" of a certain tradition, is not likely to be transparent. For the present purposes, however, it may prove useful to indulge in a metaphor, which has already been implied in an earlier metaphorical use of the word "ingredient." If a work of literary art is compared with a work of culinary art, all sorts of unexpected connections begin to appear. One begins with a certain intention; say, for example, to bake a cake. The first concrete step is to consult a recipe, to see how someone else has done the thing before. Then one assembles the ingredients, which are combined and processed in certain prescribed ways to make the finished whole. These particular ingredients can be compounded in different ways and in different proportions; and they obviously vary among themselves, too, in how essential they are to the achievement of a particular result. If we take flour, eggs, sugar, milk, and a leavening agent, combine them in a pan, and bake them, the result is generally a cake. This set of ingredients, then, may properly be called constitutive, in that omitting one or more of them is likely to result in something other than a cake. Most cake recipes, of course, contain many more ingredients than these, especially flavorings of some sort. In fact, what makes the difference between one cake and another is usually a certain variation in the proportion of the ingredients, the inclusion of additional ingredients unique to a given recipe (spices and the like), and particular techniques of mixing and baking. (Naturally, the skill of the baker is also an important factor.) The same techniques, of course, and even some of the same ingredients, can be employed with other recipes altogether, but the result is ipso facto something other than a cake, although it may be more or less like a cake, depending on its ingredients. Conversely, the very same ingredients that one might use to bake a cake can, if handled differently, be made into something else: cookies or pancakes or a pie crust or what-have-you.

For a literary text an author begins with a certain intention, to write a particular kind of work, in a certain genre; thus an author's intention to write a novel corresponds, in terms of the metaphor, to a cook's intention to bake a cake. Seldom, of course, does any author set about this task in entire innocence or disregard of previous endeavors along the same line, any more than most cooks set out to bake something utterly new, without reference to a received recipe.[21] The literary "recipe" is the tradition. Due allowance must be made for individual insight, of course; just as the best cooks seldom follow a recipe slavishly, without some effort to improve it, so the best authors add things of their own to the tradition as they have received it. But there are very definite limits. Our hypothetical baker might decide to depart from the cake recipe so completely as to bake eggs, milk, cheese, and asparagus in a pastry shell; but while the thing might be perfectly edible, no one will mistake it for a cake. In literature the tradition has largely the function of a recipe, in that it tells an author what things to include and how to handle them, so as to produce a result that fits within a recognized genre.

The "themes" of a text, then, are its ingredients. Certain of them are thus constitutive of the tradition, in that a text without them is ipso facto something else. For example, a long narrative poem that lacked a hero, or some sort of struggle, would have a hard time claiming to be an epic. Other themes are added for individuation and spice, some very commonly, others only now and again; and this even allows for a region of ambiguity, ingredients (themes) that are important enough to a certain cake (text) that it is unclear whether they should be viewed as constitutive of the recipe (tradition) or not.

Finally, the techniques of mixing and baking correspond to literary technique, including form and narrative mode. Thus a certain text might contain whatever themes one might think of as constitutive of an epic; but if the text in question is not a long narrative poem, the result, though it may be something worth reading, is not an epic. This raises some interesting questions, of course, which will be dealt with in due time; but for now, we must turn our attention back to themes, and the effort to discover at least some of the themes that are clearly constitutive of the ancient Greek novel.

The one theme with which any list would necessarily begin is what we would now call "romance." All of these novels revolve around a love affair between two amiable young lovers. To be even more exact, the central characters are young lovers, well-born and beautiful, who fall in love with each other at first sight, usually when they catch a glimpse of one another on some public occasion. Their mutual passion is immediate and intense.[22] Their immediate goal is marriage, but there is a certain variation in how this is handled: Chariton and Xenophon Ephesius marry their protagonists early on, and proceed from there, while Achilles Tatius and Heliodorus make the marriage itself the consummation of the plot.

In each of these four novels, the lovers are at some point separated from one another. Their efforts to be reunited provide, in fact, the engine which drives most of the novel's action. Thus Chaereas, in a fit of jealous rage, kicks Callirhoe in the stomach; believed dead, she is duly buried. As it turns out, however, she is not really dead and is carried away by pirates (who have taken to grave robbing to supplement their income). Chaereas learns of this, sets out to recover his lost wife, and we are off and running. When Anthia and Habrocomes are sent on a voyage, pirates appear and carry them off; various vicissitudes conspire to separate them, so that Habrocomes must spend much of the rest of the novel searching for Anthia. Much the same is true of Leucippe and Clitophon, at least in general outline. Heliodorus's lovers spend rather more of the novel in each other's company, but there are still vitally important periods of separation.

To whatever extent the lovers are separated, then, there is still a "Great Voyage" that the lovers must undertake, whether or not separation is the cause or the consequence thereof. Implicit in all this is a great deal of travel, usually to exotic locations.[23] Our protagonists are likely to be flung hither and yon around the Mediterranean basin, and sometimes even further. Thus Chaereas and Callirhoe end up far from Syracuse, in the very heart of the Persian Empire; and the dénouement of the novel takes place in Egypt. The latter, in fact, turns out to be the locale of choice. Heliodorus opens his story in the Nile delta and ends it in Ethiopia; Achilles Tatius contrives to bring Leucippe and Clitophon to Egypt; Xenophon Ephesius uses the merest of pretexts to send Anthia and Habrocomes off on a voyage, first to Rhodes, then (not entirely as planned) to Egypt. The *Liebespaar* must make their way in a strange and exotic land, far from their home and their kin.[24]

And there are always pirates (or brigands, the distinction between robbery at sea and robbery on land being not so clear in
the Greek term ληστής), who either precipitate or interrupt the
voyage. One or another (or both) of the lovers will stand in peril
of his or her life, but will (of course) be spared, albeit only to be
sold as a slave. Some of these pirates become full-fledged characters in the novel, while others have only a walk-on role; but
whether the part they play is large or small, their appearance is
de rigueur. That they somehow represent lawlessness and savag-
ery is patent; but the differences in the way they are handled by
the various authors should make us wary of any further gener-
alizations about their significance.

Pirates are not, however, the only peril likely to be faced by
the protagonists in an ancient Greek novel. Threats to the virtue
of either or both of the lovers are a constant feature; but (with
one outstanding exception, which will be discussed in a moment)
both the man and the woman remain faithful to one another
and successfully resist force and seduction, in spirit if not always
in the flesh. They are, in fact, models of probity, with due allowance for the somewhat looser sexual mores of antiquity. This
raises another issue, however. Given those mores, it is one thing
to expect these young lovers to abstain from sexual relations
with anyone other than the beloved; but it is quite another to expect them to abstain from premarital relations with each other.
Of course, Chariton and Xenophon Ephesius avoid the problem
by arranging an immediate marriage between the protagonists;
but Heliodorus confronts it squarely. Charicleia refuses to marry
Theagenes until she has completed her mysterious errand in
Ethiopia, despite their great mutual passion. Unlike the young
lovers in the other novels, Theagenes and Charicleia are together perhaps more than they are apart, which gives them the
opportunity to anticipate the ceremony. Indeed, Theagenes is
driven to importune her more than once, but she resists, and in
the end he respects that resistance. So pristine is Charicleia's virtue, then, that she resists not only the seduction of rivals for her
affection but even the seduction of her lover.

Leucippe and Clitophon appear to be an obvious exception to
all this. It is clear, really, that neither of them is precisely innocent from the outset. Both are engaged to others, and both en-

gagements are broken, none too gently. Their experience in
these matters is manifest in how they respond to their mutual
attraction: not by pining away but by arranging an assignation in
Leucippe's bedroom. And they would have carried the thing off,
too, if it had not been for the untimely arrival of Leucippe's
mother. It is precisely this, in fact, which motivates the "Great
Voyage" of this novel: Clitophon must flee the wrath of an out-
raged mother, and he takes Leucippe along. As if this were not
outrageous enough, an even more patent flouting of the usual
moral standards occurs later on, after Clitophon has been given
good reason to believe that Leucippe is dead. A lusty widow conceives a grand passion for him, and at length he agrees to marry
her; but after the wedding, he makes excuse after excuse to
postpone consummating the marriage. Eventually he discovers
that Leucippe is still alive—and at once gives in to the widow's
sexual advances. As for Leucippe, she does indeed pass a "chastity test" at one point, but no one is more surprised than she at
the outcome.

Something here is clearly amiss; but in many ways, Achilles
Tatius is the exception that proves the rule. For on this and
many other grounds, it seems clear that *Leucippe and Clitophon* is,
in intention and execution, a parody.[25] Achilles Tatius does not
so much discard the received theme of chastity as turn it on its
ear. And in the very process of mocking the conventional chastity and fidelity of the hero and the heroine, he reveals all the
more clearly that chastity and fidelity are just that, conventional.
Otherwise the joke has no point.

Some mention was made in passing just now of a moment at
which Clitophon had reason to suppose that Leucippe was dead;
and this might very well remind us of how Callirhoe, too, was at
one point presumed dead. This leads us to the last theme to be
considered here, the *Scheintod,* or presumed death, some form
of which occurs in each of the four texts under consideration.[26]
Chaereas is convinced by disappointed rivals bent on revenge
that Callirhoe has been unfaithful to him (which is untrue, of
course); he storms home and kicks her in the stomach, sending
her into a coma that everyone mistakes for death. Chaereas discovers the mistake when he goes down to Callirhoe's tomb in de-

spair, with the intention of committing suicide, only to learn that she is (*a*) not dead but (*b*) in the hands of pirates. Anthia is parted from the imprisoned Habrocomes, assuring him as she leaves that she plans to commit suicide; Habrocomes searches for her after his release, but it is her corpse that he expects to find, not her living self. Anthia, for her part, assumes that Habrocomes has not survived prison, and desires only to live long enough to visit his tomb. Theagenes, in the robbers' cave, stumbles over the body of a young woman in the chamber where Charicleia was being held captive and naturally assumes that she has been murdered by her captors. He is on the point of committing suicide, when he suddenly realizes that the body beneath him is not Charicleia, after all. All these scenes are naturally followed by melodramatically joyous reunions when the truth is discovered. The pattern, then, remains consistent: a presumption that the lover is dead; despair; intention to committ suicide; and a last-minute reprieve.

It is Achilles Tatius, however, who takes the prize for *Scheintod* scenes. There are two in *Leucippe and Clitophon,* and they are remarkable indeed. In the first instance, Clitophon is a helpless and horrified witness as two pirates disembowel Leucippe, cook her entrails, and make a feast of them. But—mirabile dictu—it is all a hoax. The two pirates turn out to be friends in disguise, who have rigged up an elaborate mechanism to extract sheep entrails from a bag under Leucippe's clothing, so as to convince the enemy that she is dead. A joyous reunion follows, but the relief is short-lived. Leucippe is snatched by another villain, who escapes in a ship; Clitophon pursues in a ship of his own and is on the point of overtaking the fugitive, when, to his horror, the villain stands Leucippe up where Clitophon can see her and beheads her. The pursuing ship stops to retrieve the headless trunk (the head is lost), and the villain makes good his escape. It is after this sad episode that the despondent Clitophon falls in with the widow Melitte. Once again, however, things are not as they seem. This time, it was not Leucippe, but a hapless slave girl dressed in her clothes, who was beheaded. Leucippe herself ends up in slavery and is finally bought (in perfect ignorance of the true state of affairs) by none other than Melitte.

By now, it should be clear what is going on here. This baroque excess in the handling of the *Scheintod* is clearly part of the parody that characterizes the whole novel. This time, instead of inverting or subverting a conventional theme, Achilles Tatius has pushed the theme up to and quite beyond its reasonable limits. The effect, in spite of the gruesomeness (perhaps even because of it), is clearly comic.

In summary, then, some six common themes, six "ingredients," recur in each of the texts at hand, with both sufficient regularity and sufficient prominence to justify our considering them to be constitutive of the tradition.[27] Listed in the order in which they have been discussed, these themes are as follows:

1. The *Liebespaar,* two beautiful and amiable young lovers, of relatively high social status, who fall in love at first sight.
2. Separation of the lovers, and their efforts to be reunited.
3. The "Great Voyage."
4. Pirates and brigands.
5. Chastity and fidelity in the face of force or seduction.
6. The *Scheintod.*

LONGUS THE NOVELIST

The arguments advanced by some scholars for the isolation of *Daphnis and Chloe* from the tradition of the ancient Greek novel prove upon examination to be primarily thematological and proceed from a premise which seems safe enough, on the face of it: namely, that Longus, in giving his novel a pastoral setting, manages thereby to omit or avoid most of the constitutive themes of the Greek novel. The prima facie case is hard to deny. It rather looks as though Longus has used different ingredients, for the most part, and so produced, *ex hypothesi,* a different sort of text. But a closer examination of *Daphnis and Chloe* yields surprising results. In one way or another, the traditional ingredients are all there; but they are worked into the text with such subtlety that the effect of discovering them is almost shocking. That very shock, however, will take us yet another step closer to understanding what *Daphnis and Chloe* is about.

To begin with, there is surely a romance between two young lovers in *Daphnis and Chloe*; but the problem is that Longus's protagonists are not true to type. The other young lovers are well-born city folk, as we saw. Daphnis and Chloe, on the other hand, are of the rural poor, and Daphnis is a slave. Even within the hierarchy of his closed pastoral world, Daphnis is near the bottom of the social ladder, since he is a goatherd, and thus outranked, according to well-known pastoral conventions, by shepherds (like Chloe), and especially by cowherds, who are always the elite in that milieu. At the very beginning of the novel, however, the reader is let in on a secret, that Daphnis and Chloe are exposed infants of apparently aristocratic (or at least upper-middle-class) birth. By the end of book 4, we have learned the true identity of our lovers, who are the lost children of two of the most prominent and wealthy families of Mitylene. Throughout the novel, then, Daphnis and Chloe have looked, talked, and acted like people from very near the bottom of the social order; but they turn out in the end to be from backgrounds very like what is expected of the hero and heroine of a Greek novel. Longus has had some fun with this, and only the humorless will fail to understand or appreciate it.

In the other Greek novels, as we saw, the protagonists fall in love at first sight; they have never met or even seen one another, until a sudden chance encounter, usually on the occasion of a festival, enkindles their mutual passion. The fact that they are lovers is thereafter manifest and settled.[28] Daphnis and Chloe, by contrast, are raised in the same vicinity and are companions and playmates well before they become lovers. Each falls victim to erotic passion for the other but at different times and in quite different ways: Daphnis is undone by Chloe's kiss after the speech contest, while it was the sight of Daphnis's nude body, several days before, that has already smitten Chloe. Neither of them has the slightest idea what is going on, and it is not until early in book 2 that Philetas comes along to tell them who Eros is. Not until near the end of book 3 does Daphnis find out what one does about erotic passion, and the actual, physical consummation of their love is delayed until the very end of the story. Only in the very last sentence of *Daphnis and Chloe*, with the newlyweds in their nuptial chamber, does Chloe find out what Daphnis has known since Lycaenium lured him into the woods: καὶ τότε Χλόη πρῶτον ἔμαθεν ὅτι τὰ ἐπὶ τῆς ὕλης γινόμενα ἦν ποιμένων παίγνια ("And then Chloe first learned that the things that happened in the woods were shepherd's games" [4.40]). Thus what takes a few paragraphs at most in the other Greek novels, the arousal and recognition of erotic passion, is here extended to fill the entire novel.[29]

The separation of the hero and heroine and their consequent efforts to be reunited motivate much of the plot in the other Greek novels. There are separations in *Daphnis and Chloe*, to be sure, but Longus subjects this theme to severe compression. Thus the protagonists are actually separated on various occasions, several times in a way that might tempt the reader into supposing that we have at last ventured into familiar territory; but none of these separations turns out as expected. Thus, near the end of book 1, Daphnis and Chloe are indeed separated by marauding pirates—who kidnap, not Chloe, but Daphnis. And they get no farther than one hundred yards offshore before their ship is destroyed by, of all things, a stampede, whereupon Daphnis rides to safety on the horns of swimming cattle. In book 2, it is Chloe's turn to be kidnapped. But she is gone less than twenty-four hours before the god Pan arranges her rescue. In book 3, Daphnis and Chloe are separated by winter, but Daphnis quickly contrives a means to spend time at Chloe's house. Finally, in book 4, Chloe is kidnapped by the brutish Lampis; but she is promptly rescued by Gnathon before she suffers anything more than a few bumps and some anxious moments. Thus each book contains a separation, but none of these lasts more than a page or so, at the most. The theme of separation is present, then, but in an almost tantalizing way, in that it never leads in the direction a reader of the other ancient Greek novels would have expected. Here, even more markedly, Longus is playing with the tradition, evoking it only to dance around it and surprise us.

As for travel, Daphnis and Chloe leave the estate where they grew up only once, briefly, late in book 4; they are conveyed only a few miles to Mitylene, after which they return to their old haunts at the earliest opportunity. The setting of *Daphnis and*

Chloe is thus as concentrated as that of all the other novels is diffuse. Longus has made a point of confining the action within incredibly tight constraints, a confinement which would not be nearly so interesting if his audience had not reasonably expected just the opposite. In this respect, again, the traditional theme has not so much been overlooked as turned on its ear.

When the prologue of Daphnis and Chloe mentions λῃστῶν καταδρομή, πολεμίων ἐμβολή ("an incursion of pirates, an invasion of enemies"), the ancient reader would very reasonably have expected that he or she was about to read the same kind of adventure story so familiar from *Chaereas and Callirhoe* and the like. We do meet pirates, but they are ineffectual and are quickly disposed of. We meet enemies, but they, too, end up looking rather ridiculous. On the other hand, we meet unscrupulous men (Dorcon and Lampis), who serve to advance the action by lusting after Chloe; but they are shepherds, not pirates. They may act abominably, but they are not outlaws. On the contrary, they are the ones who really belong in this pastoral world, while Daphnis and Chloe do not. There is also Gnathon, who also precipitates important developments by his lust, and who is not a shepherd. Then again, he is no pirate. He has a place in society, however unseemly, and we have already seen that his contribution is not inconsiderable.

With the glaring exception of Clitophon and Leucippe, the young lovers of the other Greek novels are chaste and faithful to each other, and much of the action of the novel revolves around their attempts to preserve their often endangered virtue. Daphnis and Chloe do in fact abstain from premarital intercourse but not because of a committment to bourgeois morality. What keeps Daphnis and Chloe from anticipating the ceremony of marriage is their unbelievable naiveté: they do not make love because they do not know how. Daphnis will finally learn the necessary techniques in book 3 (from another woman, interestingly enough); but he then refrains from applying his newfound knowledge to Chloe, because of Lycaenium's warning (that Chloe, because she is a virgin, will bleed and cry out the first time). In this way, then, Longus gives us chastity and fidelity (more or less), in the oddest of guises and for the oddest of reasons, de facto rather than de jure. Had Lycaenium come around in book 1, instead of waiting until the middle of book 3, the "shepherd's games" (ποιμένων παίγνια) of the novel's last sentence might have been played by different rules.

Though the examples of Longus's ironic handling of various conventional themes of the Greek novel could be multiplied beyond the six with which we began, only one more is necessary here.[30] The *Scheintod,* the apparent death, seems at first glance to be missing in *Daphnis and Chloe,* at least in its usual form: at no point does either of the protagonists believe that the other is dead. As might be expected, however, there are several scenes in which Longus seems to play with this theme. Most striking is the exposure of both Daphnis and Chloe, whose parents, because they have chosen to expose these two babies, naturally believe them to have died; thus the main action of the novel transpires while both protagonists are thought (elsewhere, by characters almost as unknown to the reader as to the protagonists themselves) to be dead. It might even be argued, on these grounds, that the *Scheintod* theme is not missing in *Daphnis and Chloe,* or even attenuated, but rather that, like the development of erotic passion, it has been expanded to fill the whole novel. This expansion paradoxically results in a fascinating transformation of the theme. It has been, in a sense, turned inside out, so that we, as readers, experience the *Scheintod* from the point of view, not of the party who grieves for the specious loss, but of those wrongly presumed dead.

Even without the elaboration of further instances, it should be clear by now that Longus has not really abandoned the conventional themes of the ancient Greek novel but rather transformed them, turned them inside out and upside down, constantly alluding to them without ever evoking them in a simple or obvious manner. Nor is this allusive play merely incidental; on the contrary, it at least implies that *Daphnis and Chloe* is meant to be a critique of sorts. Playing with a tradition, after all, means nothing other than not taking it seriously. Then, too, we have already noticed that Achilles Tatius, for his part, does not want to take the tradition seriously, though his way of signaling this is rather different. What can one say, then, about a tradition, represented by five extant texts, of which two are clearly mocking the tradition itself, one quite overtly, and the other on the sly?

At this point, some students of the modern novel may feel a shock of recognition. *Pamela,* after all, was followed almost immediately by *Tom Jones* and *Moll Flanders,* both of which have great fun at the expense of the former and its ilk, and both of which are also far more important for the history of the novel than "serious" works like *Pamela.* Cervantes, too, wrote *Don Quixote* in a spirit of mockery, ridiculing the pretensions of the chivalric romances so much in vogue in his time. It is often said of *Quixote,* in fact, that its greatness surprised no one more than Cervantes himself. After all, he took far more pride, and invested far more labor, in his last novel, *Persiles y Sigismunda,* which he wrote in an avowed effort to imitate Heliodorus. But almost no one reads *Persiles y Sigismunda* (which has never been translated into English), precisely because, for all its great seriousness, it is completely overshadowed in literary history by the not entirely serious *Quixote.* So it seems that our original question about the ancient Greek novel, and its tendency at a rather early stage in its growth to turn on itself, may well be a much larger question. What is it about novels, that they seem to grow best by biting the hand that fed them?

Thematology has led us to the point of asking this question, but it really does not provide us with sufficient means to answer it. For there is more to understanding the tradition of the ancient Greek novel than thematology, just as a cake is more than a pile of ingredients. Much depends on how the cake is cooked; much depends, too, on how the story is told. It has already been suggested that the ancient Greek novel, as a genre, had a certain problem in establishing itself within the much larger and broader tradition of Greek literature; and this problem is not thematological. Very few of the themes we have just discussed do not occur in one form or another in much older and more respectable literature. In its starkest terms, the problem is that no such thing as an ancient Greek novel should even exist. Examining what that really means will be the topic of the next chapter.

Chapter 9

The Novel and History

Nothing in the previous literary history of classical antiquity quite prepares us for *Chaereas and Callirhoe*. Even today, students with some experience of ancient Greek literature who are assigned to read one of the Greek novels, perhaps especially Heliodorus, often refuse to believe at first that this is an ancient book they are reading. Yet it would be perverse to argue that no one ever thought of telling long stories about young lovers and their adventures and tribulations before the latter half of the Hellenistic Age. The telling of stories is surely as old as speech itself; and storytelling, in prose, can hardly have been the invention of the first century B.C., even if it did not become a literary genre in the West before then.[1] It might be fair to say that at the time of its first appearance in the Graeco-Roman world as a literary genre, prose fiction was at once very old and very new.

The greatest obstacle to the admission of the novel into the mainstream of respectable literature was not that stories compounded of the thematic ingredients discussed in the previous chapter were inconceivable in terms of their content. The real problem cuts much deeper. "Prose fiction," from the classical point of view, is an egregious oxymoron, a contradiction in terms. In antiquity, any narrative written in prose was ipso facto a "true" story, in fact a history. What is more, even poetic nar-

rative kept for the most part within certain bounds of referentiality, though the lines may have been drawn a little more
generously for poets than for historians. In verse as much as in
prose, a "true" story means a story which represents real persons
and real events, things that are accepted or believed by both
author and audience to have actually occurred. Whatever is not
true, in this referential or representational sense, is a fortiori
false, and what is false is a lie. Only the comic poets are allowed
to invent characters and events, and even there the most likely
explanation for this license to fabricate persons and events is
that, by their very raison d'être, comedies are not to be taken
seriously.

What we are here calling a "novel," from this point of view,
would thus be an extended prose lie and therefore either erro-
neous or deceptive or both. Even Homer cannot get away with
that fundamental an untruth. In book 1 of the *Peloponnesian
War*, to be sure, Thucydides expresses a degreee of skepticism
about Homer's account of the Greek expedition to Troy and suggests that Homer, as poet, embellished his tale; but it does not
occur to him to suggest that the Trojan War itself never really
happened, or that there never was an Agamemnon. Thucydides
himself, later in book 1, admits without a blush that he has put
words into other people's mouths, so that we will sometimes hear
from him what was actually said on a particular occasion, and at
other times what should have been said.[2] There is a subtle but
vital difference, however, between inserting speeches that *should*
have been given or *might* have been given into a basically accurate account of actual events, on the one hand, and fabricating
not only the words of the speech but even the occasion and the
speaker on the other. Even when, absent reliable witnesses,
Thucydides conjectures what someone is likely to have said on a
particular occasion, he is certainly not imagining the occasion itself. Only the deficiency of certain knowledge about what was actually said makes it necessary for him to put words into other
people's mouths.

Poetry is often taken to be a different kettle of fish in this regard, in that the poets tell stories that can often be quite fantastic
and contrary to the audience's lived experience of reality. But

then, the stories are told about people and events from a very remote past, when it seems very likely that "reality" was rather different. They may be fantastic, then, but they are or purport to be "true" stories, none the less. If Homer says something that seems even to an ancient reader not to be strictly true, that is either because he was mistaken or because he had no way of knowing exactly who did what when. Thus he is "filling in the cracks," so to speak, in a story which remains true, taken as a whole. The idea that anyone could tell an entirely invented story, out of his own private imagination, which he would then expect to mean something to anyone other than himself, was almost literally unthinkable. Embellishment, exaggerration, yes; but outright fiction, no.

Some modern readers may object, of course, that the *Iliad* and the *Odyssey* are qualitatively or generically different from Thucydides' history; that is, the Peloponnesian War is a real historical event, but the Trojan War is mostly or entirely mythical, which is something altogether different. It is clear, however, exactly from Thucydides' handling of Homer, and even clearer from the first books of Herodotus, that the line between myth and history was not so sharp and clear in antiquity as it seems to be now. The Greek words μῦθος (*mythos*) and ἱστορία (*historia*) are not regularly, if ever, put in direct opposition to each other in Greek diction. Still, it is Thucydides himself who first brought into focus this tension between myth and history; for in that same famous passage in which he explains his reasons for inventing some of the speeches, he says this:

καὶ ἐς μὲν ἀκρόασιν ἴσως τὸ μὴ μυθῶδες αὐτῶν [sc. τῶν ἐμῶν λόγων] ἀτερπέστερον φανεῖται· ὅσοι δὲ βουλήσονται τῶν τε γενομένων τὸ σαφὲς σκοπεῖν καὶ τῶν μελλόντων ποτὲ αὖθις κατὰ τὸ ἀνθρώπινον τοιούτων καὶ παραπλησίων ἔσεσθαι, ὠφέλιμα κρίνειν αὐτὰ ἀρκούντως ἕξει. κτῆμά τε ἐς αἰεὶ μᾶλλον ἢ ἀγώνισμα ἐς τὸ παραχρῆμα ἀκούειν ξύγκειται.

(To the hearing, perhaps, the unmythical nature of these things will appear rather unpleasant. But such as wish to examine the reality of what happened, and of the same and very similar things which will someday occur again, in accordance with human nature—it will be enough [for such people] to judge them useful.

And one may now hear [something that is] a possession for all time, not a competition piece for the moment.)[3]

For Thucydides, then, there is something in the mythical (τὸ μυθῶδες) repugnant to a purely "scientific" understanding of the past. Not that even Thucydides thought of himself as a historian in the modern sense, interested in the past for its own sake. The ancient historian used his material, the events and persons of the past, to create a literary text, the meaning of which often, if not always, referred as much to the present or the future as the past. Thucydides makes it clear enough that his goal is more to edify than to inform. The past as past was not the subject, or better yet the object, of history.

We must not be misled by this line of reasoning into the facile conclusion that the ancients were so credulous as to suppose that Homer and Thucydides were equally reliable witnesses. The real point is that the Trojan War was to Homer essentially what the Peloponnesian War was to Thucydides: not an object of study per se but a subject around which and through which certain eternal truths about human nature could be revealed. For that matter, the rules which guided Thucydides in dealing with his subject are not at all unlike those Sophocles had to follow in telling the story of Oedipus in *Oedipus the King*. Neither author is at liberty to change the essential data: Sophocles can no more keep Oedipus from killing Laius and marrying Jocasta than Thucydides can keep Athens from losing the war. Both are retelling a story that they received from some particular source, whether it be from eyewitnesses or from an ancient tradition. From this point of view, the only real difference between the historian and the tragedian is that Sophocles, because his story is much more remote in time, is freer than is Thucydides to add and subtract details, even sometimes to alter the sequence of events.

There is this difference, then, between myth and history, that the former takes its stories from a remoter period of time, perhaps even from across a great gulf of time, which means that these stories come from a world where the "rules" of human and divine action and interaction are often taken to be quite different from the lived reality of teller and audience. But it is absolutely essential to realize, at this point, that neither myth nor history, even myth at its most fantastic, or the most embellished history, is at all the same thing as fiction. In fiction, by definition, the story is not being retold at all. It never existed before the individual author told it, and so its characters and events have only a contingent reality: they do not exist outside the text which has created them. This is not true of the characters of history, or even of myth. To the ancient Greeks, Achilles is as real as Pericles, even if certain aspects of the former's story have elements of the fantastic about them.

Now, anyone who has spent any time at all with Greek literature knows how thoroughly it is dominated by the myths. The whole corpus of myths provides the stuff out of which almost all narrative, especially poetic narrative, is built. It may even be accurate to say that history is to the ancient Greeks nothing more or less than a certain rather special sort of myth, which is another way of explaining why that line between myth and history can be so hard to draw. The Greek word μῦθος, after all, does not mean exactly the same thing as the English derivative, "myth." In Aristotle's *Poetics*, for example, it means nothing more or less than "plot." The μῦθος of *Oedipus the King* is the story of the tyrant of Thebes who killed his father and married his mother; the μῦθος of Herodotus's *Histories* is the story of the conflict between Greece and Persia; and so forth. What it boils down to is that the proper definition of μῦθος is really nothing more than "story"; but where modern audiences may tolerate stories that are "brand new" when they are heard for the first time, and often even prefer them that way, ancient audiences did not. Thus Kirk's definition of myth as "traditional tale" needs the qualifier "traditional" more from the modern point of view than from the ancient.

Myth, then, is something that exists in tradition and is not anyone's particular creation or property. History exists in the concrete particulars of the past, and so it, too, is no one's private creation. And the inescapable fact is that no one tells a story in classical Greek prose unless it is drawn from history or myth—which is to say, that there is no room for fiction, as something distinct from ordinary mendacity, in ancient narrative. It is not that the imagination has no play. The mythical or historical datum is the clay, so to speak, ready to be fashioned by the author into whatever he can make of it. (Aristotle called this τὸ πλάσμα [to plasma]; we might be inclined to say, "poetic license.") But what no one in antiquity seems to have done, or have thought of doing, is to do what Melville does when he writes *Moby Dick*— that is, invent a story, essentially from whole cloth, and people it with invented characters. No one in antiquity can say, "Call me Ishmael," unless his name *is* Ishmael, or unless he at least wants his reader to think so. The ancient Greek reader always wanted to have some sort of authority for his story, some identifiable source; absent such a grounding, a truly fictional story would be as meaningless as the fantasies of a lunatic.[4]

It was not to be expected, then, that when the novel first appeared in ancient Greek literature, it sprang, Athena-like, fully armed from the head of Zeus. From the beginning, the genre betrayed its indebtedness to history, from which it took its external form, and comedy (especially the Middle and New Comedy), from which it seems to have borrowed a certain amount of its thematic raw material. Still, the novel is in no sense the child of these older forms. Rather, it represents the opening of a narrative door, which the older forms had discovered, in a sense, perhaps even peeked through, but never opened. The novelist sets out to tell a myth of his own devising, even if, for whatever reason, he finds it expedient to conceal that from his readers. And if "a myth of his own devising" sounds rather like a counterfeit coin, that may be why there was something disreputable about novels in antiquity.

Up until about twenty-five years ago, the prevailing wisdom on the subject held that the ancient Greek novel arose as the result of a process of amalgamation, by which bits and pieces of various other literary genres had somehow accreted to produce a new genre. It was rather as though the Greeks, culturally shipwrecked by the Roman conquest, had put together a new vessel from the flotsam and jetsam of various old ones. Just what bits and pieces were involved in this process was, to be sure, never entirely clear. Erwin Rohde, in his magisterial *Der griechische Roman und seine Vorläufer*, suggested that the Greek novel was a fusion of the Alexandrian erotic elegy with travel literature (*die Reisefabelistik*). Eduard Schwartz demurred, being unconvinced, perhaps rightly, that any such identifiable genre as *Reisefabelistik* even existed in antiquity. Schwartz thought that historiography, having somehow acquired from the Alexandrian elegy an unseemly interest in the erotic, was the primary form from which the novel devolved. Later scholars, such as Martin Braun, saw no need to posit some second influence to account for a certain type of, so to speak, erotic history, since a taste for such things, apparent in Herodotus, became endemic in Hellenistic historiography.[5]

Theories such as this are now out of favor. Not only are there problems with the details of the individual theories, which may be apparent even in so summary a sketch as has just been given; but in fact, ever since Ben Perry's *The Ancient Romances*, the whole conception of "development" on the literary plane is highly suspect. According to Perry, the novel did not evolve, or devolve, from some other form; such things, he thought, simply do not happen. Rather, the novel was invented "on a Tuesday afternoon in July," as he put it, by some particular person, with a particular project in mind, for which the old forms would somehow not suffice.[6] The nature of this project, for Perry, had much to do with changes in the culture and society within which the ancient Greek novels were written. One can see, in much of the scholarly work on the Greek novel since 1967, how profound and pervasive has been Perry's influence, even in the work of those who disagree in detail. No one has much to say these days about any supposed "development" of the Greek novel from the flotsam and jetsam of other forms.[7]

It is with no small trepidation, then, that we should here approach the subject of the relationship between historiography and the ancient Greek novel, since the last people to go down this particular road seem to have gotten rather lost. Still, certain facts seem unavoidable, even if their implications are uncomfortable for those given to favoring Perry's nominalist approach to literary genre. The first such fact is one of which no classicist really should need to be reminded. The ancients were very conscious of form as a determinant, not only of genre, in a purely taxonomic sense, but also of content and substance. The adoption of a particular form imposed certain presuppositions about what one meant to say, or even could say, within that form; and these presuppositions had to be addressed, even when an author intended to subvert or bypass them.[8]

The second fact is that the Greek novels, whatever else one might say of them by way of description, are extended prose narratives, a form hitherto reserved for historiography. That is why a novelist, either in antiquity or the present, could easily be mistaken for a debauched historian. (In the end, however, he proves to be something quite different.) The story told in a novel cannot be true in the same sense that a historian's narrative is, or ought to be, true. Thus the writing of a novel involves something that, even if we make allowances for the plasmatic license generally given to historians in antiquity, is still repugnant to the very premises of the genre. Perry, even if he may have been wrong about much else, was quite right about this: "[H]istoriography cannot become romance without passing through zero, that is, through the negation of its own *raison d' être*, that which defines it as historiography."[9] No matter how many liberties a historian may take with his subject, he is still constrained to write about what really was, else he is not writing history; the novelist, on the other hand, ordinarily writes about what never was but might have been.[10] It is necessary, even if in some ways inconvenient, to recognize clearly that there is a logically unbridgeable gap between these two projects. So if we find authors using the form of historiography to do something all but antithetical to history, we are entitled, indeed required, to ask some searching questions about the relationship between these two genres.

Where, then, to begin looking for some answers? The most obvious recourse, of course, is to interrogate the texts themselves. The problem is how to recognize the answers when we find them. We really need to know, rather precisely, where to look.

OPENING GAMBITS

In ancient literature generally, no small importance is attached to the opening words of a given text. This is at least partly for practical reasons. The ancient reader expected to learn from the first words, the first sentence, the first paragraph, much of what we expect today to learn from the title of a book: to wit, what kind of a book it is, and something at least of what it is about. In fact, it seems clear that a given literary text was not infrequently known not by what we consider to be its title but by its first few words, a practice still prevailing in official documents of the Roman Catholic church.[11] Indeed, the role of opening words in establishing content and genre is apparent as early as the Homeric epics, each of which begins with a single word of great thematic resonance. Some scholars are increasingly sensitive to the openings of Plato's dialogues; legend has it, after all, that Plato revised the first sentence of the *Republic* on his deathbed.[12] "Well begun is half done" may be a Jewish proverb, but the Greeks would surely recognize the sentiment, and approve.

A certain difficulty arises, of course, in deciding exactly what constitutes the "beginning" of a work. Some works have formal prologues, others do not. Thucydides devotes half of book 1 to getting under way, while Herodotus launches into his story with his second sentence. Fortunately, a term and a concept borrowed from classical rhetoric is available to control what begins to look very confusing. The rhetoricians, after all, are the ones who made most explicit in their teaching the vital strategic importance of opening moves and even provided their students with a whole taxonomy of possibilities, rather like a chess master sharing his favorite gambits with a promising young player. The term used for "opening" by the Romans, in discussing the formal arrangement of speeches, was "exordium," a term which denotes the function as well as the position of the very first part of a discourse. From this point on, then, we shall borrow this Latin term, and speak of "exordia."

If we are looking for a particular genre to provide examples in support of the general rule that exordia play a significant role in identifying a work as to genre, history will serve rather well.[13] Consider, for example, the first sentences of Herodotus and Thucydides, respectively:

Ἡροδότου Ἁλικαρνησέος ἱστορίης ἀπόδεξις ἥδε, ὡς μήτε τὰ
γενόμενα ἐξ ἀνθρώπων τῷ χρόνῳ ἐξίτηλα γένηται, μήτε ἔργα

μεγάλα τε καὶ θωυμαστά, τὰ μὲν Ἕλλησι, τὰ δὲ βαρβάροισι
ἀποδεχθέντα, ἀκλεᾶ γένηται, τά τε ἄλλα καὶ δι᾽ ἣν αἰτίην ἐπολέμησαν ἀλλήλοισι.

(This is the exposition of the inquiry of Herodotus of Halicar-
nassus, [undertaken] so that neither should what has happened
among men in this time go unnoticed, nor should the great and
marvelous deeds done both by Greeks and barbarians be lacking
in renown. Among other things, [we shall especially consider] for
what reason they made war on one another.)

Θουκυδίδης Ἀθηναῖος ξυνέγραψε τὸν πόλεμον τῶν Πελοπον-
νησίων καὶ Ἀθηναίων, ὡς ἐπολέμησαν πρὸς ἀλλήλους, ἀρξά-
μενος εὐθὺς καθισταμένου καὶ ἐλπίσας μέγαν τε ἔσεσθαι καὶ
ἀξιολογώτατον τῶν προγεγενημένων, τεκμαιρόμενος ὅτι ἀκμά-
ζοντές τε ἦσαν ἐς αὐτὸν ἀμφότεροι παρασκευῇ τῇ πάσῃ καὶ
τὸ ἄλλο Ἑλληνικὸν ὁρῶν ξυνιστάμενον πρὸς ἑκατέρους, τὸ μὲν
εὐθύς, τὸ δὲ καὶ διανοούμενον.

(Thucydides, an Athenian, has written a narrative of the war between the Peloponnesians and the Athenians, how they fought
against one another, having begun as soon as the war broke out,
in the expectation that it would be a great struggle and most
worthy of the telling of all that has gone before, reasoning that
both combatants were at a peak level of preparation for it, and
seeing that all the rest of the Greek world took sides with one or
the other, some right away, others after some deliberation.)

The overall similarity is patent. Each author begins with his
name and provenance; then tells quite directly, though in general terms, what his subject is; and then proceeds to say why he
thinks this subject worth reading and writing about. As most
readers know well, both authors go on from these exordia to
reach far back into mythology, though for different reasons and
in different ways. Herodotus's exposition is basically linear, and
his reason for beginning with Io is that he has traced the story of
the enmity between East and West back just that far. The myths
with which he begins, then, are part of his story, however digressive they sometimes seem. Thucydides, on the other hand,
discusses the Trojan War and other events of almost equally

hoary antiquity, only to say that none of these was of the magnitude of the war between Athens and Sparta. About halfway through book 1, the investigation of mythology reaches its conclusion; at that point, after a few pregnant remarks about his methods of exposition (which we have already examined), Thucydides gets down to business, with the affair at Epidamnus.

Xenophon, in the first sentence of the *Anabasis*, gives us a pattern rather different from what we have just seen in the two older historians: Δαρείου καὶ Παρυσάτιδος γίγνονται παῖδες δύω, πρεσβύτερος μὲν Ἀρταξέρξης, νεώτερος δὲ Κῦρος (Two sons were born to Darius and Parysatis, the elder Artaxerxes, the younger Cyrus).

Here is what looks to be a narrative without any sort of prologue at all, almost an in medias res beginning. Still, note that the first Greek word is the name, Darius, which tells the attentive reader, in no uncertain terms, that we will be hearing something about the Persian monarchy. The rest of the first paragraph actually gives us the background of the dynastic struggle that brought the Ten Thousand into the heart of the Persian Empire and tells us something, too, of the important geography involved. Time and place are thus well, if indirectly, established, so that no reader will go beyond the first few sentences with any substantial doubt that this is a history and that it is about a dynastic struggle in the Persian royal house.

A third identifiable type of traditional historical exordium starts off with geography. It may be well to recall here that history before Herodotus may have been little more than geography. Absent any more than the merest fragments of Hecataeus, it is hard to be sure about this; but a certain relationship between history and geography comes into play in Herodotus, too, which is something to be borne in mind as we proceed. We may notice, for example, how Appian begins his survey of the history of Rome: Τὴν Ῥωμαικὴν ἱστορίαν ἀρχόμενος συγγράφειν ἀναγκαῖον ἡγησάμην προτάξαι τοὺς ὅρους ὅσων ἐθνῶν ἄρχουσι Ῥωμαῖοι ("In starting out to narrate Roman history, I have deemed it necessary to lay out the boundaries of such people as the Romans rule over").

That such beginnings were well established in later historiography, even before Appian, is attested by the opening sentences of Caesar's *De Bello Gallico* and of Tacitus's *Germania*:

Gallia est omnis divisa in partis tris.
(All Gaul is divided into three parts.)

Germania omnis a Gallis Raetisque et Pannoniis Rheno et Danuvio fluminibus, a Sarmatis Dacisque mutuo metu aut montibus separatur.
(All of Germany is divided from the Gauls, the Raetii, and the Pannonii by the Rhine and Danube rivers, and from the Sarmatians and the Dacians by mutual fear or mountains.)

The foregoing is by no means an exhaustive survey, but it will serve the purpose. For the choice of history to illustrate the function of exordia was not, of course, accidental, since the starting point for this whole discussion was the need to find a way of interrogating the ancient novels about their relationship to historiography. It follows from the preceding arguments, then, that any novel which exhibits an exordium resembling the exordium of a history is implicitly claiming to be essentially historical. The procedure is simple and obvious. If we examine carefully the exordia of the five texts we have so far been talking about, we may well find a pattern that will answer a number of questions.

Here is the opening sentence of Chariton's *Chaereas and Callirhoe*: Χαρίτων Ἀφροδισιεύς, Ἀθηναγόρου τοῦ ῥήτορος ὑπογραφεύς, πάθος ἐρωτικὸν ἐν Συρακούσαις γενόμενον διηγήσομαι. Ἑρμοκράτης ὁ Συρακοσίων στρατηγός, οὗτος ὁ νικήσας τοὺς Ἀθηναίους . . . ("I, Chariton of Aphrodisias, secretary to the advocate Athenagoras, will narrate a love affair which transpired in Syracuse. Hermocrates, the general of the Syracusans, the one who defeated the Athenians . . ."). No great acumen is required to see how closely Chariton follows the pattern laid down by Herodotus and Thucydides. This has been noticed by most scholars who have worked on *Chaereas and Callirhoe*.[14] Name, provenance, and subject first; then the genealogy of the heroine—the daughter, as it seems, of Hermocrates, the Syracusan general known to us from Thucydides and responsible for the disastrous defeat of the Athenian expedition against Syracuse in the Peloponnesian War. From Plutarch and Diodorus we hear vague stories that Hermocrates' daughter (never named in these sources) was once kidnapped and later became the wife (or mother) of Dionysius I, the founder of the dynasty.

How "historical," then, is Chariton's narrative? As it develops, hardly at all; the action is centered on that love affair, after all, and the grand movements of history are entirely subordinate thereunto. Chariton plays fast and loose, in fact, with whatever historical dates, events, and persons appear in his narrative. To begin with, the denouement of the story is all bound up with historical events (namely, the Egyptian revolt against Persia in 486/485 B.C.) that considerably precede the date when the story purportedly begins (413 B.C.); and these are dates that anyone with even a moderate interest in the history of fifth-century Greece ought to have known.[15] What is more, if *Chaereas and Callirhoe* is a serious history, one quite naturally presumes its subject would have to be, *ex hypothesi*, the antecedents of the Syracusan tyrants. But if Chariton intends us to identify Callirhoe's baby with Dionysius I, he is remarkably coy about it. One notices the hints, of course, especially in the name of Chaereas's rival, Dionysius, and in the odd fact that Callirhoe leaves her infant son by Chaereas with Dionysius. But Chariton's Dionysius is not Dionysius I; in fact, there is not a single explicit mention of Dionysius I or his descendants in the text. Even the inference that Callirhoe's son by Chaereas is in fact the future tyrant remains just that, an inference.

The result of all this is that no one can seriously suppose *Chaereas and Callirhoe* to be anything but fiction. Still, one wonders, given the "historical" exordium and the newness and strangeness of the whole concept of prose fiction, exactly how an ancient reader would have reacted. It seems, in fact, as though at least one ancient reader, Philostratus, thought Chariton to be something of a fraud.[16] If *Chaereas and Callirhoe* is history, it is very bad history, and worse than bad, mendacious. We may find ways of excusing Chariton, but we must acknowledge that he has tempted the accusation by his very manner of dressing fiction in the borrowed clothing of history.

Chaereas and Callirhoe turns out to be the only surviving ancient Greek novel to begin in precisely this fashion, so closely following the model of Herodotus and Thucydides. This does not mean, however, that there are no more historical exordia to be found. Of the major classical Greek historians, Xenophon was the one who most went in for sensation and sentiment, at least so far as the tastes of a later age were concerned; and his *Education of Cyrus* (*Cyropaideia*) is often adduced, not without plausibility, as the paradigm of a certain strain of romanticized biography, which coexisted with (and perhaps intermingled with) the novel.[17] It is probably in this context, then, that we should interpret the nom de plume of the second novelist in our list, "Xenophon Ephesius" (that is, "the Ephesian Xenophon"). When *Anthia and Habrocomes* begins in a manner not at all unlike that used by the "real" Xenophon, it becomes even clearer that this author is out to present his particular fiction as a history, and, as such, a true story. Ἦν ἐν Ἐφέσῳ ἀνὴρ τῶν τὰ πρῶτα ἐκεῖ δυναμένων, Λυκομήδης ὄνομα. τούτῳ τῷ Λυκομήδει ἐκ γυναικὸς ἐπιχωρίας Θεμιστοῦς γίνεται παῖς Ἁβροκόμης (There was, in Ephesus, a man, among those who were influential there, by the name of Lycomedes. To this man, by his wife, a local woman named Themiste, is born a son, Habrocomes).

There is a religious dimension to this novel, absent or attentuated in Chariton; as it develops, the hero and heroine are saved only at the last by the providential intervention of Isis/Artemis. It is just at this point, however, that history rears its head again, when we hear, in the very last paragraph, that Anthia and Habrocomes put up a votive tablet at Ephesus detailing their adventures. This sounds suspiciously like a source, rather as though "Xenophon" were saying, "If you doubt my story, look it up." At any event, this most unsatisfactory of all the Greek novels is precisely the one that goes to the greatest lengths to garb itself as history.

At first blush, it rather seems as though Achilles Tatius means to fall into line with his predecessors, in that he, too, begins with something rather patently modeled on a certain kind of historical exordium.[18]

Σιδὼν ἐπὶ θαλάσσῃ πόλις· Ἀσσυρίων ἡ θάλασσα· μήτηρ Φοινίκων ἡ πόλις· Θηβαίων ὁ δῆμος πατήρ. . . . (1.1.2) Ἐνταῦθα ἥκων ἐκ πολλοῦ χειμῶνος, σῶστρα ἔθυον ἐμαυτοῦ τῇ τῶν Φοινίκων θεᾷ· Ἀστάρτην αὐτὴν οἱ Σιδώνιοι καλοῦσιν. περιιὼν οὖν καὶ τὴν ἄλλην πόλιν καὶ περισκοπῶν τὰ ἀναθήματα, ὁρῶ γραφὴν ἀνακειμένην γῆς ἅμα καὶ θαλάσσης. . . . (1.2.1) Ἐγὼ δὲ καὶ τἆλλα μὲν ἐπῄνουν τῆς γραφῆς, ἅτε δὲ ὢν ἐρωτικὸς περιεργότερον ἔβλεπον τὸν ἄγοντα τὸν βοῦν Ἔρωτα, καὶ "Οἷον," εἶπον, "ἄρχει βρέφος οὐρανοῦ καὶ γῆς καὶ θαλάσσης." ταῦτά μου λέγοντος, νεανίσκος καὶ αὐτὸς παρεστώς, "Ἐγὼ ταῦτ' ἂν ἐδείκνυν," ἔφη, "τοσαύτας ὕβρεις ἐξ ἔρωτος παθών."

(Sidon is a city on the sea. The sea belongs to the Assyrians; the city is the mother of the Phoenicians; the demos is the father of the Thebans.[19] . . . Having arrived there after a fierce storm, I offered a sacrifice in thanksgiving for my deliverance to the goddess of the Phoenicians; "Astarte," the Sidonians call her. So, as I was walking around the rest of the city and looking at the various offerings, I caught sight of a painting hanging there, a seascape and landscape combined. [There follows a lengthy ecphrasis of the painting, which is a depiction of the rape of Europa.] I had much praise for the rest of the picture, too; but because I am a distinctly erotic person, I looked at Eros urging on the bull, and exclaimed, "How that child rules over sky, land, and sea!" When I said this, a young man who was also standing there said, "I could have shown that myself, having suffered such outrages at the hand of Eros.")

We begin, then, with geography, though the elaborate Asianism of this opening sentence, virtually impossible to render accurately, does suggest from the very beginning that something a little different is going on here. But when we meet a first-person narrator in the second paragraph, we are at once thrown into a different world; and when we proceed immediately into two or three pages of ecphrasis, the savor of historiography, even debauched historiography, is lost. The authorial first-person narrator meets a young man, who is Clitophon and who narrates the rest of the novel, in the first person. Sidon, with which the novel opened, turns out to be irrelevant; in fact, we never return to the mise-en-scène, and the balance of the narrative is Clitophon's first-person narration. We never even find out why Clitophon is in Sidon.

The author's failure (or tacit refusal) to return to what seemed at first to be a framing narrative denies us the opportunity of deciding whether or not Clitophon (or the author) is telling the truth. As Perry notes, any story that is primarily narrated in the first person calls into question the narrating character's veracity, not the author's.[20] The only external "authority" for the truth of this particular story is the personal veracity of the teller, who in this case is otherwise unknown, who is himself the protagonist of his own story, and who unabashedly represents himself as a liar more than once. If we are correct in supposing, on the basis of the extant texts, that some sort of insistence on the historicity of the narrative (however patently spurious that claim might be to the critical reader) was a well-nigh obligatory topos of the early Greek novels, then the parodic intent of *Leucippe and Clitophon* becomes manifest even in the way it sets out to verify itself.[21] Thus even the trappings of historiography affected by Chariton and Xenophon Ephesius are, for Achilles Tatius, objects of satiric subversion, in a way quite consistent with what we have already seen. The effect can be humorous, as with much else in *Leucippe and Clitophon*; and now we can see that the parody begins with the opening, where Achilles Tatius deliberately sets up certain expectations that he will proceed to defeat. We think, precisely because of the solemn opening, that we are reading a work of serious literature, and perhaps initially we might suppose it to be historical, in the sense that *Chaereas and Callirhoe* is presented as history. But then the author rather abruptly disabuses us of any such misconception. We may be either annoyed or amused at all this, but it certainly does not appear to be inadvertent. Achilles Tatius seems to be straining at the leash of history, perhaps even, so to speak, biting at it. He is thumbing his nose at convention, in a way; but in another way, he is respecting the very conventions he flouts in the way he goes about flouting them. Rather than assert that his story is fiction and that a fictional story is not the same thing as a lie, he allows himself to be caught in the act of lying.

Nowhere is the nascent independence of the ancient Greek novel more apparent than in Heliodorus's *Theagenes and Charicleia*, and perhaps most strikingly so in its exordium.[22] It may come as no surprise, then, to learn that Heliodorus, of all the ancient Greek novelists, had the most palpable influence on the earliest European novels. And one of the most visible marks of that influence is precisely the exordium.

Ἡμέρας ἄρτι διαγελώσης καὶ ἡλίου τὰς ἀκρωρείας καταυγάζοντος, ἄνδρες ἐν ὅπλοις ληστικοῖς ὄρους ὑπερκύψαντες, ὃ δὴ κατ᾽ ἐκβολὰς τοῦ Νείλου καὶ στόμα τὸ καλούμενον Ἡρακλεωτικὸν ὑπερτείνει, μικρὸν ἐπιστάντες τὴν ὑποκειμένην θάλατταν ὀφθαλμοῖς ἐπήρχοντο καὶ τῷ πελάγει τὸ πρῶτον τὰς ὄψεις ἐπαφθέντες, ὡς οὐδὲν ἄγρας ληστικῆς ἐπηγγέλλετο μὴ πλεόμενον, ἐπὶ τὸν πλησίον αἰγιαλὸν τῇ θέᾳ κατήγοντο. (2) καὶ ἦν τὰ ἐν αὐτῷ τοιάδε· (Day had just begun to smile, and the first rays of the sun were lighting up the heights, when men in pirate gear looked over the top of that mountain which rises over the outlets of the Nile and over the mouth called "Heracleotic." Moving forward a bit, they scanned the sea below them and looked out to the edge of the open ocean; but when nothing by way of piratical prey at sail presented itself, they made their way down to the nearby beach. And this is what was there.)

G. N. Sandy has compiled a list of seventeenth- and eighteenth-century French novels that begin with some variation on a theme of "It was dawn, and . . ."[23] One can see this going right on into the English Gothic novel and thence becoming such a cliché that it lends itself to satire.[24]

What may also have struck some readers, upon reading this exordium, is how very unhistorical, not to say unclassical, it is. To be sure, Heliodorus tells us where we are in the first sentence; and one might even suppose that the ancient reader, confronted with pirates in this way, would have known from the beginning what kind of story lay ahead. But in fact, we do not learn the names of the protagonists and what their actual relationship is until much later. For they are lovers, not brother and sister as they represent themselves to be; and indeed, we will not learn the whole background until more than half the book has gone by. It is only slowly filled in, as the chance remarks of some characters and the narratives of others (who only know part of the whole story) provide the reader with the pieces of the puzzle.

It is certainly true, of course, that the in-medias-res beginning is not new; on the contrary, it is a commonplace of the heroic epic from Homer on. But here we do not even have so much as a Μῆνιν ἄειδε ("Sing the wrath"), an Ἄνδρα μοι ἔννεπε ("Tell me of the man").[25] There is, in fact, no prologue at all. We plunge immediately into the action, though from an oblique point of view. Readers of modern novels may be forgiven for being somewhat blasé about all this, since the technique is now so familiar to us; but how would this strike the ancient ear? What other work from ancient literature plunges so abruptly into its narrative? This is more than mere innovation; it is revolution. Heliodorus tells his story in his own way, without apologizing for it, or pretending that he is a historian who is passing on some information he derived from some other source. This is not to say that the redolence of historiography is altogether missing; but *Theagenes and Chariclea* does not begin as a history, and it is not constructed along historical lines.[26] Heliodorus, in other words, implicitly acknowledges his real calling, that of a novelist.

LONGUS AND THE HISTORIANS

What we have seen so far represents a fairly coherent movement. The two earliest novelists, Chariton and pseudo-Xenophon, make themselves out, in the very form of their respective exordia, to be historians, who mean to illuminate some heretofore obscure sidelight of history. Both authors have their merits, Chariton probably more than Xenophon Ephesius, but both place themselves in an uncomfortable position, from which they can be true neither to the ideals of historiography nor to those of the novel. After these two comes Achilles Tatius, who seems to have been perspicacious enough to see what the problem was, and who attempts to extricate himself from the predicament by laughing his way out of it. He makes a sort of burlesque of this process of dressing in borrowed clothing and to some extent gets away with it, if we are prepared to recognize and accept his clowning. But this is a solution of limited scope, and one cannot imagine that many more successful novels could have been written along this line. If the modern English novel had never gone beyond Fielding making fun of Richardson, it is hard to imagine that the genre would ever have amounted to much. Somewhere between Achilles Tatius, of whom it was said that he seemed to be "straining at the leash," and Heliodorus, who has little of the specious historian about him, something seems to have happened to make it possible for the novel, in its birth throes, to cut the umbilical cord that had bound it to history.

Now it was during this very period, between Achilles Tatius and Heliodorus, that *Daphnis and Chloe* was written. It is not possible to assert with any confidence that Longus could have had some direct influence on Heliodorus; but *Daphnis and Chloe* was almost certainly written at the right time to reflect what may have been going on. Even a cursory glance at the prologue reveals that the issue of history is indeed one of its preoccupations. But this emerges as a preoccupation in a very interesting way.

The prologue of *Daphnis and Chloe* is in no way, not even remotely, a historical exordium. Indeed, there is nothing quite like it in all of ancient literature. There are, to be sure, certain resemblances to the exordium of *Leucippe and Clitophon*, in that both authors begin in the first person and use an ecphrasis to explain how they came by the stories they are about to tell. But the ecphrasis in *Leucippe and Clitophon* is ultimately peripheral or tangential to the main narrative; Eros is important, of course, but anyone who expects the theme of Europa and the bull to be developed, as either sign or signified, will be disappointed. Longus, on the other hand, puts the themes of his ecphrasis at the very heart of his narrative, as we have seen. What Longus does with his exordium is to make the literary and imaginative nature of his text manifest, which results in setting his story at least one remove from reality.

We have already had much to do with the prologue, of course; but we are now in a position to examine it from a different perspective and to ask a different question: to wit, what stance does *Daphnis and Chloe* assume, in its exordium, vis-à-vis historiography? Clearly, Longus does not dress his novel as a history in any formal way. He does not introduce himself by name or explain the genesis of his story in terms that suggest history; nor does the prologue fit any of the historiographical paradigms. He does use the word ἱστορία itself in the very first sentence. But what is distinctly odd about his diction here is that, first of all, the word is used, not of a narrative, a written text, but of a painting. Second, the subject thereof is not the usual stuff of history, kings and battles and speeches, but Eros. This is history in a very unusual guise indeed, and we will miss the point entirely if we fail to notice just how unusual. Longus gives us, in fact, the clearest possible signal that *Daphnis and Chloe* is not a history, that it is, in fact, a piece of fiction. Not that he is apologetic about this. On the contrary, the fruits of his labors are suitable to be an offering to the gods, and a delightful possession, a κτῆμα τερπνόν, for all humanity. What we are seeing here is little less than a declaration of autonomy for the novel, which is no longer going to go about dressed in borrowed clothing but stands ready to take its place as an important species of literary composition.

Ironically enough, however, it is precisely in the very words with which he stakes this claim to autonomy that Longus most directly alludes to a historian. Ever since the eighteenth century, at least, it has seemed clear that the operative phrase, κτῆμα τερπνόν, is a deliberate allusion to Thucydides, who (in the passage at 1.22 quoted just above) calls his own work a κτῆμα ἐς αἰεί.[27] But one of the striking things about this allusion is that Longus's very phrase, "κτῆμα τερπνόν," would surely have seemed to Thucydides an oxymoron. The latter, after all, asserts that his work is perhaps ἀτερπέστερον, precisely because in composing it he has consistently avoided τὸ μυθῶδες, by which he seems to mean the element of storytelling. We have already seen, however, that Longus is preoccupied with myth, and that in fact he casts his entire work, his own κτῆμα, in the form of a self-creating myth. His whole project is thus mythopoetic, in a very literal sense: he is "making a myth." What is more, Longus almost perversely takes every opportunity to remind us of Thucydides' qualms about τὸ μυθῶδες and its attendant pleasure: throughout *Daphnis and Chloe*, some form of τέρπω or τέρψις occurs almost every time the word μῦθος is used. And that is precisely the point of the apparent oxymoron κτῆμα τερπνόν: that the novel somehow manages to be, at one and the same time, historical (κτῆμα) and mythical (τερπνόν). The novel, after all, is a narrative prose genre with manifold and manifest connections to the literary tradition of historiography; but it also incorporates and transforms the imaginative power of myth, which was always, in classical antiquity, the *métier* of poetry. Like poetry, then, the novel both instructs and delights. Classical prose, on the other hand, can delight only at the expense of instruction, at least in Thucydides' not inconsiderable opinion. A history can be a κτῆμα, a poem can be τερπνόν, but only a novel can be both.

It should almost have been expected that this allusion would prove to be as pregnant as it is. Both the alluding passage and the passage alluded to, after all, occur in programmatic positions in their respective contexts. The relevant paragraph from Thucydides comes from the climax of his long proem, just before he begins to recount the conflict between Epidamnus and Corcyra (the beginning of the narrative proper), with a brief description of the city of Epidamnus. Thucydides goes on to say—this near the end of his prologue—that his work will instruct future generations, since human beings are likely to do again what they have done before. The alluding sentence from *Daphnis and Chloe*, in turn, comes near the end of the prologue and is clearly programmatic, whatever one takes that program to be. Notice how similar are the claims that Longus makes: his work, his κτῆμα, will likewise instruct, because its subject matter is likewise universal. And Longus, too, begins his narrative proper, after the prologue, with a bit of geography, in the description of Mitylene—a city, we should recall, not without importance to Thucydides. But the city turns out to have rather little to do with the story, as Longus shifts the scene from Mitylene to a small farm, where almost all of what remains of the novel takes place. Once again, Longus invites us to think about history but will not allow us to mistake what we are reading for history.

There may well be a great irony, then, in the prayer with which the prologue ends: ἡμῖν δ' ὁ θεὸς παράσχοι σωφρονοῦσι τὰ τῶν ἄλλων γράφειν ("May the god permit us, so long as we remain prudent, to write the things of the others").[28] On one level, Longus is asking Eros to help us (himself and his readers, one might suppose) keep our wits about us in dealing with an emotionally powerful subject; he is praying, in other words, for objectivity, as a historian might. On the other hand, can we be so

sure that "the others" whose "things" he is going to write (γράφειν, again, with all its write/paint ambiguity) are the lovers of
the story? Could it be that he is simultaneously apologizing (in a
very ironic way) for his appropriation of a métier (i.e., prose narrative) that really belongs to "others"—that is, historians? Some
may find this farfetched; but the language of this sentence is capable of meaning many things all at once, and it is unwise to suppose that any one reading of it is privileged.

One final reflection on this allusion seems appropriate here.
Both Thucydides and Longus, in context, use the word κτῆμα as
an antithesis to something else. For Thucydides, that same absence of τὸ μυθῶδες, which renders his work ἀτερπέστερον, is
also what makes it a κτῆμα ἐς αἰεί, rather than an ἀγώνισμα ἐς
τὸ παραχρῆμα. Longus, on the other hand, asserts that his work
is both a κτῆμα τερπνόν and an ἀνάθημα, to Eros, Pan, and
the nymphs. But Thucydides' κτῆμα/ἀγώνισμα antithesis is not
forgotten. Later on, as the story of Daphnis and Chloe un-
folds, the reader in fact encounters two obvious ἀγωνίσματα:
the speech contest between Daphnis and Dorcon at 1.15–17,
and the kangaroo-court trial of Daphnis at 2.14–17: that is, the
declamations. Thus Longus's κτῆμα (which is also an ἀνάθημα)
contains various ἀγωνίσματα; and both cult and rhetoric are
fully as repugnant to Thucydides' literary project as is τέρψις.

We have come full circle, now, in a perhaps unexpected way,
back to the subjects of myth and rhetoric. For the gap between
the ineffable world of the numinous and the distinctly human
(and not infrequently profane) world of rhetoric is filled in many
ways by myth, a linguistic production with divine resonance.
Rhetoric and myth, history and cult, all prove now to be inter-
twined in a way that Thucydides, the great rationalist, would
never have understood. But before we can really come to terms,
once and for all, with the meaning of this peculiar dialectic,
there is one more tradition which must be taken into account:
namely, the pastoral. For the one thing that sets *Daphnis and
Chloe* most clearly apart from either of the traditions we have
considered so far, the novel and historiography, is Longus's
adoption of the pastoral mode. And it is here, finally, that we
shall find the key to the interpretation of *Daphnis and Chloe*.

Chapter 10

Longus's Prose Idyll

The first six words of *Daphnis and Chloe*, Ἐν Λέσβῳ θηρῶν ἐν ἄλσει Νυμφῶν ("While hunting in Lesbos, in a grove of the nymphs"), pose no small paradox to the reader with sufficient background in the classics. For the ancient reader (absent a particular personal association with the island), a reference to Lesbos might mean several things. Lesbian wine, for one thing, was highly regarded in the ancient world. The island's two major cities, Methymna and Mitylene, were thought to be among the loveliest of cities in a lovely part of the Greek world and were on the "must see" list of any ancient traveller in the Aegean. Even more than that, however, Lesbos was famous as the home of two of the greatest poets in the Greek lyric tradition: Sappho, and her kinsman Alcaeus. Of these, the former in particular was almost a paradigm of the erotic poet; so much so, in fact, that any reference to Lesbos in erotic poetry was usually a reference, direct or indirect, to Sappho.[1]

Lesbos was not, however, a likely place to go hunting, and it was not a likely place to find oneself in an idyllic grove consecrated to the nymphs. It is certainly among the unlikeliest settings for a pastoral that could be imagined. We are entitled (required, really) to ask why Longus has chosen it.[2] To some, the only possible reason seems to be that Longus knew the island well, or was even a native of it, and chose to write about what he knew; to at least one other, Longus chose Lesbos because it was somewhat exotic, a "Wünschland."[3] Most readers will have no difficulty in recognizing the biographical fallacy at work here, and such arguments as these need hardly be refuted in detail. To others, who believe that *Daphnis and Chloe* is an allegory, the setting itself must be of some cultic significance; but the only items of proof worthy of mention are, first, that there was a famous temple of Dionysus in Mitylene, and second, that the singing head of the dismembered Orpheus is said to have floated ashore at Lesbos.[4] But both of these religious associations with Lesbos are simultaneously (taken together) associations with poetry, and point to religious allegory only if allegory is an a priori postulate.

What no one seems to have suggested before, however, is that Longus has set his pastoral on Lesbos *for no other reason than that it is an absurd setting for an idyll.* Several aspects of *Daphnis and Chloe* point in that direction. To begin with, there is the whole matter of realism. Much ink has been spilt in the effort to determine whether Longus's pastoral world is a Theocritean one (that is, realistic, or at least down-to-earth) or a Vergilian one (that is, spiritual or idealized).[5] Upon reflection, however, this turns out to be a logomachy. Longus's pastoral world is neither Theocritean nor Vergilian in toto; but then, it is not merely a happy medium, either, or some tertium quid. The absurdity is that both pastoral worlds are present and are not fully reconciled with one another.

Daphnis and Chloe themselves are idealized, naive, unreal, and in this sense rather Arcadian. They are also not really shepherds at all but rather nobles, exposed as infants and raised as shepherds, who will eventually be restored to their rightful position. They are comfortable in this pastoral world, and they bear names that could hardly be more typically pastoral; but in reality they are outsiders.[6] Both are endowed with beauty that is κρεῖτ-τον ἀγροικίας ("greater than rusticity" [1.7.1]), a fact which is alluded to more than once. In book 4 they both respond symbolically to the revelation of their true identities by making votive offerings of their pastoral accoutrements, an action which clearly suggests that they consider their pastoral lives to be at an

end. By contrast, most of the other inhabitants of the countryside in which Daphnis and Chloe live are rather more like real
shepherds. This is manifest very early on, in book 1, when both
Dryas and Lamon, upon finding the exposed infants, seriously
consider appropriating the valuable tokens (the γνωρίσματα)
with which they have been exposed and leaving the babies to die
(1.3; 1.6). For both men, the better angels of their natures finally
prevail, but even to consider such a course does not seem to be
very much in the spirit of Arcadia. Later on, then, we meet two
cowherds (Dorcon in book 1 and Lampis in book 4), who are
brutish, grasping, and lecherous; and Pan, who sometimes behaves toward Daphnis and Chloe as a tutelar deity, is twice depicted as a would-be rapist. In fact, when all is said and done, the
pastoral world of *Daphnis and Chloe* is idyllic, Arcadian, and unreal only in the characters of its protagonists, who, as was just
noted, do not really belong there. There is something distinctly
Hobbesian about the others.

One of the salient features of the pastoral, for Theocritus and
Vergil as much as for Longus, is that it creates a self-contained
world, simple and self-involved. Hence the term "idyll," that is,
εἰδύλλιον, "little scene." Whatever the preoccupations of the
author who writes in the pastoral vein may be, those preoccupations can be reduced to their simplest terms when they are
worked out among simple characters immersed in nature. These
characters thus reflect, not flesh-and-blood shepherds, but rather
the urbane and sophisticated people who read and write pastoral poetry.[7] Neither Theocritus nor Vergil write allegory, insofar as allegory means that each character and event in a given
narrative are really standing in for others; but for both of these
men, however different their treatment of the pastoral world,
the very closure of that world makes it possible to explore within
it issues that are not really germane to actual rural life. The
ancient reader, who lives in a very different world (whether
Alexandria or Rome), peeks into a miniature poetic world, an
εἰδύλλιον, and sees the conflicts in his or her own life played out
in miniature. This accounts for the preciosity and artificialness
of the pastoral, characteristics that may, depending upon the
tastes and predilections of a particular era, make pastoral poetry
either much in vogue or much neglected.

There is, to be sure, much in *Daphnis and Chloe* that is precious and artificial, and some that by contrast seems rather coarse. But the whole issue is in fact rather a tangent. There are at least two significant aspects of Longus's prose idyll that neither Theocritus's realism nor Vergil's idealism can account for. The first is that Longus's idyll is not entirely as self-contained as it sometimes seems to be. The pastoral poets tend to involve the outside world in the idyll only by implication or reference, as, for example, in Eclogue 1; but Longus not infrequently breaks the illusion of isolation and closure. From time to time, someone from the outside world penetrates the pastoral world in which the protagonists live. For one thing, Daphnis and Chloe themselves, as we have seen, are really outsiders. In book 1, Etruscan pirates try to cart off Daphnis as a prize. In book 2, a group of Methymnean youths, bent on a good time, intrude on the peacefulness of the countryside; later on, an army from Methymna, sent to avenge the rough handling their young men get from the locals, kidnap Chloe. In book 3, Lycaenium, a woman from the city, initiates Daphnis into the mysteries of sex. In book 4, everything is set topsy-turvy by the visit of Dionysophanes, who is both the master of the estate and Daphnis's real father, along with his entourage. And we have already seen how important is Gnathon, the very embodiment of urbane decadence, to the resolution of the story.

What is really remarkable about the theme of intrusion from the city is the ambivalence with which it is treated. It would almost seem, without going any further than this into the interpretation of the novel, that the whole dynamic of the plot is provided by the dialectic between the country and the city. Daphnis and Chloe are of urban origin but are raised in the country; they encounter threats from both worlds, and they are taught by both; and in the end they choose to live a life that combines the best of both. It is tempting to conclude at once that this must be part of what Longus means to say, so that *Daphnis and Chloe* becomes yet another vehicle for a lesson on *aurea mediocritas* (literally, "golden mediocrity"). There is more to all this, however, than merely the golden mean—which is, after all, rather trite, even for the second century of our era. The antithesis between the city and the country is not the only antithesis that Longus explores; it is, rather, only one of the more obvious in a whole series of antitheses (or really dialectics), most of which should quickly come to mind at this point. The dialectic between city and country thus takes its place alongside other dialectics (male and female, myth and rhetoric, history and fiction, divine and human, and so forth); and the pastoral milieu of the whole novel is itself in dynamic tension with its setting on Sappho's island.

The second problem with Longus's prose idyll is precisely that *Daphnis and Chloe* is in prose. Although the pastoral mode is not unexampled in prose, the pastoral qua genre had heretofore been strictly a poetic one.[8] Certainly Longus's prose style has something of the poetic about it, which may be why Goethe found it appropriate to call *Daphnis and Chloe* a "Gedicht."[9] But the uncomfortable fact that this is a prose narrative simply will not go away. Once again, then, we are up against something that does not fit. Longus seems to be a pastoral poet who has chosen a medium singularly ill-adapted for what one would take to be his intentions: namely, to compose an idyll. If we then call to mind that the prologue makes the whole novel out to be an extended ecphrasis, and that the γραφή which will be thus described is a ἱστορία ἔρωτος, then we may well begin to feel that we are going around in circles, from painting to writing to painting to writing, and so on ad infinitum. There seems to be no fixed point of reference, no privileged layer. But underneath the vertigo is a serious point. The novel paints a picture which is a story; hence it can do things which neither painting nor traditional stories (either myth or history) can do. The novelist has the imaginative license of the painter but employs that license with all the scope and authority of narrative. Implicit in the prose idyll of Longus, then, is the whole project of writing fiction, of making up stories and telling them, with some intention that they be worth the hearing, that they be, in other words, κτήματα τερπνά.

All this suggests that Longus's choice of a pastoral milieu for *Daphnis and Chloe* may have been motivated as much by his literary preoccupations as by some sort of escapism. This is not inherently unreasonable. One of the characteristic topics that pastoral poetry was often used to explore was poetry itself. In part, this is because shepherds were thought (accurately or not) to spend a good deal of their time singing, and indeed one of the staples of ancient pastoral poetry is the singing contest (which provides yet another perspective on that "declamatory" speech contest between Daphnis and Dorcon in book 1). On another level, too, the closure of the pastoral world lent itself to reflection by poets on poetry. Indeed, the founder of the whole pastoral tradition was one Philitas of Cos, whose name is sometimes spelled "Philetas" and who, along with his followers, rebelled against the poetic decorum of his day (the third century B.C.) by dressing as a shepherd and writing the first pastoral poems. Thus when Longus introduces into *Daphnis and Chloe* a character named Philetas, who acts as a preceptor of love, it is hard not to see an allusion to the father of pastoral poetry. To some, this has led to the conclusion that Philitas (most of whose poetry is lost) was somehow Longus's source; but that is a fruitless line of inquiry.[10] What Longus has clearly done is indirectly to allude to a poet who founded a school of poetry and whose poetic form was the direct result of a certain polemical stance on the nature of poetry. Since Longus himself, as we have seen, has by implication taken a very definite stance on certain issues involving the nature and function of the novel, its seems clear that Longus's adoption of a pastoral setting is programmatic and points to a preoccupation with literature.

We have not yet arrived, however, at a conclusion; the pastoral mode of *Daphnis and Chloe* still has things to teach us. At some point the two dialectical streams of writing and painting, and of city and country, do in fact begin to converge. But to understand that, we shall have to range a little farther afield.

Viewing the world as divided between city and country, between urban and pastoral, is in some ways an oversimplification.[11] It may be more useful, and more accurate, to speak of three worlds. There is, first of all, the city, the πόλις, built by human hands and controlled by human institutions; hence Aristotle's famous dictum that man is by nature a political animal, πολιτικὸν ζῷον. Then there are the cultivated lands outside the city, which belong to the city but are not part of it, the world of cultivated fields and domestic livestock: that is, the world of the pastoral. And then there is the wilderness, a world quite outside of human control, the mountains and forests, which are full of wild animals and either hostile or indifferent to the human. Each of these three worlds has its own inhabitants, its own divinities and daimons, and its own nature. Together, they constitute the whole economy of that part of the cosmos to which human beings have access, which thus begins to look like a series of concentric circles: the city at the center, surrounded by the pastoral world, which is itself surrounded by the wild. From the standpoint of the city, to be sure, the latter two can seem indistinguishable; but from the pastoral world itself, there is no mistaking the world of fields and flocks for the world of wolves and bears.

In the most immediately apparent way, then, the pastoral world exists as a kind of buffer, a mediation between the savage and the civilized. That, as much as anything, may explain the peculiar configuration of the pastoral god, Pan. It may also explain why the pastoral world provides a context in which certain issues in the life of civilized people can be abstracted and examined. Shepherds survive, after all, by keeping things at bay. On the one hand, they must contend with wolves and lions; on the other, with city folk, often their masters, who exploit and misunderstand them. At a much deeper level, however, this in reality is the plight of every human being. The city and the wild fight for the soul of us all, in one way or another; and we can really understand ourselves, and the world, only when we are successful in keeping both at bay. The pastoral world is the battleground in which this is fought out. Its beauty and simplicity, the clear air and clear water, serve to make it easier for us to see clearly what is at stake in that battle.

Applying this to *Daphnis and Chloe* is not terribly difficult. Brutish nature attacks Chloe, in the form of Dorcon and Lampis, just as Pan attacks Syrinx and Echo. On another level, there is a real wolf from the forest, a false wolf (Dorcon, who is actually a shepherd), and a "she-wolf" from the city (Lycaenium), with all of whom Daphnis and Chloe must contend. Each wolf poses a threat, but at the same time each has a major contribution to make, so that simple judgments about "good" and "bad" turn out to be singularly impossible or useless or both. A cicada, fleeing an eminently natural demise, is suddenly imprisoned, and sings; and the singing elicits a story, from which a great lesson is learned. Even in the story, and in its successors, there is a confrontation with the wild, and a transformation. "Raw" nature is neither good nor bad, but rather, in a literal sense of the word, "awful."

City dwellers, too, are ambivalent figures. The Methymnean hunters (and the Methymnean army), Lycaenium, Astylus, Dionysophanes, Gnathon—none of these is wholly good, or wholly bad. Each poses a certain threat, but that threat is often an opportunity, also, for Daphnis and Chloe to learn certain invaluable lessons. For the pastoral world, even though its clear air and clear water may make it possible for one to see truth and beauty, is not itself the exclusive abode of truth and beauty. The truly pastoral characters in *Daphnis and Chloe* are either brutish (Dorcon and Lampis) or terribly limited and inadequate (Dryas, Lamon, even Philetas). Only the intruders make it possible for Daphnis and Chloe, themselves outsiders, to learn who they really are.

That, of course, is what is needful. Daphnis and Chloe need to learn just who they are: not shepherds, not native-born residents of this pastoral world, but something κρεῖττον ἀγροικίας ("greater than rusticity"). After the dramatic revelations, however, Daphnis and Chloe do not simply transpose themselves into the city; instead, they choose to live out their lives in the same context in which they were raised. The real changes take place in the terms under which they inhabit the pastoral world. They still live in a world, then, to which they were not born; but while before they were blissfully unaware that they were not born here, now they know just who they are. That makes all the difference. They are not shepherds and not city folk but autonomous human beings, who are free now to choose to live how and where they wish.

All this was made possible by the intervention of various persons from outside their temporary home in the fields, both from the wild and from the city. But of all these people from outside, the one who is absolutely essential, without whom none of this would happen, is Longus himself, the hunter who becomes an author. For it was ἐν Λέσβῳ θηρῶν ("hunting in Lesbos") that the author tells us he saw a remarkable painting in a most unusual setting, which inspired him to produce four books of erotic fiction in honor of Eros, Pan, and the nymphs, for the edification of all humanity. Longus is the demiurge of this world, without whom neither Daphnis nor Chloe nor any of these characters nor their pastoral enclave on Lesbos would even exist. That they exist at all, then, is due entirely to the fact that Longus has written an erotic history set in the country, through which he means to explore various dialectics: city and country, male and female, myth and rhetoric, innocence and experience.

PLATO'S *PHAEDRUS*

The time has come, it seems, to bring to the surface what may already have occurred to some readers. For Longus is not the first classical author to bring together in one text a whole constellation of concerns, among which are myth, rhetoric, truth, storytelling, Eros, and nature, and examine all these things in a pastoral setting. It is in Plato's *Phaedrus* that we may find a thread that will tie together the major themes and preoccupations that we have so far uncovered in *Daphnis and Chloe*.[12]

There is, to begin with, the whole matter of myth. Early in the dialogue, Phaedrus asks Socrates if the place where they are standing is the very spot where Boreas is said to have carried off Oreithyia. As it happens, though, Phaedrus is mistaken, and Socrates sets him straight: the place is actually several hundred yards down the river, though some say that the whole thing happened on the Areopagus. This motivates Phaedrus to ask Socrates if he "believes" in the old myths, a question which leads into a brief (but fascinating) excursus on myth. Socrates rejects what will come to be called "euhemerism," the ruthless rationalizing of the myths. Why he does so becomes clear later on, when Socrates himself uses myths to nail down the arguments he has been building. Thus we learn that myth and reason—that is, μῦθος and λόγος—are neither synonymous (in that error arises when one mistakes the one for the other) nor antithetical (in that conclusions reached by discursive reason often require a certain validation or clarification, imparted by narrative myth). Rather, they engage in a constant dialectic within the mind of the thinker, who comes to an understanding of things as they really are—that is, of the truth—only insofar as he can learn from both.

We should recall, at this point, how very important it turned out to be that Daphnis and Chloe were unable to distinguish Philetas's *logos* about Eros from a *mythos*. One might say, in fact, that it required the rest of the novel, and the telling of several more *mythoi*, before the lesson is really learned at last. What is more, the particular *mythoi* in question bear a marked resemblance to the story of Boreas and Oreithyia, at least in that all these stories begin with a maiden pursued by a lusty male. In *Daphnis and Chloe*, however, Longus makes explicit what is only implicit in the *Phaedrus*: namely, that such stories contain within their awfulness some profound truths about Eros.

The mention of Boreas and Oreithyia in the *Phaedrus* serves, then, to introduce the subject of Eros, with which much of the dialogue is concerned. The theme is not immediately developed in the form of myths, however, but in speeches—that is, in rhetoric. Socrates listens to Phaedrus reading a speech by Lysias, delivers his own speech in defense of Lysias's thesis (to wit, that boys should give their favors to nonlovers rather than lovers), then repents of his own eloquence and delivers a second speech refuting the first two. This leads Socrates and Phaedrus into a lengthy discussion of the art of rhetoric, from which we learn that the ability to tell the truth and the ability to lie are actually inseparable. The awful paradox is that the liar cannot really lie unless he first knows the truth and chooses to conceal it; but conversely, anyone who possesses the capacity to tell the truth can also lie. Mastery of rhetoric, then, means the ability to tell the difference. Thus Socrates, who knows the truth about Eros, shows in his first speech how very effectively he can lie—more effectively, indeed, than can Lysias, who is merely mistaken about these things. But as a lover of the truth, Socrates is compelled by his δαιμόνιον, that much-discussed divine voice within him, to show that the same resources which make him a successful liar can also be put to the service of the truth.

The handling of rhetoric in *Daphnis and Chloe* may at first blush seem to contradict this teaching in certain ways. It is Daphnis who "wins," after all, in the first two declamations, without actually knowing how to lie or really understanding very much at all, as yet, about who he is or what is really at stake. But we should remember that Daphnis's "victories," in each case, turn out to be specious, or at least to have unforeseen consequences, precisely because of Daphnis's lack of understanding. Then, in book 3, it is Chloe who "wins" the λόγων ὁμιλία τερπνή (pleasant exchange of speeches). She does not yet know everything she needs to know; but she understands more than Daphnis does, and so she has a certain rhetorical power over Daphnis, clearly displayed on this occasion.

The particular truth at issue, of course, is the truth about Eros. It is in the *Phaedrus*, more than in the *Symposium*, that Plato's teaching about love deals most directly with the ambiguity of love, with the fact that its carnal manifestations are somehow inseparable from its nobility, much as falsehood is peculiarly interwoven with the truth. This is manifest in the myth of the charioteer, in that cutting loose the black horse cannot really be the solution to the problem of controlling the chariot of the human soul. For Longus, too, an ascetic denial of physical love is not the solution to anything. The carnal appetite (ἐπιθυμία) which Gnathon represents cannot be rejected, denied, or destroyed. Rather, Gnathon must be received, reconciled, and allowed to expend his energies in the service of the good, overcoming the mere brutishness of Lampis. He is, after all, a θεατής, an observer of Daphnis's beauty; and the action he takes under the influence of Eros to unite himself with that beauty brings much to fruition, even though it all works out in such unexpected ways. Nothing might ever have happened, after all, if Gnathon had not seen Daphnis and desired him.

At the end of the novel, then, Daphnis and Chloe finally understand, in the bridal chamber, what everything that has happened to them really means. The nature of Eros, his name and his works, are finally manifest. The physical love between Daphnis and Chloe can now, and only now, be consummated, as Daphnis has gradually learned how to rein in the black horse of his passion while giving rein to the white horse; and Chloe has learned what she properly ought to fear and what not to fear in the sexual nature of the man to whom she is now married.

What bearing, then, does the setting have on all these matters, either in the *Phaedrus* or in *Daphnis and Chloe*?

The *Phaedrus* is by no means the only dialogue in which Plato is careful to situate the dramatis personae in a particular place. The *Republic*, for example, is given a particular setting in the house of Cephalus, on a particular occasion; and the dialogues of the first tetralogy, too, are set, for obvious reasons, in places well known to Plato's reader. In none of these other dialogues, however, does the setting function in quite the same way. To begin with, this is the only dialogue that takes place both outdoors and outside the city; it is, in other words, the only dialogue given an essentially pastoral setting. That we are to understand this as a pastoral setting is made abundantly clear by numerous pastoral images and allusions, including the singing of cicadas, the numinous presence of local nymphs (to which Socrates is almost preternaturally sensitive), the nearby shrine of Pan, and even Socrates' fear that passersby will mistake Phaedrus and himself, conversing in the shade of a tree at midday, for lazy shepherds. Nor is this pastoral setting merely an incidental detail. Socrates and Phaedrus talk about where they are and where they are going throughout the dialogue; and Socrates in particular frequently adverts to their physical surroundings in a peculiarly emphatic and empathetic way. What is especially important is that Socrates seems a stranger in this place, or so Phaedrus thinks:

ΦΑΙ. Σὺ δέ γε, ὦ θαυμάσιε, ἀτοπώτατός τις φαίνει. ἀτεχνῶς γάρ, ὃ λέγεις, ξεναγουμένῳ τινὶ καὶ οὐκ ἐπιχωρίῳ ἔοικας· οὕτως ἐκ τοῦ ἄστεως οὔτε εἰς τὴν ὑπερορίαν ἀποδημεῖς, οὔτ' ἔξω τείχους ἔμοιγε δοκεῖς τὸ παράπαν ἐξιέναι.

ΣΩ. Συγγίγνωσκέ μοι, ὦ ἄριστε. φιλομαθὴς γάρ εἰμι· **τὰ μὲν οὖν χωρία καὶ τὰ δένδρα οὐδέν μ' ἐθέλει διδάσκειν, οἱ δ' ἐν τῷ ἄστει ἄνθρωποι** (emphasis added).

(PHAEDRUS: And you, my amazing friend, seem to be the most absurd person. For really, as you say, you look like someone who needs a guide, and not a native. In fact you do not go on vacations

into any foreign country, nor does it seem to me that you so much
as take a walk outside the walls.

SOCRATES: Forgive me, oh best of men. For I am a lover of learning; *and the countryside and the trees do not want to teach me, while the
people in the city do* [emphasis added].) (*Phaedr.* 230c–d)

Socrates, then, like Daphnis and Chloe, is a stranger in the
pastoral world. But despite his apparent diffidence, he will indeed learn something out here, something that he could not
learn in the city. For the *pharmakon* (roughly, "potion") that will
lure him away from the city is, ironically enough, his love of
λόγοι, of speeches. Here he will confront the truth, head on; and
he will tell Phaedrus a salutary myth. In the interchange between myth and rhetoric, outside the city of Mitylene, Daphnis
and Chloe learn who they are, who Eros is, and what it really
means to be a man and a woman.

We are not yet finished, however, with the setting. It has come
to the attention of more than one scholar that, given an ade-
quate knowledge of the topography of ancient Athens, including the locations of various shrines and landmarks mentioned in
the text, one can almost fix the very spot, on the far bank of the
Ilissus, where the plane tree must have stood, under which Socrates and Phaedrus had their long discussion. What is fascinating about this is that the spot in question is at the foot of a particular hill, known by various names in antiquity but originally
as Helicon. It was on another Helicon, of course, that another
shepherd, Hesiod, had a fateful encounter with the Muses, re-
counted in the opening verses of the *Theogony*. The beautiful
singing of the Muses instructs Hesiod as to how things got to be
the way they are, and what the hierarchy of the cosmos is. But
they preface their song by warning Hesiod (in a couplet already
quoted in a previous chapter), that they know how to tell the
truth, and they know, also, how to tell many things that look like
truth but are not. What is really disturbing is that they do not
give Hesiod, or he does not give us, a means by which to tell the
difference. Hesiod is instructed to begin and end his song with
praise of the Muses; he does so, and for the rest we are all at
their mercy.

What seems to be occurring in the *Phaedrus*, if we take this pastoral setting at its full value, is some kind of reconstruction, or refiguring, of Hesiod's encounter with the Muses. The crucial issue of that encounter, the reason that it needs refiguring, is the difficulty in distinguishing the beautiful singing of truth from the beautiful singing of deception. This, in turn, is the great preoccupation of the *Phaedrus*, which works itself out on many levels. Socrates knows what the Muses know, how to lie and how to tell the truth. With myth and reason, true and false rhetoric, base and noble love, Socrates confronts Phaedrus with an awful truth which he (and we) would as soon not face. In each case, things we would rather think of as separate and separable are in fact inextricably entangled with one another. Truth can be had only at the price of deception, love only at the price of passion, the comfortable certainty of λόγος only at the price of the riddling ambiguity of μῦθος.

An answer to the question posed by the pastoral setting of the *Phaedrus*, and of *Daphnis and Chloe*, now begins to take shape. Socrates is a stranger outside of the city, as we saw. Oddly enough, however, it is Socrates, not Phaedrus, who knows exactly where Boreas carried off Oreithyia. Socrates is disoriented on one level, it seems; but at another level he understands the significance of this place very well indeed. This particular dialogue must take place in that space of mediation between the wild and the city. No place else but at the foot of Helicon can the absurd shepherd Socrates reencounter the Muses. So, too, it seems that Daphnis and Chloe must be taken from the city and placed in a pastoral setting before they can learn the necessary lesson about myth and rhetoric.

But why is it necessary to do this, to go away from the city? For the *Phaedrus*, the answer lies in the ostensible subject of the dialogue, rhetoric. What requires Socrates to come to terms with rhetoric is the activities of the sophists and their students. As Aristophanes knew, sophistry (and the attendant demagoguery) had brought Athens to the brink of moral, political, and social collapse, because the traditional foundations of the society had been radically undermined. What everyone once knew to be true was now open to argument and proved unequal to the challenge. Aristophanes did not understand, however, that the traditional foundations of society could not be recovered. Socrates did and thus became for Aristophanes an even more fearsome enemy than the other sophists. In fact, the great paradox of Plato's Socratic dialogues is that Socrates, who was put to death for corrupting the young and for impiety, was guilty as charged. He corrupted the young by showing them how to live outside the traditional structures of the πόλις; and he undermined their fidelity to the received religion by showing that the gods of Olympus were inadequate to the task of governing an orderly cosmos. And he did all this by the power of argument, which enabled him, from a conservative point of view, to make the worse appear the better cause.

In the *Phaedrus*, then, what is really at issue is the strength of that tradition represented by Homer and Hesiod, which is being assaulted by the sophists. And the conclusion to which we are forced is that this assault must succeed. The beautiful singing of the Muses contains within itself the seeds of its own destruction, because, in the end, it cannot really tell the truth from a lie. Plato may not have known, of course, exactly how the conquests of Philip II of Macedon and Alexander (which he did not live to see), and finally the advent of the Romans, would bring the day of the autonomous polis to an end. But that it would end, and soon, he saw clearly enough. So Socrates must leave the city to grapple with rhetoric and with myth, with the tradition embodied by the latter and the antinomian tendencies of the former. Plato, in other words, must draw for us an εἰδύλλιον.

All this may seem to have little to do with Longus, who wrote more than half a millennium after Plato. But if we look, even in a brief and general way, at the classical world in Longus's time, we may be able to see that here, again, is a world on the brink of great change, a world in crisis. Once again, the received ways of understanding the world do not seem to work anymore. The nature of this crisis is properly, then, the subject of the next and final chapter.

Chapter 11

Longus the Sophist

On the title page of his 1605 edition of *Daphnis and Chloe*, without comment or explanation, Gottfried Jungermann styled Longus "the Sophist" (that is, Λόγγος Σοφιστής). It is hard to be sure where Jungermann got this epithet; there is no ancient evidence for it, nor does it appear in any of the surviving manuscripts. Nevertheless, it has stuck, to such an extent that Italian and Spanish classicists in particular are likely to refer to the author of *Daphnis and Chloe* as "Longo Sofista." It is not that hard to see why: even without reflection, "Sophist" seems somehow to fit Longus, especially if one is not too unfavorably impressed by the resonances of the term itself. But there is more to this epithet than would be implied by the apparently casual way in which Longus seems to have acquired it. It is the purpose of what follows, in fact, to explore more deeply what it might mean to call Longus "the Sophist."

THE TEMPER OF THE TIMES

If all of Roman history between the two watershed battles of Actium and the Milvian Bridge were to be placed on a time line, the year A.D. 200 (which, plus or minus a quarter century or so, seems to be when *Daphnis and Chloe* was written) would fall a little past the midpoint. For most readers, the image of this "mid-life" period in the history of the Roman Empire is likely to be indistinct at best. Though it was a time that did not lack for interesting personalities and dramatic events, it still somehow seems to be a sort of waiting time.[1] By the beginning of the second century, the Augustan world of the Julio-Claudians was gone. The Antonines ushered in a renaissance of sorts, but with the death of Marcus Aurelius in 180, and the accession of his son, Commodus, things began to fall apart. The victory of Septimius Severus in 197 brought a new dynasty and a modicum of order, but upon his death in 211 disorder reigned, not to end until the accession of Diocletian in 285. The Christians were still in the catacombs, about to face (under Decius, 249–251) the worst of the persecutions, and so the new world they were to inaugurate after Constantine's victory at the Milvian Bridge (312) was as yet unimagined—even, one supposes, by the Christians themselves.

Whatever else one may say about the period in question, it is beyond doubt the twilight of pagan antiquity. And this is especially true of the Greek world.[2] Whatever remained of the old Hellenic culture, of παιδεία, remained for no other reason than that the Romans, the conquerors of Greece, had both the will and the resources to keep some shadow of Hellenism alive. Both Hadrian and Marcus Aurelius endowed chairs of philosophy and rhetoric in Athens and Rome; without their patronage, it seems at least conceivable that the Academy, and most of the other ancient schools of philosophy, would have folded during the second century. It does not follow from this, however, that the Greeks of the time viewed their Roman protectors and patrons with any particular respect or affection.[3] Plutarch, to be sure, had in the previous century found some complimentary things to say about certain individual Romans; and the second-century Greek rhetorician Aelius Aristides wrote a fulsome panegyric of the *pax Romana*, which has survived.[4] Still, most of the Greek literature and art of this period reflect a nostalgia for (and idealization of) the remote past, the fifth and fourth centuries B.C., when the cities of Greece were free and independent and the Romans were still living in huts on the Tiber.

All this is not to say that the spirit of rebellion was abroad in Greece during this time. Revolution was not in the air; no cries of "Aux barricades!" were to be heard. The freedom of the polis was lost beyond all recovery. What is more, no sensible person would even want it back; the price tag was just too high. Submission to the Romans meant order and prosperity, stable government, and protection from the barbarians lurking not so very far away, to the north or the east. Even if revolt against Roman power were possible, then, life without that power would be harder by far than life with it. As it was, Roman support, protection, and patronage could be had, at the price of a certain submission, a submission which did not require or entail the loss of Hellenic language and culture, and which could be exacted by force of arms in any event. That is why, even when dynastic chaos in Rome left the empire apparently vulnerable to revolt, such revolts seldom actually happened, in Greece or elsewhere.[5]

This does not seem to be the picture of a vital or dynamic culture. And yet there was no lack of Greek intellectual and literary activity during the second and third centuries, even if much of that activity does not seem to us (or to them, for that matter) to meet the high standards of the fifth and fourth centuries B.C.[6] Lucian, by most reckonings the best Greek author of the period, merits inclusion on most graduate reading lists in the classics. Ptolemy, the astronomer, and Galen, the physician, both lived and wrote during this period. So did the arch-skeptic, Sextus Empiricus, as well as two of the most eloquent spokesmen for Stoicism, Marcus Aurelius and Epictetus. These are not inconsiderable talents, and one might well wish that our own age were graced with the like of them. Still, it is unlikely that any of these men would have ranked himself as highly as we may be inclined to do or have brooked comparison to those authors whom their own age already considered to be the classics. It was not an age that thought highly of itself, and in fact its keynote, its hallmark, is pessimism and doubt.[7] Lucian was brilliant, but he was a curmudgeon who looked upon the world around him with cynicism and disgust. Sextus Empiricus was as thoroughgoing a skeptic as the ancient world produced. The two great Stoics taught a grim perseverance in the face of overwhelming adversity—a theme which was always a part of Stoic ethical teaching but which in the works of the emperor and the slave came to dominate over all else.[8]

Another measure of the temper of the times, its prevalent disenchantment with the dreary present, can be found in its religious climate. The second and third centuries are the crucial formative years of Christianity, with its promises of redemption from sin and everlasting life—not life on this earth, of course, but somewhere else, in a better world. Nor were the Christians the only ones making such promises; the pagan religious milieu teemed with cults, old ones and new ones, many of which promised some variation on the themes so familiar to modern readers from our common Christian heritage. The Eastern cults of Isis, Cybele, and Mithras flourished side by side with, and often in syncretic fusion with, the Greek mysteries of Demeter and Kore, of Dionysus, and of Orpheus. To be sure, these latter cults were by no means new inventions. The cults of Orpheus and Dionysus, and the mysteries at Eleusis, were already ancient in the second and third centuries of our era, and many of those that came from the East were of even greater antiquity. The period in question saw, not the origins of the cults, but rather their profusion and elaboration, as well as a certain intensification of that syncretic fusion always characteristic of pagan polytheism. All of the larger and more familiar cults had, after all, a great deal in common with each other: a central myth about the god or goddess who was the focus of the cult; an emphasis on conversion and salvation; an initiation ceremony of some sort, often involving a ritualized sharing in the mythical death and rebirth of the god or goddess; and an attendant promise of life after death.[9]

What do the prevalence and popularity of such cults tell us about the Zeitgeist of the times? This is not an easy question to answer with any certainty and could easily lead us into an epistemological jungle from which we could only with the greatest difficulty extricate ourselves. Only the most general of observations seem either safe or germane here. Men and women who find comfort in myths and rituals of conversion and salvation are clearly not very happy with their lives here and now. Dissatisfaction may well be, of course, the common lot of humanity. But there is a further, deeper implication of the mystery cults: that their devotees, in general, do not look for or expect any temporal remedy for their misery. Their consolation lies in the promise that their burdens will be lifted somewhere else, at some other time. The Roman Empire was too powerful to be directly opposed with even a prayer of success, and, on the whole, too beneficent to drive its subjects to desperation. This was an age of boredom and anxiety, not of revolution. The cults promised changes hereafter, not now, and in another world, not here.[10]

That some scholars have read *Daphnis and Chloe* as an allegory of initiation into a cult has already been remarked. While we have found several good reasons to resist that conclusion in its most extreme (which is to say, reductionist) form, it is still very much true that such religious currents as have just been described were in the air in Longus's day and that they could hardly fail to have exerted some influence on the tenor and preoccupations of *Daphnis and Chloe*.[11] The cults are themselves a symptom of the world-weariness of a culture that, a little over a century after Longus wrote, collectively embraced Christianity—and stopped writing novels. These are people no longer satisfied with the tragic view of life and death that there is something inherently beautiful in our losing battle against mortality.[12] The old answers no longer satisfy, but the search for new answers is fraught with peril, and no one can really know where it will lead.

Whenever large numbers of people within a given culture are so disaffected with the present that all avenues of escape are being simultaneously explored, a cultural crisis, even a revolution, is clearly at hand. It is of no small significance in this context to note that the second century A.D. was also the century of Clement of Alexandria and Origen; Christianity was on its way out of the alleys and the catacombs, with consequences that few of Longus's contemporaries (or Longus himself, for that matter) would have been likely to guess. Still, the manifest fact that classical pagan civilization was on its last legs must have been apparent to any acute observer, and we have already seen reason to believe that it was apparent to Longus. The very obsession of some of the major figures of the second century with preserving the heritage of the past reflects a deeply rooted fear that the heritage of Hellas might be lost. Longus is adept at alluding to the whole range of classical literature, and he does so with both subtlety and sympathy; but at the same time, all this play of allusion is occurring in a text that itself, by its very ethos, profoundly subverts the classical understanding of the profound difference between truth and falsehood. Great changes must have taken place before the same literary tradition that produced a Thucydides and a Sophocles could produce a Longus.

All this may give a new significance to McCulloh's suggestion that *Daphnis and Chloe* is "the last great creation in pagan literature." It is not an altogether unfitting or accidental coda to the great symphony of classical antiquity. The realization that the truth really lives in the strangest of places is a thread, subtle but strong, which leads from Hesiod to Plato to Longus. Plato answers Hesiod's Muses in one way, Longus in another. This, of course, may be precisely why the *Phaedrus* turns out to play so important a role in understanding *Daphnis and Chloe*, why Longus may have turned back to Plato to find a frame for his own understanding of things. For the fact is that despite vast and important differences in their situations, there are equally vast and important similarities between the fourth century B.C. and the third century A.D. In each case, the most fundamental questions about human existence, human society, and the limits of human intelligence, questions which an older generation had thought settled (or had never thought to ask), were for various reasons asked again, with increasing urgency. The process is infinitely various and subtle, but the inevitable result is that the world must be somehow taken apart and then put back together.

The significance of the appearance of prose fiction in the classical world is really explicable only in such terms as these. Fiction sets out to explore the truth by telling a lie in which author and reader collude. It does so by telling a story—heretofore the province of myth or history—which is constructed not from tradition but from the mind of the reader. Here, then, is where rhetoric enters in; for rhetoric teaches us how to assemble words into a persuasive construction, for whatever end. Hence, the dialectic between myth and rhetoric, which we saw controlling the narrative structure of *Daphnis and Chloe*, provides a means by which the emergence of prose fiction itself can be understood. This is not to say that these last observations could stand as a diachronic account of the history of the ancient novel; for (pace Perry) some development had to take place. The novel had to take its first steps before it really could know what it was and where it was going. With Chariton and Xenophon of Ephesus, one wonders if they really knew what they were doing, or what it meant to make a claim for fiction in the classical world, which had always believed that what was true, was true, and that an understanding of the world involved sorting out what was true from what was not. Achilles Tatius, then, seems to have better understood the project; but then, he also seems in certain ways to be mocking it. It remained for Longus to write a self-aware, self-conscious novel, and to do so in full awareness of what he was doing. Like Plato in the *Phaedrus*, he encounters the tradition, and in a profound way loves and respects it; but he situates himself clearly outside that tradition and both signifies and foretells its imminent loss of potency.

At the same time that *Daphnis and Chloe* somehow rings down the curtain on pagan antiquity and its way of looking at the world, it also clearly anticipates and foreshadows the future of European literature, even down to our own day. The novel is still a form much preoccupied with searching for the truth in fiction, even if the paradoxical nature of that search is not as apparent now as it was in the second century A.D., and even if neither myth nor rhetoric looks quite the same today as either one of them looked then. The novel is still given to looking at itself, though the modern world may yet fancy that, in the modern "self-conscious" novel, it has invented something very new. For Longus wrote at the end of a long period of literary development, in a context of profound cultural crisis. He wrote with consummate skill, and with no small sensitivity to the issues that affected his contemporaries. But he wrote, to the detriment of his reputation, in a period that is postclassical but premedieval, in a métier that is not part of the usual province of classical scholarship; and he has somehow contrived to keep his personal identity a profound secret. It is our fault, rather than his, that he has lain in such obscurity for so long.

THE DEATH OF THE ANCIENT GREEK NOVEL

But if this is so, if *Daphnis and Chloe* is indeed a novel, how are we to account for the millennium and more which elapsed before the novel was reborn in the West? Why did such a promising beginning remain largely unexploited for so long? Some readers, surely, will have a ready answer. A moment's thought about when the ancient novel vanished and when the modern novel emerged reveals at least one possible solution to this puzzle. For the premature demise of the ancient novel coincided, as it seems, with the rise of Christianity, while the reemergence of prose fiction seems, for its part, to have coincided with the collapse of the medieval theological synthesis. Whatever date one fixes for the "first novel," whether it be *Don Quixote* or *Pamela*, the form clearly came to life somewhere between the Reformation and the Enlightenment. Western Europe, between Augustine and Luther, seemingly had no place for novels.

A superficial explanation for this is not hard to come by. To some, it will be enough to say that the ancient pagan novels were erotic in theme, and that eroticism was anathema to the Church. But such an explanation, though not inherently implausible, ultimately fails to satisfy. To be sure, the fathers of the Church had their problems with sexuality; but then, the conjugal love of man and wife, which is so much celebrated in the pagan Greek novels, was a symbol and sign of Christ's love for the Church as early as Testamentary times. It would not have taken all that much doing to "baptize" Heliodorus, to write a Christian novel. In fact, we have two ancient Christian texts which might reasonably be taken as efforts to do something like that: the *Acts of Paul and Thecla*, and the *Recognitiones* attributed in antiquity (probably spuriously) to Clement of Alexandria. We might also recall that the Byzantines took to writing novels again several centuries before Cervantes, apparently without incurring the wrath of at least the Eastern church. And finally, those all too eager to blame the censoriousness of the early Church for the disappearance of the novel will somehow have to explain the absence of any hard evidence that the Church, even in the West, ever set out in any systematic way to suppress the pagan novels.[13]

If the Church did not actually or consciously suppress the ancient novel, why did the Edict of Milan apparently sound the death knell for prose fiction? A full answer to that question would have to be another book; but perhaps the results of the present study may point out a road down which some such book might go.

The heart and soul of Christianity is a story not quite like any other. On the one hand, it has something of the cult myth about it: we hear about a divine action, which explains to us who we are and why we do what we do. We break bread in a certain way, because we have heard a story about the breaking of the bread on the night of Christ's betrayal; we believe our action to be full of significance because of that story, which in fact we retell every time we break the bread in that special way. On the other hand, there is something of history about the story in question. These events did not occur in the "Dream Time," in a world so far removed in time as to be utterly unlike the reality we know. On the contrary, Jesus was born when Quirinius was governor of Syria, and died when Pontius Pilate was procurator of Judea. The miraculous nature of this birth and death, and the supernatural significance of them for believers, should not be allowed to obscure their essential historicity. The worship of the resurrected Christ was first spread by men who had known him, who had walked and talked with him.

So this story, the gospel of Christ Jesus, is neither myth nor history but something that is both and neither. Now much the same thing was said before of fiction; but no Christian imagines the story of Jesus to be fiction. To suppose that the apostles made up the story of the Resurrection is to invalidate the gospel, even if the story as told is still invested with some symbolic or artistic significance. "If Christ Jesus did not rise from the dead," Saint Paul says, "your faith is in vain." Thus the gospel, like the ancient Greek novel, speaks to a world accustomed to myth but somehow grown weary of it; but what the gospel does is not to "de-mythify" the culture, as Longus seems to do, but rather to "re-mythify" it. The story of Jesus is a new myth, one which commands belief in a way the old ones never did. It subsumes myth and history, claiming the prerogatives of both.

As for rhetoric, its importance for Christianity need hardly be belabored here. What the Christian preachers did, beginning with Saint Peter on the Day of Pentecost, was to embody their new myth in rhetoric. Precisely because this myth required not just acquiescence but belief, the Christians had to persuade their listeners of the truth of the story they were telling, on two levels: first, that the alleged events really did occur and, second, that the reality of these events had some significance for the lives of everyone, and especially of all those who believed. Without rhetoric, the means of persuasion, the "myth" of Jesus would remain nothing but a story—interesting, perhaps, but still a story. We may be deeply moved by watching the myth of Oedipus acted out on the stage, but we are most unlikely to surrender our lives to Oedipus. That which we might call the "rhetoric" of *Oedipus the King* is verbal artistry; but a Christian homilist, retelling the story of Jesus, is out to persuade, which is the proper meaning and province of rhetoric. Here again, then, myth and rhetoric are brought to bear on each other, and the result is a new world.

All this suggests that both Christianity and the novel arose in response to the cultural collapse of pagan classical civilization. But they are not at all complementary solutions to that collapse. It was not the eroticism of the ancient novels that banished them from the new order but the fact that the idea of fiction was as fundamentally antithetical to Christian culture, or at least to Augustinian and Thomistic Christian culture, as it had been to the dominant pagan intellectual culture from which it had emerged. Not until the medieval synthesis began to break down and Christianity began to ask more questions of itself than it could answer did the issue of truth take on the kind of complexity necessary to the genesis of fiction. To the medieval world, the difference between the true and the false was clear enough; there was a way of knowing what the truth was, even if it was not always easy to understand or apply. But by the time of the Reformation, these things were no longer so clear, or at least did not seem so to many people. By a somewhat parallel path, then, the novel arises from the dying embers of a disintegrating world, in A.D. 200, and again some 1,300 to 1,500 years later.

This is why *Daphnis and Chloe* seems to be so thoroughly dominated by antitheses, on so many levels. The urbane world is set off against the country, innocent lovers against various brutes and voluptuaries, male aggression against female understanding, and myth against rhetoric. In each case, however, these are not mere antinomies, or Manichaean dichotomies of good against evil, light against dark, life against death. What we discover, instead, is a consistent dialectic. We are not allowed to follow one straight path to the truth; all is indirection. The common thread that binds together all these antitheses as antitheses is the disintegration of culture; but precisely because dialectic is possible, the dialectic which is pointed to by the structure of the novel, on one level, and by the marriage of Daphnis and Chloe, on another, we discover that reintegration is also possible. What is needful, Longus tells us (as Plato did), is that we know who we are and where we are.

We have come to the end, then, of our inquiries. We began by asking what *Daphnis and Chloe* is about, and have been about the business of answering that question. The result, as so often, may well be more questions. But that is very much how it should be.

Appendix 1

Author and Date

Whatever importance Longus may have had for the history of the ancient novel, he apparently attracted little notice in his own day. That we have no certain knowledge of even who Longus was, or exactly when or where he wrote, is a notorious and indisputable fact. For all practical purposes, *Daphnis and Chloe* might as well be anonymous. Not only that, but whoever Longus was, his work had no measurable influence on other authors until centuries after he wrote; indeed, no one can prove that any other ancient author ever read *Daphnis and Chloe*. It is not merely that Longus was personally obscure, then; he and his novel escaped the notice of classical antiquity so completely that the very survival of a manuscript tradition seems hard to explain. Someone in antiquity must have enjoyed *Daphnis and Chloe* enough to have it copied, but that is all that can safely be said about its reception before the Byzantine era. Longus's novel may *represent* a turning point in literary history, but it did not *cause* any immediate changes that we can detect from this distance in time.

There are various ways of responding to this dearth of information about the author of *Daphnis and Chloe*. Some scholars will be content simply to accept the isolation of this text from any synchronic context and to proceed to read it diachronically or without any particular reference to any context at all.[1] Others, operating from quite different presuppositions, have tried to squeeze some solid information out of whatever bits of internal or external evidence can be found (or created). Scholarship, like nature, abhors a vacuum. L. Herrmann, for example, has recently argued that the author of *Daphnis and Chloe* was one Velius Longus, a Latin grammarian and intimate of Hadrian.[2] Herrmann's case is hardly compelling, however, unless we are so desperate for an identification that we are ready to grasp at any straw. The following will suffice for example: Velius Longus is known to have written a lexicographical treatise in which one lemma involved a wolf's hide; thus the reference to a wolf's hide at 1.20–21 proves, according to Herrmann, that the author of *Daphnis and Chloe* is Velius Longus. What more can we say? So little of substance has been accomplished from so much effort that we end up where we began: not knowing anything about Longus as a historical, flesh-and-blood person.

There is, of course, a certain unspoken premise behind much of this futile effort to pin down the identity of the author of *Daphnis and Chloe*: to wit, that the virtual anonymity of *Daphnis and Chloe* precludes any useful investigation of the context in which it was written. Those who care little for context as such may well say, ἀλλὰ τύχῃ ἀγαθῇ (which means something like "So?"), and go on about their business of reading the text as a given. All the more reason to do so that the current state of the evidence, as we shall see, will not support any effort to solve this problem by reconstructing a biography for Longus from his text or from other evidence. The abandonment of any search for the context of *Daphnis and Chloe* can be justified, however, only if the unspoken major premise be granted, that knowing the identity of an author is a necessary and sufficient condition for knowing the context of his work. This premise may once have seemed self-evident (and may still seem so to some), but biographical criticism in literature is highly suspect these days, and rightly so. There are other possibilities. We do not know who Longus was, but we can find out approximately when he wrote; and even a date as approximate as this one must be does imply a context, after all. Longus, whoever he was, cannot have been altogether immune to the issues and preoccupations of his times. A great deal can be learned about the context within which *Daphnis and Chloe* was written if we refuse to let what is unknowable prevent us from dealing with what we can know.

The purpose of this Appendix, then, is to justify in greater detail an assumption made in the earlier chapters: namely, that Longus wrote *Daphnis and Chloe* sometime between A.D. 175 and A.D. 225. It may also serve to explain why certain other arguments were *not* made here, arguments that might have been possible if we knew a thing or two about the man who wrote this novel. It may seem, especially to those who know the literature on this subject, that some of what follows belabors the obvious. Nevertheless, the arguments must be worked through, even at the risk of going over some twice-plowed ground. Much of what the present study has to contribute to the reading of *Daphnis and Chloe* consists of reintegrating the text and the context, and much of that begins with an assumption of Longus's approximate dates; and a due regard for the decorum of scholarship requires that any such assumption be examined. The first task at hand, then, is to sort out the knowable from the unknowable and what matters from what does not.

THE QUESTION OF IDENTITY

There is no trace of ancient biographical or bibliographical information about the man who wrote *Daphnis and Chloe*. The *Suda* never mentions either Longus or *Daphnis and Chloe*, nor does the indefatigable Photius; in fact, we have no certain reference to either text or author before the second half of the twelfth century, scarcely one hundred years before the oldest extant manuscript was written.[3] Thus the usual ancient sources for the biographies of authors, however unreliable they may be for such other ancient Greek novelists as Heliodorus or Achilles Tatius, are in this case entirely silent.[4]

Even the name "Longus," though probably correct, is not necessarily so. The two best existing manuscripts of *Daphnis and Chloe* (Vaticanus Graecus 1348 and Florentinus Laurentius Conventi Soppressi 627, called "V" and "F," respectively, in the Teubner text of *Daphnis and Chloe*) appear to differ on the author's name, or at least on its spelling.[5] The superscription of V reads Λόγγου Ποιμενικῶν τῶν κατὰ Δάφνιν καὶ Χλόην λόγος πρῶτος, which is to say, "The First Book of Longus's Pastorals concerning Daphnis and Chloe." Hence the name "Longus." Manuscript F, on the other hand, reads **Λόγου** Ποιμενικῶν **περὶ** Δάφνιν καὶ Χλόην λόγος πρῶτος, that is, "The First Book of *Logus's* Pastorals *about* Daphnis and Chloe" (emphasis added). Neither the variant between the prepositions περί and κατά, nor F's omission of the definite article τῶν, is of any real consequence, especially in view of the ancients' casual attitude toward titles; but F's reading of Λόγου for V's Λόγγου is more of a problem. That the author of *Daphnis and Chloe* was a man named "Logus" (Λόγος) seems unlikely, since the Greek word λόγος is a common noun almost never used as a name.[6] As it stands, in fact, F's superscription is impossible, and so there must be an error somewhere. But where?

One very ingenious line of argument holds that the "Logos" of the superscription never was a name, but appears in that troublesome initial position as the result of a transposition of *logos*, "book," within the superscription, from "Book One" (λόγος πρῶτος) to the author's name. Λόγγος differs from λόγος, after all, by only the single letter γ. Presumably, then, the actual author's name was displaced at an early stage in the manuscript tradition by this errant λόγος, which was then in turn corrupted into Λόγγος, perhaps accidentally, or perhaps as the result of some subsequent scribe's effort to make a name out of that puzzling initial λόγου. Thus, the argument runs, we have lost the author's real name, and *Daphnis and Chloe* is really, literally, anonymous.[7] But this argument, however ingenious, yields a conclusion that must finally be judged implausible. Even though it must be acknowledged that many strange things happen in fourteenth- and fifteenth-century Greek manuscripts copied in the West, when many of the copiers were themselves illiterate in Greek, no such chain of scribal errors can be shown to have occurred in the manuscript tradition of any other ancient text. A much more likely explanation of the Λόγγου/Λόγου variant is that the scribe of F (or his source) inadvertently dropped a γ in writing the superscription.[8] Still, hardly anything better illustrates the futility of any effort to create some sort of biography for Longus than the fact that not even his name can be established beyond a reasonable doubt.

Even granting the name, however, does not solve all the problems. We are still very much in the dark, with little to go on but speculation. "Longus," if genuine, is a name of obviously Latin origin, not Greek; thus its owner would seem to have been either a Roman citizen (by birth or by grant of citizenship), or the freedman of a Roman family. This observation has led to some interesting conjectures. From inscriptions, we know of a family named the Pompeii Longi who lived, coincidentally, on the island of Lesbos.[9] Of (presumably) Greek extraction, they became clients of Pompey the Great after the Mithridatic wars: hence the *gentilicium* "Pompeius." That they survived the downfall of their patron and namesake is possible, perhaps likely, since a Pompeius Longus rose to the consulship in A.D. 49, under the emperor Claudius.[10] Early in this century, Conrad Cichorius suggested that the author of *Daphnis and Chloe* was a member or client of this family.[11] But though the conclusion may be tempting for many reasons, the evidence has a disconcerting tendency to evaporate under closer scrutiny. "Longus" was not an uncommon cognomen in late antiquity, and in fact the Pompeii Longi are not the only Roman *gens* with which our Longus has sometimes been identified.[12] In the final analysis, the inference that he came from the Pompeii Longi, rather than from one of the many other *gentes* who used that cognomen, is based on the assumption that, since *Daphnis and Chloe* is set on Lesbos, and since the author seems to be familiar with the island, then Longus was a native of the place, and presumably related to the Pompeii Longi.

Now if everyone could be persuaded that Longus knew Lesbos very well, the matter might be closer to resolution, and one might feel more comfortable in supposing that *Daphnis and Chloe* was written by someone named Pompeius Longus, a Romanized Greek resident of Lesbos. But one of the greatest German classicists of the nineteenth century, Ulrich von Wilamowitz-Moellendorff, said of Longus that "die Insel Lesbos

gar nicht kennt und das gleiche seinen Lesern zumutet" ("He
is clearly unfamiliar with the island of Lesbos, and presumes
the same of his readers"); he chose Lesbos as a setting, according
to Wilamowitz, only because it was a suitable "Wünschland," a
"Never-never land."[13] S. A. Naber, in 1877, backed up Wilamowitz's hunch by pointing out in the text of *Daphnis and Chloe* what
he took to be a serious topographical error: Longus says that the
distance between Methymna and Mitylene is 330 stades, some
sixty stades farther than the distance given (or rather, implied)
by the Greek geographer Strabo.[14] An accusation of geographical ignorance, coming from two eminent German classicists (especially when one of them is Wilamowitz), is no trifling matter;
but Longus's would-be detractors have not had the last word. On
the contrary, the most recent scholarship has tended to uphold
the accuracy of Longus's topographical knowledge. The stade as
a unit of measure fluctuated throughout antiquity, for one thing;
and, at any rate, Longus seems to have measured the disputed
distance by "road miles," while Strabo's measurements are based
partly on travel by ship. Two recent scholars have been convinced enough of Longus's essential accuracy in these matters
that they have even suggested possible locations, on the basis
of Longus's descriptions, for the estate of Dionysophanes on
Lesbos.[15]

Other arguments for or against the thesis that Longus was
personally familiar with Lesbos center on some of the descriptive passages in *Daphnis and Chloe*, where we might expect someone writing from first-hand knowledge of the setting to give us
accurate information, with particular attention to whatever is
unique to that setting. Two of these descriptions have posed considerable problems to those who maintain that Longus was a native or resident of Lesbos: the description of grapevines hung
over tree limbs at 2.1, and the description of a relatively harsh
winter at the beginning of book 3.[16] Though the draping of vines
over tree limbs to keep the grapes off the ground was apparently
rare in Italy and the West, the practice was not peculiar to
Lesbos and is not even certainly attested there; thus what appears to be a piece of local color may in fact be something of a
commonplace.[17] As for the winter, Longus's description, which

features snow and frozen rivers, seems to be far too harsh for what we know of Lesbos's climate in antiquity. It has been argued, then, that if what Longus says in these two passages results more from literary convention or embellishment than from strict attention to particular details (something which current literary jargon calls "overdetermination"), his knowledge of Lesbos must have been mainly or entirely derivative. In fact, however, no such conclusion is provable. It may well be true that the descriptions in question are more or less overdetermined, that they are written with an eye to literary necessity rather than to strict representation of reality; but that in itself, even if true, cannot really tell us anything about the man who wrote them.[18] Any extended literary description of even the most familiar landscape could hardly avoid some dependence on literary convention, especially in the case of an author whose wide learning and allusiveness are an integral part of his style. Much in Longus's description of young love is also conventional, but no one argues that the text is overdetermined on this point and that Longus therefore had no first-hand experience of adolescence and its passions. No one can prove, then, that Longus did not really know Lesbos; and if either Mason or Green is correct in locating an actual place near Mitylene that Longus seems to have had in mind in his description of Dionysophanes' estate, then Wilamowitz and those who have followed his lead are simply wrong.

Those who would make of Longus a member or client of the Pompeii Longi must do more, of course, than to prove that he had some first-hand knowledge of the geography and climate of Lesbos—or rather, than to disprove the converse, which is about all that can be done. That Longus apparently knew something of Lesbos, and perhaps knew one particular part of it rather well, does not prove that he was a native, as he would almost certainly be if he were indeed "Pompeius" Longus. Some have argued that, on the contrary, whether or not Longus knew Lesbos personally, he clearly represents himself in the prologue as a visitor to Lesbos, not as a native.[19] The language of the prologue has many layers of meaning, which we have only begun to probe; but what seems to matter at this stage in the argument is that the authorial persona represents himself, at least by implication, as a traveller, a stranger on Lesbos. The very words with which the prologue begins, Ἐν Λέσβῳ θηρῶν ("While hunting on Lesbos"), do not seem to be those of a native.[20] Furthermore, the author's need for an ἐξηγητής, an exegete, implies that he was unfamiliar with a story that any native of Lesbos would be likely to know. The first-person singular speaker of the prologue is, therefore, a visitor to Lesbos.

It is just here, however, that this whole line of argument reveals its fundamental weakness. A moment's thought should make us wary of accepting the unspoken premise upon which much of this argument back and forth about Longus's acquaintance with Lesbos clearly depends, which is that whatever is true of the authorial persona within the text, the first-person singular of the prologue, is also true of the author himself, the human being who once existed outside the text. Even the most recalcitrant biographical critic is likely to see the pitfalls lurking in that. Anyone who approaches even an ancient novel with such an assumption, to say nothing of a modern novel, will quickly get into intractable problems. Illustrations could be multiplied, but a brief look at another ancient novel may be sufficient.

In the very beginning of Apuleius's *Metamorphoses*, the narrative voice, the ego, is apparently that of Apuleius himself. The author promises to delight his audience with a string of stories, in the Milesian manner but with an Egyptian accent. Within a few sentences, however, and without perceptible transition, the narrator has become the protagonist, Lucius. For the next eleven books, the first-person singular is unambiguously this fictive Lucius of Patrae; but near the very end of the *Metamorphoses*, after his conversion to Isis, Lucius is suddenly, and without any apparent internal motivation, sent off to Madaura, in northern Africa: that is, to the hometown of Apuleius himself. Who is Lucius, and who is Apuleius, in the text of the *Metamorphoses*?[21] Of course, this radical and unannounced shift in the point of view might be mere perversity on Apuleius's part, or even shoddy writing; but to assume that any given difficulty in a literary text is the result of an authorial error or blunder is to run a grave risk of devaluing what may well prove to be sophisticated literary technique. That is precisely the case here. What Apuleius does with the point of view at the beginning and end of the *Metamorphoses* bears a striking resemblance to—is indeed nothing other than—a common technique in the modern novel: romantic irony, the deliberate undermining of the point of view.[22] Romantic irony subverts the classical understanding of the relationship between author and text, that the ego is always the author, who is therefore personally responsible for the truth of his narrative. But this is fiction; and in fiction, the old rules of truth and referentiality are suspended. That is the point. To attempt to sort out the difference between the Lucius-narrator and the Apuleius-narrator in the *Metamorphoses* is to miss that point entirely. The reconstruction of the biography of any author, ancient or modern, from his text, on the assumption that the narrative voice is the author's voice, is thus a very dangerous business.

And this brings up what is really the central point. That Longus was (or was not) a native of Lesbos is quite unprovable. The argument goes around in circles and ends up where it began, with nothing more than a name. But how much more than a name do we really need? To engage in some kind of critical discourse about *Daphnis and Chloe*, it is useful to have a name by which we can refer to the author, the formative intelligence behind the text. If the novel were entirely anonymous, we should have to resort to a clumsy periphrasis, "the anonymous author of *Daphnis and Chloe*," whenever we wished to say anything about the creation and formation of the text. As it is, we have only a name, and so there is little else to tempt the incautious critic into biographical criticism. Tomorrow someone may discover a papyrus or an inscription that will reveal the author of *Daphnis and Chloe* to have been one A. Pompeius Longus, who lived from A.D. 133 to 189, who owned a pleasant country estate not too far from Mitylene, who had a wife named Aurelia and three children (a boy and two girls), who had a mole over his left eye and suffered from chronic respiratory ailments that finally killed him. Such a discovery would certainly satisfy a good deal of curiosity about the man responsible for *Daphnis and Chloe*, but of all the (imaginary) facts listed above, only one would really affect our understanding of the text: the date.

THE QUESTION OF DATE

Whether or not Longus was actually familiar with the topography of Lesbos can only be incidental to the reading of *Daphnis and Chloe*. On the other hand, the question of the audience to whom the novel may have been addressed is anything but incidental. We ourselves are not, we cannot be, that audience. No amount of learning and study can transform any of us into Greek-speaking residents of the later Roman Empire. This does not mean, however, that critics and readers of ancient literature are thereby discharged from any obligation to take account of the external circumstances surrounding the creation of the text—in other words, of the context. The audience, the public for whom any work of literature is written, is always a silent partner in the act of literary creation, and its role must be considered in the criticism of any text. Date alone, of course, does not identify an audience, and we shall have to look deeper into the whole problem before we can be sure, or nearly sure, who the intended audience for *Daphnis and Chloe* might have been. Nevertheless, without at least a rough idea of the date, we can have very little notion of what possible audiences might have been available or likely at the time when Longus wrote. Thus, for example, if Erwin Rohde had been correct in assigning Longus to the sixth century of the present era, we would have to assume that *Daphnis and Chloe* was written in a Byzantine (and thus predominantly Christian) milieu and that some reaction or response to Christian dogma is implicit in Longus's unapologetic paganism. Indeed, one could downdate *Daphnis and Chloe* two centuries at least and still have to make very nearly the same assumption. This is not to say, of course, that an author writing in a Christian milieu must be a Christian. But after the reign of Constantine, at the latest, Christianity was prevalent and powerful enough to make itself felt even in the work of the most unrepentant pagan. As the dominant religion, Christianity had the power to influence, if not to define, the terms of the debate; in the sixth century, and even to some extent in the fourth, the hand and the voice of the Church could not be simply ignored. But if the majority of recent scholars are correct in assuming that Longus wrote toward the end of the second century or the beginning of the third, there is no need to search for the shadow of Christianity in the text: the Christians were still in the catacombs, and their doctrines were still largely beneath the notice of the dominant pagan culture.

That same dearth of information which precludes a biographical study of Longus makes certain dating almost as difficult. A general consensus among those interested in the subject assigns Longus to the end of the second century A.D.[23] That assumption proved useful in the final chapter of this book; but its usefulness was not its sole justification. Let us review, then, the arguments that lead to that approximate date.

Nothing in the text of the novel itself is distinctly dateable. There are no obvious topical allusions. Three thousand drachmae seem a considerable sum to the characters, and that has led some scholars to conclude that the novel must have been written before about A.D. 250, when the rampant inflation that set in during the reign of Gallienus would have made 3,000 drachmae virtually worthless.[24] There is a certain specious plausibility to this line of argument, but it would work much better if *Daphnis and Chloe* were not so obviously set in a time rather remote from that of author and reader. On the whole, Daphnis and Chloe do live in a remarkably timeless world; but there are a few hints in the text that the novel is set in the pre-Roman past. We should almost expect this, after all: most of the other Greek novels have an easily identifiable fictive date in the Hellenistic period, before the Roman annexation of Greece, while some, such as *Chaereas and Callirhoe*, are set at an even earlier date. The mini-war between Methymna and Mitylene in book 3 of *Daphnis and Chloe*, and even the activities of the pirates in book 1, certainly imply that there is no Roman presence on or near Lesbos, since the Romans would never have tolerated such goings-on. Neither piratical raids nor intercity warfare would have been part of the actual experience of Longus's audience, unless we date Longus himself to the first century B.C. (at the latest), a date which no one is likely to accept. So the value assigned in the text to the sum of 3,000 drachmae may itself be part of a certain nostalgic aura, an evocation of the simplicity of a bygone era. In much the same way, a modern American novelist can summon up a whole complex of feelings and attitudes about the American past by treating a dollar as a fair day's wage for a day's work, and a thousand dollars as a substantial fortune. It is dangerous to use such references as these to date a work that is set in the past.

Another possible point of reference in establishing an approximate date of composition for *Daphnis and Chloe* comes from the prologue. The painting there described seems to consist of a series of scenes, arranged in an order that implies an underlying narrative. (The gist of the narrative itself must not have been self-evident, since the services of an ἐξηγητής, an exegete, are required.) Paintings of this sort were in fact popular at various periods in antiquity, especially in the latter half of the second century A.D. Perhaps Longus is describing an actual painting here (though that is by no means always the case with other literary ecphrases from antiquity); if so, it seems only reasonable to suppose that this painting would be of the style that was popular in the author's time, and thus familiar to his audience. If this is true, the style of narrative painting described by Longus suggests an Antonine date.[25]

On its face, this is a coherent and plausible line of argument. It runs afoul, however, of the same biographical fallacies that tend to enter into arguments over whether or not Longus was a native of Lesbos. To say that Longus must have been describing a real painting, perhaps a mural that was actually found by him in a grove on the island of Lesbos, is again to mistake authorial persona for author—an error which results, in large part, from a certain failure to take account of the freedom of invention essential to fiction.[26] Arguments based on the apparent style of the painting described in the prologue are also vulnerable on the same grounds as the dating based on the value of 3,000 drachmae. The possibility that Longus may well have deliberately evoked an aura of nostalgia by referring to a painting style that was already passé cannot be ruled out. Paintings do not disappear as soon as the style in which they are painted is out of fashion. In sum, the very possibility of deliberate anachronism defeats any and all such arguments right from the start.

No help, then, from the content of the novel. The next recourse would seem to be relative dating. The procedure is a familiar one to most classicists: If author A, whose date is known, can be shown to be borrowing from or quoting author B, author A's date is the terminus ante quem for author B. Conversely, if B seems at some point to be borrowing from A, the latter's date (again, presuming that it is known) is the terminus post quem for B. The logic is impeccable, but in practice the procedure is all but impossible to apply. The difficulties are many. Borrowings and imitations are seldom blatant enough to be identified as such beyond all doubt. When two authors use similar language, similes, incidents, or characters, the possibility of a common source cannot usually be ruled out on purely logical grounds. Furthermore, even in those rare cases where imitation or borrowing seems patent, it is well nigh impossible to say for sure who is borrowing from whom, especially where one of the two authors is of uncertain date. In the case of *Daphnis and Chloe*, these difficulties have proven thus far to be insurmountable. Much attention has been given, for example, to some alleged points of contact between *Daphnis and Chloe* and the *Letters* of Alciphron; but since, quite beyond all the problems just mentioned, Alciphron is also of uncertain date, we can expect no help from that quarter.[27] Both Longus and Achilles Tatius (who has been dated on the basis of papyrological evidence to the second half of the second century) tell the story of Syrinx; but even if the two authors told the tale in the same way (which they really do not), we would still not be able to tell who borrowed from whom or whether they might have relied on a common source.[28] Thus relative dating has so far come up empty.

The failure of all these various attempts to date the composition of *Daphnis and Chloe* leaves us, it must be said, with little to go on. All that we can really do is to establish some very wide termini and then use whatever legitimate evidence is available to narrow these termini as much as possible. Though any kind of precision is impossible in the current state of our evidence, we can, without unduly taxing anyone's credulity, arrive at a date that is at least specific enough to be useful.

To begin with, there is the language itself. Longus writes a literary koine, with occasional Atticisms.[29] That a work with obvious literary intentions could have been written in koine before the beginning of the present era (at the very earliest) seems almost impossible, while Longus's occasional Atticisms suggest a date no earlier than the beginning of the second century. This gives us a safe terminus post quem of A.D. 100, at the very earliest; even 150 is probably safe, on these grounds.

A consideration of the history of the genre to which *Daphnis and Chloe* belongs leads to very nearly the same date. Prose fiction did not begin to appear on the Greek literary scene, as we have seen, until late in the Hellenistic period. The earliest extant fragments of what may have been a Greek novel (the "Ninus Fragments") date from about 100 B.C., and the oldest extant complete novel, *Chaereas and Callirhoe,* is now generally dated, on papyrological evidence, to sometime after A.D. 50. Longus, as we have seen, is a self-conscious novelist who delights in subtle play with the conventions of his genre. It seems very unlikely, then, that he wrote when the form he was playing with was still new and indistinct. A form must have a certain history before any flouting or subversion of its conventions and topoi can be meaningful. On these grounds, Longus is not likely to have written earlier than Chariton or Xenophon of Ephesus; the latter of these can with some confidence be dated to the mid- to late second-century A.D., which can accordingly be postulated as a fairly firm terminus post quem.

The opposite terminus can also be narrowed. Longus shows no sign of the tendency toward rhythmic clausulae that began to be felt in the earliest Byzantine prose, from about A.D. 350 onward.[30] This terminus ante quem can be pulled back further if some account is taken of the fact that the period between about 235 (the fall of the Severi) and 283 (the accession of Diocletian) was a period of military anarchy in the Roman world, during which very little of the patronage essential to literary productivity in the ancient world was available. That fifty-year period is, in fact, a kind of watershed for the late Roman Empire, which is to say, for Graeco-Roman civilization; Diocletian's reestablishment of order was followed within a fairly short time by the triumph of

Christianity under Constantine and the beginning of the end of pagan classical civilization. Everything about the style and ambience of *Daphnis and Chloe* suggests that it was written before, not after, that third-century hiatus.

When all roads, even those not taken, seem to point in the same direction, to the last quarter of the second century A.D. or the first quarter of the third, it is only perverse to resist, especially when not even one road seems to lead compellingly in any other direction. The process of elimination thus leads to a date that is neither unattractive nor inherently implausible. Longus's fondness for balanced antithetical clauses (that is, as some readers will know, for the Asianic style), the elegance and polish of his rhetorical displays, his wry wit, the mantle of learning he wears lightly but convincingly—all these point to that revival of Greek rhetoric that is now generally known as the Second Sophistic, which reached its highest point of development at precisely the time in question. There is no compelling reason to struggle against this date, and more than one reason to embrace it.

The Second Sophistic often comes in for passing mention when Longus's date is under discussion, since his "sophisticated" style is one of the few pieces of would-be evidence that cannot be explained away.[31] Conversely, discussions of Longus's style characteristically begin with a reference to his presumed date and to the Second Sophistic.[32] From neither direction, however, has the relationship between Longus and the Second Sophistic been fully explored.[33] It was not for nothing that Gottfried Jungermann (or a lost source) gave Longus the epithet "Sophista," by which he is still called in some languages (especially in Italian and Spanish), as well as in the title of the last chapter.[34] That Longus had a career or reputation as a sophist or declaimer parallel to those enjoyed by Aelius Aristides and Herodes Atticus, the leading lights of the Second Sophistic, could not be maintained, for reasons that should be obvious by now. If the Second Sophistic is defined in strictly historical or biographical terms as a group of specific persons who were gathered around or patronized by the imperial court and who made their livings as declaimers and teachers of rhetoric, then Longus cannot rightly be called a part of it, at least so far as our evidence permits. But

Longus is, as we have seen, extraordinarily sensitive to rhetoric, perhaps even preoccupied with it. The title of the last chapter suggests, then, that there may be more substance in the epithet "Sophista" than might be inferred from the apparently casual way in which Longus acquired it. Whether or not Longus was a "sophist" in literal fact, he certainly breathed the spirit of his times.

We have finally arrived, then, after a long and sometimes tortuous journey, at an approximate date for the composition of *Daphnis and Chloe*. But A.D. 200 is just that, approximate, and may be wrong by a quarter century or so either way. That Longus wrote sometime during the period that elapsed between the accession of Marcus Aurelius (161) and the murder of Alexander Severus (234), dates which correspond rather precisely with the high point of the Second Sophistic, seems a safe enough conjecture; but that is about as specific as we can be. This lack of specificity means, naturally, that nothing can be said about the strictly historical context of *Daphnis and Chloe* with quite the degree of precision or detail that would be possible if we knew more exactly who Longus was, and when (or where) he wrote.[35] It might be interesting to know, for example, whether Longus wrote under the Antonines or the Severi, or whether he wrote at a time and place where that mattered much. The cold fact remains, however, that in the present state of the evidence there is no way to know these things.

But to acknowledge that precision in these matters is not possible is not to say that nothing of value can be said about the synchronic context of *Daphnis and Chloe*. Again, even a broadly approximate date can have important implications for the reading of a text. If all our knowledge of Shakespeare's life were somehow to be wiped out, except for an approximate floruit, the loss would not do irreparable damage to our understanding of his plays. Knowing that he wrote during the last years of the Tudor dynasty and the first years of the Stuarts is of far greater significance than knowing that he left his second best bed to his wife or why he did so. Even if it were to be proven that Francis Bacon actually wrote the plays, *Hamlet* would still be *Hamlet*; but our reading of the play would be dramatically altered if we were to discover that it was actually written a century before or a century after the reign of Elizabeth. There are things worth saying, then, about the general state of the world in the second and third centuries of the present era, and even more important and apposite observations to be made about certain intellectual and cultural currents that would have influenced almost anyone writing within the period in question. We can know nothing for certain about the tree under which Longus sat to write *Daphnis and Chloe*, but that does not prevent us from looking at the forest.

Appendix 2

Scholarly Interpretations of the Ancient Novel

Even though critical tastes and theories have evolved and changed considerably since 1876, when Erwin Rohde wrote his monumental study of the Greek novel,[1] much of the scholarship on the subject has not, until rather recently, gone beyond the questions he asked or the implicit critical stance he assumed. What, Rohde asked, were the antecedents, the *Quellen*, of the ancient Greek novel? How, when, and by whom were the *disiecta membra* of old literary forms reassembled into this new one? And (more or less implicitly), how could Greeks write such trash? It is hard not to admire the meticulous scholarship Rohde displays in the process of answering these questions, in the great tradition of German philology. Indeed, a certain awe and admiration may itself be enough to explain why Rohde still exercises so potent an influence over the terms and limits of the discussion, or why, over the years since *Der griechische Roman*, many new answers to these old questions have been advanced but very few new questions have been asked.

That may be why so many of those who have set out to discuss the nature of the ancient Greek novel seem to get no farther than the tangled issue of origins. The matter is not without interest, of course; but it seems to have so absorbed the attention of scholars that matters of perhaps far greater import have gone by the board. Somehow the study of the novel per se has been almost entirely subsumed by the study of its beginnings. It may be that a certain proclivity toward identifying the essence of a thing with its origin has been inherited from the Greeks themselves: the ἀρχή (*archê*) of a thing, in Greek, is at once both its organizing principle and its beginning, its province and its provenance. Or perhaps this confusion between essence and genesis can be explained in Heideggerian terms, in the movement from Greek φύσις (*physis*) to Latin *natura*. Whatever the reason, we are left with a body of scholarship that, with some notable exceptions (and those relatively recent), tells us much more about where the ancient novel came from than about what it is.

The rise of the novel in antiquity has been explained in many different ways; but although the various theories adduced by several generations of classicists are of great diversity in detail, the theoretical paths by which they have arrived at their individual conclusions can be reduced, without unacceptable violence, to two. Some scholars, especially (but not exclusively) in the nineteenth and early twentieth century, have begun by assuming that the novel arose as the result of a certain evolutionary process in ancient literature and have accordingly set out to trace what we might call the "literary pedigree" of the form. Others, mostly of more recent date, have looked for the key to the origins of the ancient Greek novel in the social history of later antiquity; that is, they have gone outside of literature and literary history. What divides these two groups and has tended to send each individual scholar down one path or the other is a great and fundamental disagreement over the nature and province of causation in literature.

The terms of this debate are familiar to anyone who has followed the course of developments in literary theory over the past three or four decades. Is a text created or determined by other texts, or is it the literary effect of nonliterary causes? How autonomous is literature? What constitutes "literariness?" These fundamental theoretical issues, though they sometimes seem to have gotten little explicit or systematic attention in the classical academy, have governed the peculiar history of scholarship on the ancient novel. Each theory to be considered here is conditioned by, and predicated upon, a certain critical stance, which is seldom articulated. The task at hand, therefore, is to articulate the unarticulated, to bring out of hiding the presuppositions of a previous generation of scholars on the ancient novel.

Replacing one set of presuppositions with another may not seem, at first, to have much point. Would it not be better, or more legitimate, to dispense with presuppositions altogether, so as to deal with things as they really are? The inescapable fact is, however, that no human being will ever succeed in reading without presuppositions; complete objectivity is beyond our grasp, and might not be worth having even if it were obtainable. The purpose of the survey that follows is not to claim a superior position, from which the putative "blindness" of older scholars may be contemned. The problem is not that Rohde (or anyone else) was blind, but rather that he read the ancient novels through lenses, as it were, of a certain thickness, curve, and color; and these lenses, though they may have been perfectly appropriate for him, no longer seem to work very well for us. We have other lenses, other interests and other preoccupations; and these require that we set aside the old ones, even though we do so with all due respect for the scholarship that ground them so very fine. This is an important step forward. To understand presuppositions is to control them, and to control our own presuppositions is to make them our servants instead of our masters.

The next few pages will consist of an outline of the terrain over which previous critics have traversed, in roughly chronological order. We shall first briefly examine several theories that have attempted to trace the literary pedigree of the ancient novel; and then we shall turn our attention to those scholars who have looked elsewhere (that is, outside of literature per se) for the causes of the novel's appearance in the ancient world.[2] Once we have sifted through all this, and gleaned from it whatever still seems sound and usable, we can go forward, with some chance of making real progress.

THE "ASIAN" THEORY

Perhaps the earliest effort to account for the genesis of the ancient novel is to be found in a seventeenth-century essay by a

French cleric, Msgr. Pierre-Daniel Huet. His *Lettre à M. Segrais de l' origine des romans*, published in Paris in 1678, put forward a theory which has been remarkably persistent: that the ancient Greek novel was not of Greek ancestry at all but came from the Orient.[3] The peoples of the ancient Near East (the Egyptians, the Mesopotamians, the Persians, and others) had traditions of literary fiction in prose that were already old when the Greeks were still illiterate. The fact that several of the Greek novels are set in the East lends a certain plausibility, perhaps, to Huet's main idea, that Greeks living in the twilight and decadence of classical literature began to look to the even older (and presumably more decadent) literary traditions of the East for both form and content. Huet's theory was eclipsed for many years by the preponderant influence of Rohde's very different model, which will be considered shortly; but the demolition of the latter's chronology, and the concomitant discrediting of his theory, opened the door for a revival of sorts.

Huet's "Asian" theory—after a long dormancy, and not without significant changes—was resuscitated earlier in this century by Martin Braun, who advanced the thesis that the antecedents of the Greek novel were to be found in efforts to preserve their respective national identities on the part of various Oriental peoples, whose historical fate it was to be continually subjugated, first by the Persians, then by Alexander, and finally by the Romans.[4] According to Braun, the basic plot line to be found in almost all the Greek novels originated in these nationalistic (but highly localized) myths and legends, which were picked up by Greek authors, and then modified, elaborated, and embroidered to such an extent that their nationalistic origins and purposes were all but entirely obscured.[5] The case that Asia somehow played a direct and formative role in the genesis of the Greek novel has also been argued in articles by Moses Hadas, in 1952, and by J. W. B. Barns, in 1956; and now Graham Anderson has given the whole theory a much more detailed exposition, along with a new twist.[6] According to Anderson, the plots of the Greek novels, though they came from the East, are not of post-Alexandrian date at all but are rather based on incomparably older Near Eastern originals; in demonstrating this, he goes into much greater detail than did Huet, even to the extent of identi-

fying the "sources" of each of the surviving Greek novels. Thus
Daphnis and Chloe, for example, is based on *Dumuzi's Dream*, a Su-
merian tale about a shepherd boy who falls in love with his sister.

There are, however, serious difficulties with this whole theory. Although some (not all) of the Greek novels have a certain
flavor or aura of the mysterious Orient about them, all that can
be demonstrated is just that: a flavor or aura. No one, including
Anderson, has yet succeeded in proving the existence of any
conscious borrowing by any Greek novelist from any presumed
Oriental model. It is one thing, after all, to say that similar
stories are told in one place and in another; it is quite another to
say, let alone prove, that some sort of transmission has taken
place. The whole Asian thesis rests, in fact, upon scant evidence
and owes what plausibility it has to an a priori notion (a preju-
dice, really) that whatever is nonclassical is non-Greek. The fact
that the trials and tribulations of young lovers appear as favorite
themes in both Oriental and Greek texts, in and of itself, proves
nothing. These characters, and the ordeals and passions they experience, are so much the nearest thing to universals in human
life that it would be surprising if we did not find parallel texts,
mutatis mutandis, in different cultures and different eras. No
one will argue, of course, that Greek culture, even in the days of
Marathon and Salamis, was ever hermetically sealed against influences from the East, or that the Greek novels in particular
were not susceptible to such influences; but to go beyond this
and argue that the novel was a direct borrowing from the East is
to make an impermissible (or at least very dangerous) logical
leap from "influence" to "cause" and to dismiss a priori, without
examination, the possibility that the origin of the novel might
be explicable without any such deus ex machina. The novel is
indeed nonclassical, as we have seen, but there are other and
better ways of explaining that.

LOCAL MYTHOGRAPHY

The theory that local or eponymous myths may have been trans-
muted into novels does not necessarily depend upon the Asian
thesis, in the course of which it was first worked out. An analo-

gous line of argument can be found in influential studies by Bruno Lavagnini and J. Ludvíkovsky, who argued that the kind of localized myths preserved for us by Pausanias (and, to some extent, by Parthenius) provided the seed from which the Greek novels grew.[7] Again, the Greek novelists are presumed to have taken stories that originated as myths and then "novelized" them, so that their mythic origins are all but unrecognizable. Therein, of course, lies the difficulty: even if there are mythical sources for the plots of some of the ancient novels, the connection between the novels and their presumed mythical models are so tenuous as to be meaningless, from a critical standpoint. Myth is one thing, fiction another, as we have seen. If the ancient novel is mythography, then it represents mythography so entirely transformed as to be unrecognizable. The continued pursuit of mythical antecedents for the plots of the ancient novels is, in fact, nothing other than *Quellenforschung*, a "source criticism" that amasses data of virtually no use.

Unlikely as it may seem to the uninitiated, source criticism has in fact been brought to bear on *Daphnis and Chloe*. According to one view, to which Schoenberger and others have apparently subscribed, the "source" of Longus's narrative is purported to be a certain local legend that Longus has elaborated into a novel. There was, in fact, a spring known as Daphnis's Spring (cf. "Jacob's Well") on Lesbos, and some have supposed that the "myth" of Daphnis and Chloe is an eponymous legend about that spring. Others have tried to connect Longus's story with the temple of Dionysus, or the country district in the eparchy of Mitylene called "Napaios," or some such geographical reference.[8] Those who maintain positions along this line naturally construe the "interpreter" (that is, the ἐξηγητής) of the prologue as a local man, learned in the lore of the place. Longus apparently went hunting on Lesbos, found in a lovely grove a painting that told a myth associated with the place, sought out a local expert to tell him the story, and then worked the whole thing up into a novel.

All this presupposes, of course, that the prologue is literally autobiographical. Naturally, there are good reasons to be skeptical of such an assumption; certainly the easiest way to dispose of some Lavagnini-style reading of *Daphnis and Chloe* is to label it "biographical" and discard it. But that is probably too easy. The real difficulty with source criticism, after all, is that it does not help us to read the text. Geographical myths from Lesbos are no more illuminating for the reader of *Daphnis and Chloe* than are Syracusan legends about the daughter of Hermocrates and Dionysius I for the reader of *Chaereas and Callirhoe*. Even if the existence of such legends could be proven—which is not easy—we would not necessarily be any the wiser for it. Any school edition of *Moby Dick* is likely to mention that Herman Melville had shipped on a whaler and had probably heard many stories about ferocious whales who attacked their persecutors, and perhaps about albino sperm whales, as well. This cannot be much more than an interesting footnote, however, and does not, in any useful way, explain *Moby Dick*, or facilitate the reading of it.

We have not yet quite done, however, with "mythological" readings of *Daphnis and Chloe*. One rather different tack is to assume that our protagonist, Daphnis, is somehow to be connected with the mythical shepherd of the same name. If indeed there were one particular myth associated with the name Daphnis, its exegesis might be at least a starting point for some investigation of a possible mythical source for *Daphnis and Chloe*. Theocritus's Daphnis might then be to Longus's hero what Homer's Aeneas is to Vergil's. The fact is, however, that any compilation of references or allusions to the name Daphnis in Greek literature will simply not support any contention that there is one basic mythical persona denoted by that name.[9] The ill-fated shepherd of Theocritus's first idyll is indeed evoked once in *Daphnis and Chloe*, though lightly and playfully; but it is very hard to find anything of substance that the two Daphnises actually have in common.[10] The solution to this whole conundrum should be obvious: by Longus's time, the name Daphnis had become almost a "generic" name for a herdsman. The same can really be said for the name Chloe, which is also unmistakeably but very broadly pastoral. Longus could not have chosen any two more likely names for a herdsman and his bucolic lover than Daphnis and Chloe.[11] If he were writing today, he would accomplish much the same thing by calling his novel "Bobby Joe and Thelma Lu."

This very lack of particularity should give the lie to any notion that the story Longus tells is a hoary old myth, modernized.

THE NOVEL AND HISTORY

The novel, ancient and modern, shares much of its form and method with historiography. The earliest English novelists were notoriously fond of playing with the close narratological relationship between fiction and history, and we have seen how several of the ancient novelists, too, tried to borrow the respectability and verisimilitude of history for their fiction. Many, over the years, have tried to prove that this resemblance of technique is actually, in the case of the ancient novel, a family resemblance.[12] A certain taste for sensational or pathetic episodes in historical writing was at least as old as Herodotus; and Xenophon, especially in his *Cyropaideia*, had already explored the possibility of building an entire history out of such episodes.[13] What we have of Hellenistic historiography suggests that later historians gave free rein to this predilection for pathos and sensationalism.

The usual form of the "historiographical" thesis on the origins of the Greek novel holds, then, that by a gradual process of decay, as veracity became subordinate to sensation, the novel emerged from history. Often other genres are supposed to have interacted with this kind of debauched history to produce the novel; such theories were especially popular after Rohde set an important procedural precedent. History, as we shall see, did not play an important role in Rohde's own theory, but his premise that the novel could be explained as the result of some sort of chemical reaction ($x + y \rightarrow$ the novel) was capable of almost infinite adaption and variation. Thus Eduard Schwartz, in his *Fünf Vorträge über den griechischen Roman*, argued that decadent Hellenistic historiography and the Alexandrian erotic elegy had somehow amalgamated to produce the novel; many years later, Otto Weinrich revised Schwartz's version of the Rohdian formula by substituting the epic for the elegy.[14] The presumed process is much the same, in either event: certain Hellenistic historians, no longer capable of writing history in the "scientific"

Thucydidean mold, began to draw their narrative materials from poetry rather than history, and so produced what they themselves may not have realized was a new genre, the novel.

The argument that the novel thus devolved from historiography was strenuously attacked by B. E. Perry, who insisted that "historiography cannot become romance [i.e., novel] without passing through zero, that is, through the negation of its own *raison d' être*, that which defines it as historiography."[15] There are problems with this, of course. Perry seems to be accepting on its face an ontological equivalence between history as we know it and history as the ancients understood it. Still, what separates the historian from the novelist, then and now, is that the former is held to the test of referentiality: his narrative must be about something that actually happened or is at least purported to have actually happened. Thus, although he may make the story signify one thing or another, he cannot far depart from the accurate representation of actual persons and events without losing all claim to the reader's attention. The novelist, on the other hand, is free to invent, by the very definition of his genre.[16] His task is not to retell a story that already exists, in whatever form, but rather to call a story into existence, precisely in and through the act of telling it. The perceptive reader will read any text identified as history with the presupposition that the narrative is substantially true, in the baldest referential sense, but must presume precisely the opposite in order to read a novel intelligently. Thus the whole devolutionary process that Schwartz and the others presume to have taken place is inherently implausible. That a certain "poetic license," Aristotle's τὸ πλάσμα, was available to ancient historians from Herodotus on, of which even Thucydides availed himself, is beyond dispute; but a genre cannot be made out of a tendency. Since both history and the novel are narrative genres, a certain sharing of technique between them is inevitable, and we may even ultimately conclude that this sharing is not without significance. It does not necessarily follow from this, however, that history "begat" the novel. Whatever Perry's other shortcomings, he was probably right about this: one literary genre does not "beget" another.

ROHDE

So much has already been said about the influence of Erwin Rohde on the criticism of the ancient novel that rather little remains to be said now. The cornerstone of Rohde's edifice was his belief that the Greek novel was invented during the Second Sophistic, by writers who melded together two preexisting genres: the travel narrative (*die Reisefabelistik*) and the Alexandrian erotic elegy. The method by which he arrived at this formula was simple and straightforward: he read all the ancient novels, decided that the predominant themes were love and travel, and then searched out "forerunners" (*Vorläufer*) for each of these. Those familiar with the typically German source criticism (*Quellenforschung*) of the late nineteenth and early twentieth centuries will recognize the procedure and can almost certainly anticipate the recital of its faults. The salient fallacy implicit in almost all source criticism is *post hoc, ergo propter hoc*: the invalid inference of a causal relationship from a chronological one. The whole procedure is, as Perry puts it, "a popular philological game, but not much more profitable than the working out of a crossword puzzle." [17]

Rohde's emphasis on *Reisefabelistik* presents more specific problems for his thesis. Even if the existence of travel literature as an autonomous genre be granted (a concession which can hardly be forced), most scholars now agree that Rohde's selection of travel as an architectural component of the novel was somewhat arbitrary. Travel is only one of many themes that repeat themselves in many of the Greek novels; it is somewhat attenuated in *Leucippe and Clitophon* and occurs in *Daphnis and Chloe* only by indirection. One might as well postulate that the true antecedents of the novel were tales of piracy and shipwreck, or of kidnapping and mistaken identity.

Now the importance of the love theme for the ancient novel cannot be gainsaid. Giuseppe Giangrande has even attempted on that basis to salvage that half of Rohde's formula: he concedes the irrelevance (or better, nonexistence) of *Reisefabelistik*, but suggests that the forerunners of the novel were certain prose summaries of the "plots" ($\mu\hat{v}\theta o\iota$ [*mythoi*]) of Alexandrian elegies, done by both students and teachers in the rhetorical schools of late antiquity.[18] Giangrande's efforts are valiant but in vain. Only in the broadest outlines is the erotic theme handled in the same way in both the elegy and the novel. The latter's heroines are never prostitutes or married ladies of easy virtue, as they almost invariably are in the elegies; and the lovers in the novels seldom quarrel and though separated are always reunited in the end. The whole milieu in which the lovers interact is entirely different in the two genres, which are really connected only by the importance that each attaches to the personal and sexual relationship between a man and a woman.

The game could go on like this indefinitely. Almost any genre of ancient literature, prose or poetry, contains themes that are also handled in the ancient novel. Common themes could thus be used to trace the literary pedigree of the novel back to any genre that one might choose; but nothing of value will be learned, either from the results or from the process. Perry has clearly identified for us the central fallacy: the mistaken belief that literary genres are analogous to biological species.[19] Again, one literary form does not beget another. We shall soon see that Perry pushed his conclusions too far and that his sociological theories produced a taxonomy of the ancient novel that has outlived its usefulness; but his telling criticism of the "biological fallacy" remains a valuable contribution to the study of the genre. Source criticism had to be set aside before other, more fruitful lines of inquiry could be pursued.

It is somehow instructive, in a grim and cheerless sort of way, to note that what actually dethroned Rohde's thesis was not so much the invalidity of his premises as his errors in establishing the chronology of the genre. Rohde postulated that the "sophistic novels" (so-called because of their highly rhetorical style) of Achilles Tatius and Heliodorus were the first fruits of that putative synthesis between elegy and travelogue effected by the sophists, and that the novels of Chariton and pseudo-Xenophon were thus "postsophistic," early Byzantine imitations. Papyrus discoveries about the turn of the century upset this whole schema, however, by proving conclusively that both *Chaereas and Callirhoe* and *Anthia and Habrocomes* are earlier than the "sophistic" novels, so that the former are now conventionally known as the "pre-sophistic" novels. The prevailing wisdom now has it that the pre-sophistic novels reflect the real antecedents of the genre, while the sophistic novels, now including *Daphnis and Chloe*, reflect its somewhat premature decadence.[20] At any event, the demolition of Rohde's chronological schema brought down his taxonomy of the ancient novel, and with it his theory of the genre's origins, like a house of cards. Thus his thesis has been rejected, but not on theoretical grounds, with the result that his premises continue to have some influence on the way the history of prose fiction in antiquity is seen.

THE INITIATION THESIS

The "biological" approach to literary history, which characterized the work of Rohde (and of most of the others who have so far been given a hearing here), is now rather out of fashion. But finding alternatives to the biological fallacy has not been easy. To some, the search has led into issues that reach far beyond the merely literary, into the religious and social history of late antiquity. Though the theories on the genesis of the novel advanced by Merkelbach and Perry are quite diverse in content, it should be recognized at the outset that the impulses which motivated both scholars were broadly similar. The novel is not to be explained as the outgrowth of an evolution (or, one suspects, a devolution) in the literature of late Greek antiquity, but rather from social forces and changes that originated outside the literary sphere.

Though Reinhold Merkelbach is now generally recognized as the chief exponent of what we shall call here the "initiation thesis," he was not the first to bring forward arguments that the ancient novels somehow originated in the mystery cults of late antiquity. That distinction belongs to Karl Kerényi, who was an associate of Carl Jung and appealed to the latter's theories to account for the genesis of the ancient novel.[21] Jung's theory of the collective unconscious, which entails a criticism based on the search for universal archetypes in myth and literature, accounts for much of what Kerényi's extremely difficult book was trying to do. The stereotypical plot line of the Greek novels (from which *Daphnis and Chloe* substantially deviates) led Kerényi to suppose that an archetype might be lurking there under the guise of lack of imagination; and the particular outlines of that familiar plot (a hero and heroine in love, separated, wandering about in search of each other, and finally reunited), along with certain often-repeated motifs and themes (especially the "apparent death," or *Scheintod*, motif), suggested a source for that archetype: the Egyptian myth of Isis and her brother-cum-husband, Osiris.

The outlines of this myth are, greatly simplified, somewhat as follows: Isis, a mother-goddess, whose earliest Egyptian representations give her the head of a cow, is married to her brother, Osiris. Together, they preside over a sort of Golden Age, until the evil god Set (= Satan) ambushes Osiris, dismembers his body, and conducts his soul to the underworld, where he becomes the king of the dead. Isis goes about the world (that is, Egypt) collecting the pieces of Osiris's body, with the help of their son, Horus; she then reassembles Osiris, thereby freeing him from the power of Set. He remains, however, the king of the dead, and the Golden Age is over. This myth became the center of a powerful and popular cult in antiquity, which spread far beyond Egypt, subsuming many other cults along the way. Initiates devoted themselves to the service of Isis, and expected, as a reward, to share in the resurrection of Osiris. Though the Egyptian milieu was never lost sight of, the syncretic tendencies of ancient polytheism naturally caused both the cult and its myth to go through many changes and variations.[22] Kerényi called particular attention to the "evangelizing" techniques used by the priests of Isis, who prepared aretalogies of the doings and wonders of Isis for the edification of potential converts; he argued, in fact, that these aretalogies were the direct ancestors of the ancient novel.

Several factors contribute to the plausibility of Kerényi's thesis. It is, to begin with, inescapable that there is a certain sameness and even predictability about most of the Greek novels, particularly as regards the plot line, and that this plot does indeed have certain points of contact with the myth of Isis. More-over, two extant ancient novels arguably center on the cult of Isis: Apuleius's *Metamorphoses* (in which the eleventh and final book is an epiphany of Isis, followed by the initiation of Lucius into the Isiac priesthood) and Xenophon Ephesius's *Anthia and Habrocomes*.[23]

To some reviewers, all this made it seem as though Kerényi had finally found the key to the riddle of the ancient novel.[24] Others, however, found reason for skepticism.[25] Symbolism, es-pecially religious symbolism, is notoriously difficult to isolate. An extremely reductionist approach can solve this problem, after a fashion, by ruthlessly subordinating every image, theme, and motif to one central myth or symbol. Self-justifying systems al-ways have a certain atttraction, but they seldom stand up to de-tailed critical scrutiny. While it is clear that Isiac symbols (and a message) are to be found in the text of *Anthia and Habrocomes*, and possible that the like are also to be found in the *Metamorpho-ses*, many other novels (especially *Daphnis and Chloe*) can hardly be made to fit Kerényi's Procrustean bed.

Kerényi's failure satisfactorily to account for *Daphnis and Chloe* was especially troublesome to those inclined to favor his thesis, since Longus's text is precisely the one that seems most replete with religious language and themes. In few of the other Greek novels, if any, is the divine world so deeply and directly involved with the human characters. Indeed, Longus himself seems to say, in so many words, that his novel has a religious purpose; he wrote it, he says, as ἀνάθημα . . . Ἔρωτι καὶ Νύμφαις καὶ Πανί ("an offering . . . to Eros, the Nymphs, and Pan"). To Reinhold Merkelbach, this diction seemed to indicate, first, that some sort of religious purpose underlay *Daphnis and Chloe*, and second, that Isis was *not* the subject. Merkelbach published an article in 1960 in which he argued that *Daphnis and Chloe* was, start to finish, an allegory of initiation into the cult of Dionysus; then, in 1962, with the publication of *Roman und Mysterium in der Antike*, he extended his work to cover all the ancient novels.[26] Like Kerényi, Merkelbach was convinced that the ancient novels, both Greek and Roman, originated in the mystery cults; but unlike his predecessor, Merkelbach did not attempt to reduce all the novels to the same cult myth. Thus (according to Merkelbach) Apuleius, Xenophon of Ephesus, and Achilles Tatius were devotees of Isis, Longus of Dionysus, and Heliodorus of the sungod (best known as the object of the cult favored by the mad emperor, Elagobalus).

Merkelbach's approach is less reductionist than Kerényi's, to be sure, but it is still a self-justifying system and thus remains subject to many of the same criticisms. Many have remarked on the great virtuosity with which Merkelbach makes anything a symbol of anything.[27] An even more fundamental problem than this, however, is the circularity of the basic argument. Because relatively little is actually known about the rituals which he supposes to be allegorized in the novels, Merkelbach often ends up appealing to the novels themselves as sources for details about what actually happened when someone was initiated into a cult.

Almost any theory, even if it is finally rejected, will contain a kernel of truth, a certain number of valid interpretations or useful insights, which can be put to use, or at least should be accounted for, even by those who cannot accept in toto the theory that produced them. What often happens, however, is that the collapse of an older critical edifice seems, wrongly, to discredit each individual brick out of which it was made. Rohde's formula, for example, has already been shown to be an unsound approach to the basic critical problems posed by the ancient novel; but certain parts of Rohde's thesis, now lost in the general wrack and ruin of his critical edifice, need to be reexamined. The Second Sophistic did not invent the novel, but we still have much to learn about what the rhetoric of the Second Sophistic means for the novel's development. The "sophistic" novels may actually tell us more about the potential of the form than do those novels now thought to be prior. So it is with Merkelbach and the initiation thesis generally. Even if we conclude that the ancient novel is not the direct offspring of the cults and their aretalogies and rituals, there remain points of contact, for which some account needs to be given.

Perhaps the most useful explorations of the role that religion actually played in the development of the ancient novel are those of B. P. Reardon.[28] In all of his various articles on the subject of the ancient novel, Reardon's main point is that both the novels and the cults are reflections of their times. The novels, like the cults, are concerned with the lives and morals of private individuals, not with public affairs or political and social issues. The cults, for their part, found most of their followers among the same people who seem to have been, at least originally, the main audience for the novel: not the intelligentsia, nor the socio-economic elite, but the growing middle class, literate but not sophisticated, comfortable but not wealthy. Finally, both the cults and the novels provided distraction or release from the boredom and anxiety of their times.[29] It is not surprising, then, to find that the novels seem to reflect the influence of the cults; there was something in the air, reflected in the popularity of the cults, to which the novelists could hardly have been immune. Religion, though it was almost certainly not the raison d' être of the novel, was an inescapable part of the milieu into which it was born.

BEN EDWIN PERRY

Since its publication in 1967, B. E. Perry's *The Ancient Romances* has in many ways replaced Rohde's *Der griechische Roman* as the authoritative study on the ancient novel. Perry's approach represented a radical departure from the kind of scholarship that had previously been brought to bear on the ancient novel.[30] We have already seen how effectively he attacked the "biological fallacy." Inspired by the radical nominalism of Benedetto Croce, Perry downplayed the importance of literary development in the formation of any genre and emphasized instead the autonomy of the individual creative impulse. The discrete literary work, which was to Perry "the only logical limit to divisibility in the classification of literary forms," constitutes one individual's response to the forces at work within that individual, and within his or her society.[31] The rise of the novel thus cannot be explained as the inexorable development of a new literary form from the bits and pieces of other and older forms. One particular person, for his or her own reasons, wrote the first novel "on a Tuesday afternoon in July."[32] A new form was in order, not because of some evolutionary process within literature itself, but because the old forms did not satisfy contemporary tastes or imperatives. Borrowing a concept from twentieth-century sociology, Perry argued that the dominant narrative forms of the classical era, the epic and the drama, were the products of a "closed" society, where the individual was always part of an organic and self-contained unit, the polis. Philip II's forced unification of Greece and Alexander's subsequent conquests created a new sort of world, an "open" society. The identity of the individual was no longer to be found, as it was in the fifth century B.C., within the narrow confines of a body politic that might number no more than 15,000 souls; after Alexander, the population of the Greek world was to be counted in millions, among whom the solitary individual must find his own spot.[33]

Perry's contention, reiterated again and again throughout the first chapters of *The Ancient Romances*, is that literary forms are created by the needs of the society and so change and develop as the society changes and develops. When the classical "closed" society yielded to the "open" society of the Hellenistic Age, new literary forms were necessarily invented. Literature now had two rather disparate potential audiences: on the one hand, an educated elite, and on the other, a great mass of literate but unsophisticated readers, the "poor-in-spirit."[34] This bifurcation within Greek literary culture gives rise to what Perry insisted were two fundamentally different types of composition: the "ideal romances," produced in large quantities along certain stereotyped lines in response to a demand for entertainment from a large audience of "the poor-in-spirit," as against the "comic romances," which are more sophisticated productions, written by individual authors for their own particular literary motives and meant to appeal to a much higher level of reader than are the "ideal romances."[35] Among these latter he included all of the Greek novels (including *Daphnis and Chloe*) and the Latin *Life of Apollonius of Tyre*, while he limited the "comic romance" to Petronius's *Satyricon* and Apuleius's *Metamorphoses*.

There can be little question that Perry's reassessment of the previous scholarship on the ancient novel was a valuable contribution. The biological approach sponsored by Rohde was bankrupt, and someone had to administer the coup de grace. But the

legacy of *The Ancient Romances* itself has not been entirely unmixed. To begin with, Perry clearly overstated his case when he
insisted that social changes were the only real causes of the development of the novel.[36] Even within what must be a very limited sample of the ancient Greek novels, the signs of development on the literary plane are clearly there, and in Longus's case
there is a demonstrable preoccupation with that development, as
we have seen. No one author simply "invented" the novel one
day, on a Tuesday afternoon in July or at any other one moment.
The history of the ancient novel is more than the sum total of
the biographies of its authors. Perry's radical atomism almost
entirely ignores, on theoretical grounds, the intertextual connections that contribute so much to an intelligent reading of
Daphnis and Chloe.

An even greater problem is posed by Perry's division of the
ancient novels into "ideal" and "comic" types. Quite recently,
Graham Anderson has shown that, with the apparent exception
of Xenophon of Ephesus, all the ancient novelists, Greek and
Roman, display a certain "lightness of touch," which bespeaks a
rather higher level of sophistication than Perry supposed them
to display.[37] Perry was, in fact, fully as unwilling as Rohde was to
approach the Greek novels as literary texts worthy of study on
their own merits. His classification scheme led him to approach
those novels he labeled "ideal" as artifacts rather than as texts;
thus the chief advantage that he expected to gain from the reading of *Chaereas and Callirhoe* was the insight that Chariton gives
us into the life and mentality of the "forgotten people" of the
Hellenistic world. This is to do a serious disservice to an author
who deserves better. Gareth Schmeling has shown that Chariton
is not at all the lightweight he has been taken to be.[38] Achilles
Tatius, for another example, is a talented parodist and no poor
stylist.[39] Heliodorus, the last novelist properly considered Greek
rather than Byzantine, is a fine storyteller, whom writers now
thought to be far greater than he have not scrupled to imitate.[40]
And we have seen that *Daphnis and Chloe*, for its part, is a carefully crafted piece of work, hardly written by some anonymous
hack for whatever may have corresponded to drugstore book
racks in antiquity.

This problem cannot be solved by merely switching *Daphnis and Chloe*, or any other of the ancient novels, into the category of "comic romance."[41] Perry's whole system is faulty, in that it confronts the reader of any ancient novel with a false dilemma: is this text comic or is it naive? Thus, ironically enough, the great exponent of Crocian nominalism himself created a system of classification that has caused several ancient texts to be misread. It may well be, in fact, that the only reason why Longus is not at least as prominent a figure as Apuleius in the literary history of classical antiquity is the implicit and unexamined presupposition that all Greek novels (as opposed to the Roman ones) are jejune and sentimental. If Longus had had the sense to write in Latin rather than Greek, he might have gained a more receptive audience. For the persistence of this judgment, the influence of *The Ancient Romances* must bear a considerable portion of the blame.

GRAHAM ANDERSON AND TOMAS HÄGG

We end up where we began, then, with almost all the discussion predicated on the a priori assumption that the ancient novels are not so much literature as cultural artifacts in written form. Underlying this premise is a great trap, which waits for any critic of the ancient novel: the perceived need to justify, perhaps even apologize for, the study itself. All three of the most influential and best-known historians of the ancient novel—Rohde, Merkelbach, and Perry—fell squarely into that trap, each in his own way. Rohde thought the works to which he devoted so much of his time and energy were, at best, interesting illustrations of literary and cultural decadence. Merkelbach tried to redeem the novels by finding something serious, something σπουδαῖον, under the trivial exterior. Perry tried to do the same, this time by using the texts as a window into popular culture, much as a historian of contemporary popular culture may use the comic book as source material on the Zeitgeist.[42] None of these approaches is likely to do justice to the ancient novel, the poor stepchild of classical literature. Only if the Greek novels are conceded to be literary texts can any really serious critical work be done on any of them.

There are those, of course, who have already begun to move in this direction. All due credit should be given to Alexander Scobie, whose two books of essays on the Greek novel, though never intended to be encyclopedic, represent a conviction on the author's part that old prejudices need to be set aside and that the Greek novel deserves as much attention as its Latin counterpart.[43] Also worthy of mention in this regard is Arthur Heiserman's study *The Novel before the Novel*. Heiserman's somewhat controversial book is vitiated by a certain lack of system (which is perhaps understandable, since it was published posthumously); but its fundamental premise, as the title implies, is that the ancient novel is a part of the larger history of the novel and is therefore amenable to serious literary criticism.[44] Of all recent books on the ancient novel, however, it is the *Eros Sophistes* of Graham Anderson that most clearly signals a substantive change in the critical approach to the ancient novel. Anderson's central thesis, that the ancient novelists (with the exception of Xenophon of Ephesus) never really meant their works to be taken at face value, seriously challenges the received wisdom about both the audience and the intentions of most, if not all, of these works. For if it can be shown that Chariton, for example, did not necessarily write for a jejune, sentimental, and unsophisticated audience, then the possibility must be considered that those who wrote in this new form thought that it had at least the potential of appealing to a mature and sophisticated audience. This idea not only suggests that the prevailing evaluation of the ancient Greek novels is badly skewed; it also shakes the very foundations of Perry's taxonomy, and with it his whole approach to the genre.

The most obvious contribution of *Eros Sophistes*, then, is that it removes some serious obstacles to the interpretation of texts that may never before have seemed to require interpretation.[45] The largely false dichotomy between the "ideal" and the "comic" novel has outlived any usefulness it ever had and needs to be set aside. But Anderson has more than that to teach us. Like Tomas Hägg, and unlike so many before him, he refuses to be misled by the specious sameness of the Greek novels into the false assumption that they are all cast in the same mold. For the real problem with almost all previous scholarly work on the ancient novel is that, in one way or another, these scholars seem to be interested only or mostly in the "stuff" of which the Greek novelists constructed their plots: that is, with themes. This preoccupation with thematology has led almost inexorably to variations on a theme of source criticism, Perry not excepted. But Anderson and Hägg together have turned our attention in more fruitful directions. They have not asked, "Where did the ancient Greek novelists get their stories?" Rather, they seem to have begun by asking themselves, "How did Chariton and the rest go about telling their stories?" What this amounts to, in short, is a shift from thematology to narratology; and in that shift are the seeds of a new beginning for scholarship on the ancient Greek novel. Not that the themes found in the Greek novels can safely be ignored; on the contrary, we were much exercized with them in a previous chapter. Still, the crux of the matter is really the issue of literary fiction, which a purely thematological approach tends to obscure.

RECENT DISCOVERIES

In the last two decades, several important papyrus discoveries have made significant contributions to our understanding of the history of Greek prose fiction. Albert Henrichs's publication of the fragments of Lollianus's *Phoenician Tale* has given us, if not a complete new text to add to the corpus, at least enough of one that we may begin to see some new dimensions to the tradition.[46] The fragments, which date from the late second century A.D., seem to be part of a tale fully as "baroque" as *Leucippe and Clitophon* and in some ways may yet provide a bridge of some sort between the latter text and Petronius's *Satyricon*. Further such discoveries can only enrich our understanding of a genre, the range of which we are only just beginning to appreciate; but until some complete texts are uncovered—which may never happen, of course—much of what can be learned will perforce remain conjectural and tentative.[47]

Notes

1. *Bellum Catilinae* 3.2. For an earlier version of the thesis I am discussing here, see my article, "Quid valeat apud Sallustium historia," *Hermes Americanus* 1 (1983), 276–285.

2. For a bibliography on this, see the second chapter of my book *Plato's* Republic *in the Monographs of Sallust* (Chicago: Bolchazy-Carducci, 1981).

3. In English, the word "history" has both a subjective and an objective sense, since it can be used to denote either the past itself (object) or the study of the past (subject). In Latin, these two senses are quite distinct. *Historia* means the study of the past or, more properly, a literary genre that draws its narrative material from the past; the deeds and events of the past are denoted by some such locution as *res gestae*, literally, "things done."

4. See chapter 9 below, "The Novel and History."

5. I refer here, of course, to Erwin Rohde, *Der griechische Roman und seine Vorläufer*, 4th ed. (Leipzig, 1876; repr., Hildesheim: Georg Olms, 1960).

6. Some, of course, will question whether anything properly called a "novel" was written before the eighteenth century, in England (or in France, a century earlier, or in Spain, a century earlier still, or what-have-you). So little did the ancient novels concern or impress the scholars of their own day that the latter, assiduous taxonomers that they were, never coined a proper name for the novel, in either Greek or Latin.

7. Perhaps the most elaborate such apology is to be found in the

introduction to Petrus Moll's edition of *Daphnis and Chloe* (Frankfurt, 1660). Moll begs the reader (in Latin) to indulge the whims of an old man, who prattles on about romances because the loss of his faculties gives him nothing better to do.

8. See Edward Schwartz, *Fünf Vorträge über den griechischen Roman*, 2d ed. (Berlin: DeGruyter, 1943).

9. Johann Wolfgang von Goethe, *Gespräche mit Eckermann*, 21 May 1839.

10. Full bibliographical information for all editions of *Daphnis and Chloe* can be found in the Annotated Bibliography at the end of this book. R. L. Hunter, *A Study of Daphnis and Chloe*, Cambridge Classical Studies (Cambridge: Cambridge University Press, 1983); and William McCulloh, *Longus*, Twayne World Authors series 96 (New York: Twayne Publishers, 1970).

11. Karl Kerényi, *Die griechische-orientalische Romanliteratur in religionsgeschichtlicher Beleuchtung: Ein Versuch* (Tübingen: J. C. B. Mohr, 1927); Reinhold Merkelbach, *Roman und Mysterium* (Munich: Beck, 1962); and H. H. O. Chalk, "Eros and the Lesbian Pastorals of Longus," *Journal of Hellenic Studies* 80 (1960), 32–51. Kerényi later reiterated his arguments, in brief, in *Der antike Roman: Einführung und Textauswahl* (Darmstadt: Wissenschaftliche Buchgesellschaft, 1971). See also G. Wojaczek, *Daphnis: Untersuchungen zur griechischen Bukolik* (Meisenheim am Glan: Anton Hain, 1969).

12. For refutations of the allegorists, see Angelika Geyer, "Roman und Mysterienritual: Zum Problem eines Bezugs zum dionysischer Mysterienritual im Roman des Longos," *Würzberger Jahrbücher für die Altertumswissenschaft*, n.s. 3 (1977), 179–196; Marisa Berti, "Sulla interpretazione mistica del romanzo di Longo," *Studi Classici e Orientali* 16 (1967), 343–358; and Robert Turcan, "Le 'roman initiatique': A propos d' un livre récent," *Révue de l' Histoire des Réligions* 163 (1963), 149–199.

13. This is nearly (but not quite) how E. Rohde's approach to the genesis of the ancient novel is characterized by Ben Edwin Perry, *The Ancient Romances: A Literary-Historical Account of Their Origins*, Sather Classical Lectures 37 (Berkeley and Los Angeles: University of California Press, 1967).

14. Experience suggests that this choice largely depends upon the academic specialty of the person consulted.

CHAPTER 1: THE PROBLEM OF INTERPRETATION

1. Exceptions to the triviality of the murder mystery abound, of course: Umberto Eco's *The Name of the Rose*, for one, of which it might

safely be said that one can hardly put it down without asking all manner of serious questions. But this is in many ways the exception that proves the rule, even if Eco himself, semiotician that he is, would very likely not approve of the definition of literariness that has been advanced here.

2. The ancient attitude on this issue is clear, and remarkably unanimous: the function of literature is primarily to edify its readers, secondarily (if at all) to entertain them. As we shall see, Longus expresses himself very directly on this point (prologue 2).

3. See the Preface, n. 9. A friend and former colleague of mine, a student of Goethe and the Classical Age of German literature, once remarked to me that this often-quoted dictum was just the sort of thing that Goethe would say—in his dotage.

4. To his important and interesting study *The Novel in Antiquity* (Berkeley and Los Angeles: University of California Press, 1983), Tomas Hägg has added a delightful appendix of paintings and etchings inspired by *Daphnis and Chloe*, including many drawn from illustrated editions, which have long been a favorite of the book trade.

5. Arthur Heiserman, *The Novel before the Novel: Essays and Discussions about the Beginnings of Prose Fiction in the West* (Chicago: University of Chicago Press, 1977), p. 145, remarks that the ideas in *Daphnis and Chloe*, once uncovered, are neither compelling nor original. McCulloh adverts in his first chapter of *Longus* to a certain disdain for the ancient novel, but quite properly rejects this attitude. Hunter seems to have little respect for Longus (see *Study of Daphnis and Chloë*, esp. p. 58).

6. See the Preface, n. 12. By allegory, I mean the use of a literary text as a sort of code, in such a way that every element of the text is reducible to, or stands for, a constituent element of some other specific thing, such as a religious ceremony or doctrine.

7. Paul Turner, "*Daphnis and Chloe*: An Interpretation," *Greece and Rome* 7 (1960), 117−123. This book owes a major debt to Turner's provocative article.

8. Hunter's *Study of Daphnis and Chloë* and McCulloh's *Longus* remain, as of this writing, the only book-length critical treatments of *Daphnis and Chloe* in English.

9. "There is, of course, no necessary divorce between high artifice and real intellectual depth, and we are lucky that some ancient writers who exhibit both characteristics survive. Longus is not to be numbered in their company, because he tickles rather than nourishes our intellects. This is, however, no mean service, particularly when it is set against much else that survives from the Greek literature of the imperial period" (Hunter, *Study of Daphnis and Chloë*, p. 58). If I can succeed

in convincing even a few of my readers that Hunter is quite wrong about all this, I shall be satisfied.

10. On the other hand, Photius, the ninth-century patriarch of Constantinople and bibliophile, often calls them δράματα, "dramas."

11. Rohde's *Der griechische Roman* and Perry's *Ancient Romances* have been particularly influential; indeed, any *Wissenschaftsgeschichte* on the ancient novel would have to revolve around these two works above all others. The best recent works on the genre as a whole, in my estimation, are the following: Graham Anderson, *Eros Sophistes: Ancient Novelists at Play*, American Classical Studies 9 (Chico, Calif.: Scholar's Press, 1982); the same author's *Ancient Fiction: The Novel in the Graeco-Roman World* (London: Croom Helm; Totowa, N.J.: Barnes and Noble, 1984); and Hägg, *The Novel in Antiquity*.

12. The Twayne World Authors series has good volumes on Chariton, Xenophon of Ephesus, Heliodorus, and Longus. For a somewhat more sympathetic view of the genre as a whole, see Tomas Hägg, *Narrative Technique in Ancient Greek Romances: Studies of Chariton, Xenophon Ephesius, and Achilles Tatius* (Stockhom: P. Aström, 1971). In my own case graduate courses on the Greek novel and on the Roman novel were required for the Ph.D. in classics at the University of Iowa.

13. Hägg and Anderson have been especially insistent on calling our attention to the distinct individuality underlying the specious sameness of at least the other four Greek novels, and the serious distortions that result from overlooking that individuality.

14. See app. 1.

15. The word "context" is compounded from the Latin *con* (with) and *textus* (weaving) (cf. "textile" and "texture"), from the related verbs *tego* and *texo*.

16. Those readers familiar with T. S. Eliot's famous essay "Tradition and the Individual Talent in Poetry" will realize that I am essentially using the word in Eliot's sense.

17. *Republic* 6.504c, where the true education of the philosopher is at issue, and it is shown that no shortcuts are available, or desirable.

18. Some of what happens in the Introduction of this book was anticipated in an earlier article of mine, "Longus and the Myth of Chloe," *Illinois Classical Studies* 10 (1985), 119–134.

19. McCulloh, *Longus*, p. 15.

CHAPTER 2: THE PROLOGUE

1. Turner, "Interpretation," suggests that the pastoral setting of *Daphnis and Chloe*, taken with the pictorial language of the prologue, re-

minds us how the root meaning of "idyll," εἰδύλλιον, is "little picture." More on this later, in chapter 10.

2. The important sources for the allegorical interpretation of *Daphnis and Chloe* are Merkelbach, *Roman und Mysterium*, and Chalk, "Eros." Chalk's explication of the structure of *Daphnis and Chloe* can be found on pp. 39–42 of his article.

3. Most especially perhaps, in the middle chapters of book 3.

4. For Chalk, for instance, in "Eros," all this constitutes proof that Daphnis and Chloe are "year-spirits," numinous beings under the tutelage of the syncretic godhead whose cult is, for him, the allegorical interpretant of the novel.

5. This argument first appeared in Weinrich's appendix to R. Reymer's edition of Heliodorus's *Theagenes and Charicleia*, and was then reprinted on pp. 18–63 of his own *Der griechische Liebesroman* (Zurich: Artemis, 1962). Weinrich's arguments are amplified and strengthened by M. C. Mittelstadt, "Longus, *Daphnis and Chloe*, and Roman Narrative Painting," *Latomus* 26 (1967), 752–761.

6. In app. 1, we shall consider (and ultimately find reason to reject) the arguments advanced by Weinrich and Mittelstadt, that this apparent allusion to a particular style of narrative painting can be used to date Longus. Necessary skepticism on this score does not really obviate the usefulness of these scholars' perceptions on the structure.

7. See Kestner's article, "Ekphrasis as Frame in Longus' *Daphnis and Chloe*," *Classical World* 67 (1974), 166–171.

8. To me, this seems to read ἀντιγράψαι τῇ γραφῇ a little too literally. Longus does not say that his novel *is* an ecphrasis, and its form is not really the same. Properly speaking, an ecphrasis is a rhetorical exercise, a vivid description of a work of plastic art, and is seldom longer than a few paragraphs. In fact, book IV contains an ecphrasis, properly so-called, concerning which we shall have more to say later on. There is too much play on words here to allow the meaning of this pregnant phrase to be nailed down once and for all, as we shall see. Cf. the opening chapters of Achilles Tatius's *Leucippe and Clitophon*.

9. The usual criterion for the size of a "book" was the amount of papyrus that would be manageable on one scroll. Thus the owner of the 146 books of Livy, for example, owned (and had to manage) 146 scrolls. By Longus's day, the papyrus scroll was giving way to the codex, the bound book on the modern pattern. The sense of a longer work being necessarily divided into "books" persisted, however, long after the practical necessity had been rendered obsolete.

10. Stavros Deligiorgis, "Longus' Art in Brief Lives," *Philological Quarterly* 53 (1974), 1–9.

11. Marios Philippides, "The 'Digressive' *Aitia* in Longus," *Classical World* 74 (1980), 193–199. McCulloh, *Longus*, remarks at pp. 65–66 on the thematic connection between each of the myths and its context.

12. See, for example, *Iliad* 18.483–607, and the emulation thereof at *Aeneid* 8.625–728. Vergil also provides famous ecphrases at *Aeneid* 1.466–493 and 6.14–33; cf. Plutarch, *Moralia* 779F and Diodorus Siculus 1.98.9. In all these instances (examples could of course be multiplied), the ancient author does not merely describe the work of art as to its appearance, but goes on to supply in words the action or movement, and not infrequently the emotion, which is only latent or implicit in the object itself. At the same time, seldom are such ecphrases embroidered all the way into complete narratives, with beginning, middle, and end. Catullus 64 may be the exception that proves the rule.

13. Kestner, "Ecphrasis as Frame," is very good on this subject.

14. Some editors insert a paragraph break after πολλὰ ἄλλα καὶ πάντα ἐρωτικά ("many other things, all erotic").

15. See below.

16. Thus Anderson, *Eros Sophistes*, p. 46, who, however, seems to overstate his case.

17. The frequent use of this verb and its cognates in Euripides' *Bacchae* has often been noted; it is also used, interestingly enough, in the first sentence of Plato's *Republic*, where Socrates goes down to the Piraeus to see (θεάσασθαι, using the aorist infinitive) the festival of Bendis.

18. See Hans Georg Gadamer, *Reason in the Age of Science*, trans. Frederick Lawrence (Cambridge: MIT Press, 1981), pp. 17–19.

19. There is a textual problem here of some interest. Punctuation in an ancient text is always a matter of editorial judgement, since the ancients themselves had no punctuation marks, and the medieval scribes were rather haphazard about adding punctuation to their manuscript copies. In the Teubner edition, Reeve punctuates the phrase πολλὰ ἄλλα καὶ πάντα ἐρωτικά ("much else and all of it erotic") as though it formed a concluding summary of the images on the painting. Some previous editors, however, have taken that same phrase to be part of the following sentence, as the direct object of ἰδόντα (having seen) and θαυμάσαντα (having wondered at). The grammatical case of the whole phrase is ambiguous, since πολλά is a neuter plural substantive and can be either nominative or accusative. For myself, I rather suspect that Longus, sophist that he is, intends the ambiguity. It is clearly an *apo koinou*, and a very clever one at that.

20. Some readers may balk at the way this name is spelled here.

Spelling of this proper noun fluctuated in antiquity, between the older "Mytilene" of Thucydides and the "Mitylene" found in manuscripts of *Daphnis and Chloe*. Incipient iotacism probably accounts for the metathesis. Recently I saw a travel brochure from Greece in which the principal city of Lesbos was called "Mitilini."

21. The antithesis is at least as old as Plato; underlying it is the perception that there are two modes of speech, roughly, narrative and discursive, each of which expresses truth in a different way. See Kent F. Moors, *Platonic Myth: An Introductory Study* (Lenham, Mass.: University Press of America, 1982); and Robert Zaslavsky, *Platonic Myth and Platonic Writing* (Lenham, Mass.: University Press of America, 1981).

CHAPTER 3. BOOK 1: EROTIC *APORIA*

1. As was remarked above, myths of this sort were called αἴτια (*aitia*; literally, causes) by the Greeks; English-speaking readers may be reminded of Kipling's "Just-So" stories. Note how the Greek text here uses the adverb οὕτω(ς), which means precisely "just so," twice in the first sentence.

2. The pastoral vocabulary of English does not provide a verb as general in meaning as the Greek νέμω, which means "to herd [cattle], to tend [sheep or goats], to pasture [as a transitive verb]."

3. There is an elaborate play on words here, hard to translate, in that *pitys* (πίτυς) is the Greek word for "pine." What we have here, in fact, is an allusion to yet another *aition*, that of the pine tree; and, as Philippides has pointed out, that *aition* follows the general outline of the others told in books 1 through 3. This serves to include Pan (who will be the male antagonist in the next two *aitia*) in the present story as well.

4. The tone of the original is very hard to capture in translation, and the difficulty is compounded by the bucolic language, which is not always easy to render.

5. The noun φάττα is used in context, when the story is introduced, but not in the story itself. This is in contrast to Syrinx and Echo, who are called by name in their stories.

6. Thus Philippides, "Digressive," p. 195.

7. Philippides, "Digressive," p. 195; Heiserman, *Novel*, p. 136; Deligiorgis, "Brief Lives," p. 3.

8. According to Turner, "Interpretation," p. 120, these pirates represent, conventionally, unrestrained and untrammeled male sexual rapacity. This seems quite apposite in the present context.

9. He also asks for, and gets, a farewell kiss from Chloe, whom he

first attempted to seduce, then to marry, and finally to rape. Like Lampis, the villain of book 4, he is a sexual brute, who is, surprisingly, redeemed at the end.

10. The episode can be found at 1.20; it will be further discussed somewhat later on in this chapter.

11. At 1.13.

12. See Philippides, "Digressive," p. 196; McCulloh, *Longus*, pp. 65–66; and B. D. MacQueen, "Longus and the Myth of Chloe," *Illinois Classical Studies* 10 (1985), 125 and 131.

13. See 1.13; 1.15; 1.19. On the whole subject of erotic naivete in *Daphnis and Chloe*, see M. C. Mittelstadt, "Love, Eros, and the Poetic Style," in *Fons Perennis: Saggi critici di filologia classica raccolti in onore del Prof. Vittorio d'Agostino* (Turin: Amministrazione della *Rivista di Studi Classici*, 1971), 305–332.

14. Purists may object that the Greek word σύριγξ (*syrinx*) refers to what most readers might call, properly if awkwardly, "Pan-pipes." I concede the point; but I found in translating that the word "pipe" has so many different meanings in English that Greekless readers are likely to be confused by its use. Let the record show that the instrument herein called "flute" was made of sections of hollow reed, of uneven length and with stops cut in at various points to alter the pitch, all bound together with twine. The Greeks did have an instrument more accurately called "flute," the *aulos*, though it was not transverse and does not appear in *Daphnis and Chloe*.

15. The translation unfortunately but inevitably conceals some significant repetition of vocabulary between Daphnis's speech and Chloe's. The Greek adjective πικρός, for example, means "sharp, bitter, painful," and is used by Chloe of her heartwound, by Daphnis of the kiss, in both instances in the comparative.

16. I am struck by the resemblance between this sentence and the first sentence of Plato's *Apology of Socrates*: "ὅ τι μὲν ὑμεῖς, ὦ ἄνδρες Ἀθηναῖοι, πεπόνθατε ὑπὸ τῶν ἐμῶν κατηγόρων, οὐκ οἶδα" ("What you experienced, men of Athens, at the hands of my accusers, I do not know"). This is typical of Longus's elusive-allusive style.

17. One can easily get the impression that Dorcon is supposed to be an older rival. We know, however, that Daphnis is fifteen years old (1.7), while Dorcon, at 1.15, is called ἀρτιγένειος μειρακίσκος, which is to say, an adolescent whose beard has just begun to grow. The onset of puberty was rather later in antiquity than it is now, but even so, Dorcon cannot be more than two or three years older than Daphnis, at the most.

18. This is frag. 2 (Lobel-Page), 14–15.

19. Note, too, how similar all this is to Longus's sly and ironic appro-

priation of Thucydides in the prologue, which will be discussed in a later chapter.

20. In the third book of Heliodorus's *Theagenes and Charicleia*, the heroine, Charicleia, is afflicted with symptoms quite similar to Chloe's; while her family is baffled she knows quite well what is wrong with her but is ashamed to admit it, until the information is inveigled out of her by the Egyptian priest/mountebank, Calisiris.

21. In the ancient pastoral tradition, the three types of grazing animals (i.e., cattle, sheep, and goats) define the pecking order of their respective herdsmen. Cowherds rank higher than shepherds, who in turn outrank goatherds.

22. The rhetorical complexities of these speeches, in context, have been well and sufficiently analyzed by Hunter, *Study of Daphnis and Chloe*, pp. 91−92. Note how the vocative παρθένε, "oh maiden," stands at the beginning of Dorcon's speech and the end of Daphnis's, which suggests the same kind of specularity that we have heretofore been discussing. The same form occurs at the beginning of the Phatta story.

23. Note, however, how Daphnis urges against Dorcon's claim of superior masculinity the whiteness of the latter's skin. Ancient painters by convention always depicted female figures with markedly paler skin than male figures, who are always deeply tanned.

24. Note how Dorcon said of Daphnis that he was as "beardless as a woman," while Daphnis said of Dorcon that he was white "like a woman from the city."

25. Notice how almost all the verbs in 1.10 are imperfects, which clearly indicates that its purpose is to set the background for the narrative proper.

26. We will meet a former prostitute, whose name, Lycaenium (that is, Λυκαίνιον, *Lykainion*), is nothing other than a diminutive of "she-wolf," λύκαινα (*lykaina*).

CHAPTER 4. BOOK 2: LEARNING THE NAME OF EROS

1. At 1.8, a little boy with wings simultaneously appears to Lamon and Dryas in their dreams and commands them to set their foster children out to tend the flocks. Eros is never called by name in that passage, but the two old men at once recognize his godhead, and sacrifice to the winged boy, even though they do not know his name (!). We may also recall that Eros is chief among those to whom *Daphnis and Chloe* is an "offering" ἀνάθημα; but that, of course, is to step outside of the story itself.

2. Thus Chalk, "Eros," pp. 34−37.

3. This sentence comes near the end of book 2 and will be discussed in somewhat more detail later.

4. Specifically, at 4.2; we shall discuss this again in chap. 6.

5. Note how Daphnis, in turn, becomes a hunter at the beginning of book 3.

6. That Chloe is to be identified with Syrinx is—need it be said?—made abundantly clear by the dance scene that follows the telling of the Syrinx story, in which Chloe enacts in dance the role of Syrinx. Note also how Chloe, in her "lover's soliloquy" in book 1, expressed a wish to become Daphnis's flute, his σύριγξ.

7. The story of Apollo and Daphne (Δάφνη, which means "laurel") is the paradigm of all these etiological myths, which are, in the whole corpus of Greek myth, legion. Can it be coincidental that the name of Longus's hero is so like that of the heroine of the quintessential model for the type of *aition* he is exploiting so fully in *Daphnis and Chloe*?

There have been, incidentally, numerous discussions of the possible significance of Daphnis's name. The most useful, by far, is that found in Hunter, *Study of Daphnis and Chloë*, pp. 22–31; the author's characteristic caution is salutary, on this occasion. I share his negative opinion ("vitiated by error and rash assumption," p. 22) of G. Wojaczek, *Daphnis*, which takes as its hypothesis that "Daphnis" is a Dionysiac name. Much of this, naturally, goes back to the allegorical interpretation. For a more detailed critique of Wojaczek, see the first section of Geyer, "Roman und Mysterienritual."

8. Freudians among our readers will not fail to notice the phallic connotations of the flute; some emphasis is given to how large and powerful Philetas's flute is.

CHAPTER 5. BOOK 3: LEARNING THE WORKS OF EROS

1. See app. 1.

2. Especially *Metamorphoses* 2.10, where Fotis says, "tota enim nocte tecum fortiter et ex animo proeliabor" ("I shall do battle with you all night long, stoutly and with spirit"); and 2.16–17.

3. The term denotes a passage of dialogue in which the actors trade lines so rapidly that they divide the six iambs of each verse between them.

4. See George Kennedy, "The Sophists as Declaimers," in *Approaches to the Second Sophistic: Papers Presented at the 105th Annual Meeting of the American Philological Association*, ed. Glen Bowersock (University Park, Pa.: American Philological Association, 1974), pp. 17–22; on a

larger scale, D. A. Russell, *Greek Declamation* (Cambridge: Cambridge University Press, 1983). The idea is, of course, older than the Second Sophistic: such fifth-century B.C. texts as Gorgias's *Palamedes* and *Helen* are of exactly this same provenance.

5. We can get some flavor of this in the collection of *controversiae* and *suasoriae* preserved by Seneca the Elder, father of the philosopher. Various scenes in Petronius's *Satyricon* also seem apposite.

6. As various people have noted, the whole scene seems parallel to a well-known pastoral convention: that is, the singing contest. The parallel is patent, to be sure; but an exchange of speeches is, after all, something rather different from an exchange of songs. Longus obviously intends us to think of the pastoral singing contest, but at the same time we should think of declamation, too. This convergence of the pastoral and rhetoric will turn out to be significant.

7. The best short discussion of rhetoric in the Greek novel is, in my opinion, that of B. P. Reardon, "The Second Sophistic and the Novel," in *Approaches to the Second Sophistic*, pp. 23−29. For those desiring more, a longer discussion by Reardon is to be found in the relevant chapter of his major book, *Courants littéraires grecs des duxième et troisième siècles après J. -C.* (Paris: Belles Lettres, 1971). Giuseppe Giangrande, "The Origins of the Greek Romance," *Eranos* 60 (1962), 132−159, goes so far as to argue that late Hellenistic declamations were the source of the whole genre; few have followed him, but the influence of rhetoric on all the Greek novelists is hard to deny. We shall return to this subject in chapter 7.

8. The Elizabethan dramatists, including Shakespeare, were more familiar with Seneca than with the now more famous Greek tragedians. That Shakespeare and Marlowe (and their audiences) had a taste for sophistry and point, which they were not loathe to indulge, need hardly be documented here.

9. See below. Achilles Tatius does this also, but that particular incident in *Leucippe and Clitophon* is something else again: Clitophon betrays Leucippe in full knowledge of what he is doing, which is part of the burlesque atmsophere of the whole novel. See Mittelstadt, "Love, Eros"; and R. M. Rattenbury, "Chastity and Chastity Ordeals in Ancient Greek Romances," in *Proceedings of the Leeds Literary and Philosophical Society* 1 (1925−1928), 58−65.

10. See especially D. N. Levin, "The Pivotal Role of Lycaenium in Longus' *Daphnis and Chloe*," *Rivista di Studi Classici* 25 (1977), 5−17; and A. M. Scarcella, "La donna nel romanzo di Longo Sofista," *Giornale Italiano di Filologia*, n.s. 3 (1972), 27−36. Levin provides a useful compen-

dium of bibliographical references on this subject, though the present study, as will shortly become obvious, contradicts much of what Levin himself wants to contribute.

The spelling (or more properly, the transliteration) of this character's name is a problem, and practice varies widely. Direct transliteration from the Greek Λυκαίνιον would yield "Lykainion"; the conventional Latinization of Greek proper names (thus "Thucydides" instead of "Thoukydides" and so on) gives the result "Lycaenium," adopted here. Lately, the trend seems to be in the direction of a compromise, "Lycaenion," which strikes me as neither fish nor fowl.

11. Readers of Plautus and Terence will notice that the prostitute heroines of many of these plays are called by such names as "Glycerium," which several modern translators have rendered as "Sweety." That, of course, would turn Lycaenium into "Wolfy."

12. Cf. Livy, 1.4.7, where he alludes to an attempt to rationalize the myth of the she-wolf who suckled Romulus and Remus by suggesting that perhaps these two foundlings were raised by a prostitute named "Lupa."

13. Thus Levin, "Pivotal Role"; Chalk, "Eros"; and Merkelbach, *Roman und Mysterium*.

14. I notice, with satisfaction, that Graham Anderson, in *Eros Sophistes*, p. 47, makes the same point. Levin, "Pivotal Role," notes the difficulty, but decides that Lycaenium must have been under Eros's influence, anyway. This decision seems perverse.

15. We should probably note that there is a point at which "nature herself taught him [Daphnis] what was to be done" (3.18).

16. We shall have more to do with this sentence later on.

17. The first clause reads, literally, "The erotic pedagogy having been fulfilled." In ancient education, the "pedagogue" (παιδαγωγός, Latin *paedagogus*) was not a teacher but a slave whose task it was to take the young pupil to his teacher and see to it that he did his lessons.

18. *Republic* 6.504c.

19. Someone may object here that, according to 2.27, Eros means to make a *mythos* of Chloe; this would mean, presumably, that it is the god himself who is the final teacher of Daphnis and Chloe. But it is not Eros who makes the myth, it is Longus, as the prologue makes clear. Eros did not inspire Longus to write. We are not yet through with this issue, by any means.

20. Greek, let us recall, does not have two different words for "man" and "husband" or for "woman" and "wife."

21. This is fragment 105a in the edition of Lobel and Page. As early

as 1794, in the edition of Mitscherlich, the allusion to Sappho was recognized. See also McCulloh, *Longus*, pp. 75–76, Philippides, "Digressive," p. 197, and Hunter, *Study of Daphnis and Chloe*, p. 74.

22. Due credit for perceiving the connection between this ship and Chloe's suitors should be given to Deligiorgis, "Brief Lives," pp. 3–4.

23. This "promise-fulfillment" is the same device used to frame the story of Syrinx.

24. The simile is remarkable, in that Chloe, as we have seen, hardly plays a passive role in the colloquy.

25. All that is said is "$\tau o\hat{v}$ $\kappa\acute{\alpha}\lambda\lambda ov\varsigma$ $\mu\grave{\eta}$ $\tau v\chi\acute{\omega}v$," which is very difficult to translate: something like "having had no experience of her beauty."

26. Philippides, "Digressive," p. 196, and McCulloh, *Longus*, pp. 65–66, remark on the increasing level of violence in the *aitia*. I am not aware that anyone has previously called attention to any development on other planes.

CHAPTER 6. BOOK 4: MAN AND WIFE

1. F. Christie, "Longus and the Development of the Pastoral Tradition" (Ph.D. diss., Harvard University, 1972), argues that book 4 is a sort of graft, a denouement borrowed from New Comedy attached to an extended prose idyll. This seems to overstate the discontinuity.

2. Literally, "the paternal goats." The Greek adjective $\pi\alpha\tau\rho\hat{\omega}o\varsigma$ carries a connotation difficult to render; it really means, "belonging to that which the son is going to inherit from his father." That connotation gives point to the irony that Daphnis has been herding goats that are in fact part of his patrimony.

3. We may note that Dryas has brought the tokens first and then told how he found them, while Lamon had told of finding them first and then brought them: again, the latter scene is a specular image of the former.

4. The first of these inferences was precisely the subject of my "Myth of Chloe" article. In a footnote in that article, I suggested that each book of *Daphnis and Chloe* had what is here called a "first cycle," which would be worked out in a future article. In fact, that article turned into the present study; in the process, the subject broadened considerably.

5. This refers to the scene where Daphnis dedicates his pastoral accoutrements, then says farewell to his goats, calling each by name, and taking one last bath in the spring. The use of the word $\theta v\sigma\acute{\iota}\alpha\iota$ ("sacrificial offerings") for all this is striking, and revealing; more will be said of it later.

6. One of Heliodorus's many virtues is that he, too, eschews the "Meanwhile" device, preferring instead to use "flashback" narratives and delayed exposition.

7. At 1.27, μυθολογῶν; at 2.33, μῦθον; at 2.35, μυθολογήματος; at 3.22, μυθολογεῖν τὸν μῦθον; and at 3.23, μυθολογήσαντα.

8. Advocates of a newer and more egalitarian ideology of marriage (among whom the present author counts himself) will wince at this, and at much else herein. As scholars, however, we are obliged to report what we see, whether we approve of the whole thing or not.

9. Critics familiar with Jungian psychology will at once grasp a possible significance of all this, which I shall pursue somewhat later on in this chapter.

10. On this garden (and that of Philetas, also), see W. E. Forehand, "Symbolic Gardens in Longus' *Daphnis and Chloe*," *Eranos* 74 (1976), 102–111.

11. Notice the elaborate chiasmus here, which I have attempted to preserve in the English, though perhaps at the expense of some degree of clarity.

12. Cf. 4.8.

13. This is by no means an exhaustive list of the passages cited in support of the allegorical reading of *Daphnis and Chloe*. One of the greatest weaknesses in that whole line of argument is precisely its proclivity to reductionism. Everything that happens in the novel can be reduced to some symbol of the cult of Dionysus, and whatever fails to fit can be simply set aside: a critical Procrustean bed.

14. Anderson, *Eros Sophistes*, p. 46; Hunter, *Study of Daphnis and Chloe*, p. 38. Note the manner in which Dionysophanes privately asks Daphnis if Chloe is a virgin before he gives his consent to the marriage. One can almost hear the father figure from contemporary situation comedies on television asking his son if the girl he wants to marry is a "nice girl." One wonders, too, if we are really supposed to forgive his decision to expose the infant Daphnis quite so easily.

15. This is, of course, the version told by Catullus in *Carmen* 64.

16. One detects the hand of Athenian apologists in this version, since Theseus was always Athens's particular hero and primeval mythic king, not unlike Arthur in English legend.

17. This Lycurgus is not to be confused with the legendary lawgiver of Sparta. Note the *lyk-* (wolf) stem in his name.

18. The image of Daphnis swimming to shore on the horns of cattle has often been called Dionysiac, probably rightly; but Anderson is also correct to point out (*Eros Sophistes*, p. 42) that there is something

humorous about the whole scene, and that Longus undermines the seriousness of the imagery by at once digressing into a mock-scientific discussion about the swimming techniques of cows. Only those who entirely lack a sense of humor will miss the point.

CHAPTER 7. THE DIALECTIC OF MYTH AND RHETORIC

1. See app. 1.

2. For an overview of the Second Sophistic, see especially Albin Lesky, *Geschichte der griechischen Literatur*, 3d ed. (Bern: Francke, 1971), pp. 926–945; Eduard Norden, *Die antike Kunstprosa*, vol. 1 (Leipzig: Teubner, 1898); George Kennedy, *The Art of Rhetoric in the Roman World* (Princeton, N.J.: Princeton University Press, 1972), pp. 553–613; and Bowersock, *Approaches to the Second Sophistic*.

3. The most thorough discussion of Longus's "rhetorical" style is that of Gunnar Valley, *Über den Sprachgebrauch des Longos* (Uppsala: Berling, 1926); see also Hunter's chapter on style in his *Study of Daphnis and Chloe*.

4. Philostratus, *Vitae Sophistarum* 481.

5. *Litteris* 2 (1925), 126 (= *Kleine Schriften* 3 [1969], 421).

6. Erwin Rohde remarked (*Der griechische Roman*, p. 290) that the Second Sophistic was nothing more or less than the victory of Asianic rhetoric over Attic. This obiter dictum was attacked by G. Kaibel, "Dionysios von Halikarnass und die Sophistik," *Hermes* 20 (1885), 497–513; Rohde replied in an article entitled "Die asianische Rhetorik und die zweite Sophistik," *Rheinisches Museum*, n.s. 41 (1886), 170–190. On Atticism in general, the standard work is W. Schmid, *Der Atticismus in seiner Hauptvertreten*, 4 vols. (Stuttgart: Kohlhammer, 1887–1897).

Longus's position in this controversy should perhaps be noted here. Gunnar Valley (*Sprachgebrauch*) pointed out that Longus, although not a purist by any means, avoids the "colorful" poetic vocabulary of the Asianists. Hunter, on the other hand (in his chapter "Language and Style" in *Study of Daphnis and Chloë*) is at pains to demonstrate Longus's Asianic syntax. M. D. Reeve, on p. xiv of his Teubner edition of *Daphnis and Chloe*, and in his article "Hiatus in the Greek Novel," *Classical Quarterly*, n.s. 21 (1971), 514–539, adverts to the curious hybrid nature of Longus's style: restrained diction but exuberant paratactical syntax.

7. E. Norden, *Die antike Kunstprosa*, pp. 387–391. Naturally, this renders Longus's eclecticism in matters of style less peculiar.

8. *Vitae Sophistarum* 484. Note that Philostratus uses the archaic ξύν (for σύν), a form that was already old-fashioned in Plato's day.

9. See Philip Lacey, "Plato and the Intellectual Life of the Second Century A.D.," in *Approaches to the Second Sophistic*, pp. 4-10; and especially B. P. Reardon, *Courants littéraires grecs*.

10. Giuseppe Giangrande, in his article "The Origins of the Greek Romance," goes so far as to argue that the origins of the novel are to be found in the declamations, a conclusion he bases on some evidence that declamatory topics were sometimes drawn from *hypotheses* of Alexandrian erotic elegies. This is probably too mechanical an explanation, but it provides some food for thought.

11. I have learned much from a collection of essays edited by Keith V. Erickson, entitled *Plato: True and Sophistic Rhetoric* (Amsterdam: Rodopi, 1979).

12. See Rollin W. Quimby, "The Growth of Plato's Perception of Rhetoric," in *True and Sophistic Rhetoric* (cited just above). One of the greatest issues confronting scholars in this area is the relationship between the *Gorgias* and the *Phaedrus* as regards Plato's teaching about rhetoric. One must try not only to ascertain what Plato means in each dialogue but also to decide whether the latter represents some change of attitude from the former. The whole subject is clearly digressive here, however; what follows merely skims the surface.

13. On similar grounds, of course, rhetoric and logic (along with grammar) formed the medieval "trivium," which provided the propaideutic foundation, without which the study of the quadrivial disciplines could not even begin.

14. See Brian Vickers, *In Defence of Rhetoric* (Oxford: Clarendon Press, 1988).

15. On the quarrel between rhetoric and philosophy in antiquity, see George Kennedy, *The Art of Persuasion in Greece* (Princeton, N.J.: Princeton University Press, 1963), pp. 13-25 and 321-336. The work of such modern philosophers as Martin Heidegger and Jacques Derrida has served to reopen this debate in our own day, where, in a somewhat perverse form, it rages on.

16. *Republic* 607b. Few passages in all of Plato's dialogues have provoked so much controversy, much of which, for the most part, far exceeds our present concerns.

17. Cf. Socrates' assertion in the *Apology* that the poets are among the most significant of his "old accusers" (παλαιοὶ κατηγόροι).

18. See G. S. Kirk and J. E. Raven, *The Presocratic Philosophers* (Cambridge: Cambridge University Press, 1957), chap. 1: "The Forerunners of Philosophical Cosmogony," pp. 8-72.

19. In much the same way, our own times have seen the quarrel between "creationists" and "evolutionists" quite fail to contain itself within the confines of cosmogony.

20. Xenophanes frag. 10 (Diels-Kranz).

21. *Theogony* 27–28.

22. G. S. Kirk, *Myth: Its Meaning and Functions in Ancient and Other Cultures* (Berkeley and Los Angeles: University of California Press; Cambridge: Cambridge University Press, 1970). For the structuralists, see Jean Piaget's account in *Structuralism*, trans. and ed. Chaninah Maschler (New York: Basic Books, 1970).

23. See Moors, *Platonic Myth*, and Zaslavsky, *Platonic Myth and Platonic Writing*. We shall return to this subject in a later chapter.

24. Cf. Socrates' diatribe against the "rationalizing" of myths, in the early chapters of the *Phaedrus*.

25. See Heraclitus frag. 51 (Diels-Kranz).

CHAPTER 8. THE ANCIENT GREEK NOVEL

1. Pace those who with montonous regularity proclaim the death of the novel. It is a lively corpse.

2. Naturally, the fate of Apuleius's *Golden Ass* is another matter.

3. See Otto Bird, *Cultures in Conflict: An Essay in the Philosophy of the Humanities* (Notre Dame, Ind.: University of Notre Dame Press, 1976), esp. chap. 6, "The Quarrel of Ancients and Moderns."

4. One of the defenders, for example, is M. H. Abrams; see p. 111 of his *Glossary of Literary Terms*, 3d edition (New York: Holt, Rinehart, and Winston, 1971), s.v. "novel."

5. Northrop Frye, *The Anatomy of Criticism: Four Essays* (Princeton, N.J.: Princeton University Press, 1969), clearly had the medieval genre in mind when he identified the "romantic" as that mode of fiction which prevails between the mythopoeic and the high mimetic. Though his description of the romantic mode applies in some particulars to the ancient Greek texts in question, the analogy falls apart precisely at what is for Frye the first determinant of the romantic mode: namely, the heroic stature of the male protagonist.

6. Arthur Heiserman, *The Novel before the Novel: Essays and Discussions about the Beginnings of Prose Fiction in the West* (Chicago: University of Chicago Press, 1977), presupposes a great deal in his very title; on p. 4 (with the note on p. 221) he discusses the issue of "novel vs. romance," without settling it. Kestner, "Ecphrasis," p. 169, argues

that *Daphnis and Chloe* fits Ian Watt's criteria for a novel. Paul Turner, "Novels, Ancient and Modern," *Novel* 2 (1968), 15–24, argues very forcefully for "novel" as against "romance."

7. This may not be true of the anonymous *Life of Apollonius of Tyre*, which was indeed widely read during the Middle Ages. But this is a Latin text, which explains its promulgation. It is also rather unlike the other Greek novels in several respects; and it is most like the medieval chivalric romances precisely in those aspects in which it is most different from *Daphnis and Chloe*. At any rate, the question need not be resolved here and now for the present purposes.

8. The ultimate provenance of "novel," oddly enough, is not literary but juridical: the Roman jurists used *novellae* (sc., *constitutiones*) of legal decisions made by the emperor in special cases when applicable precedents seemed to be missing, or required correction.

9. In addition to these complete works, we have fragments and synopses of several others, including Lollianus's *Phoenician Tale*, Iamblichus's *Babylonian Tale*, and Antonius Diogenes' *Wonders beyond Thule*. One might also mention the "Ninus Fragments," ps-Callisthenes' *Life of Alexander*, the Jewish *Joseph and Asenaath*, and such Christian romances as *The Acts of Paul and Thecla* and the *Recognitions* of ps-Clement. All of these are either incomplete or otherwise marginal to our discussion, for reasons that will become apparent.

10. One even sees *Daphnis and Chloe* sometimes called the *Lesbiaca*, as by M. Philippides, "A Note on Longus' *Lesbiaka*," *Classical World* 71 (1978), 460–461. The observable ancient insouciance about titles should be enough to warn us about making too much of all this.

11. The present study will have rather little to say about the Latin novel. This is not because there seems to be nothing to say but rather because such a study would really require separate treatment. Of course, one might justify the omission of the Latin texts from what follows by adverting to that notorious ignorance of Latin texts on the part of Greek authors, which explains why the influence of the Greek tradition on the Latin will always be easier to see than any contrary influence of the Latin on the Greek.

12. My own grandmother, who was born in 1908, can remember being told in her childhood that "Nice girls don't read novels."

13. See app. 1.

14. If it is true, as some suppose, that the Latin *Apollonius of Tyre* is a translation of an older Greek original, then that would be an exception to the rule. There are some interesting issues here, but pursuing them, as noted above, would take us too far from *Daphnis and Chloe*.

15. Alonso López de Pinciano, *Philosophia Antiqua* (Milan, 1595). Pinciano was untroubled by the fact that Heliodorus's *Theagenes and Charicleia* is prose rather than verse. Whether or not this really matters in such things is, of course, still an open question.

16. For detailed information on editions and translations of *Daphnis and Chloe*, see the Annotated Bibliography following the notes. Goethe's appreciation was mentioned in the first chapter. Almost the whole entry under 21 May 1839 is given over to a discussion between Goethe and Eckermann on the merits and character of *Daphnis and Chloe*.

17. The most extended argument along this line is to be found in Christie, "Longus and the Pastoral Tradition." Some sense of this isolation may also be evident in Hunter's silence on the subject of the Greek novel generally (in *Study of Daphnis and Chloë*). Tomas Hägg, *The Novel in Antiquity*, p. 35, calls Longus "[t]he most marked individualist among the writers of Greek novels." Perry mentions Longus only passim; Rohde mistakenly believed him to be Byzantine, no earlier than the sixth century A.D., and thus part of a different history altogether.

18. Anderson's insistence (*Eros Sophistes*) on the individuality of these texts has been salutary; see also both of Tomas Hägg's books, *Novel in Antiquity* and *Narrative Technique*.

19. A brief *Wissenschaftsgeschichte* on these matters constitutes app. 2 of the present book.

20. The whole discussion that follows is heavily indebted to the general treatments by Hägg (*Novel in Antiquity*), Anderson (*Eros Sophistes*), and Perry (*Romances*). Three volumes in the Twayne World Authors series fill some serious gaps in the critical literature: Gareth Schmeling, *Chariton*, Twayne World Authors series 295 (New York: Twayne Publishers, 1974); by the same author, *Xenophon of Ephesus*, Twayne World Authors series 613 (Boston: Twayne Publishers, 1980); and Gerald N. Sandy, *Heliodorus*, Twayne World Authors series 647 (Boston: Twayne Publishers, 1982).

21. Etymology is, as often, revealing: "recipe," after all, comes from the same Latin root as "received."

22. Mittlestadt ("Love, Eros," p. 305) characterizes Eros in all the Greek novels, except for *Daphnis and Chloe*, as "uncomplicated sensual passion, *tempered with a degree of moral asceticism*" (emphasis added). The importance of the emphasized portion will become apparent shortly.

23. The prominence of travel in these texts led Rohde to suppose that travel literature was one of the older genres out of which the novel evolved. For proponents of the "mystery text" thesis, on the other hand, the tendency of the "mysterious" East in general, and of Egypt in par-

ticular, to figure in the plot is a sign of cultic significance. For yet others, all this points to an Eastern origin for the genre as a whole. See app. 2.

24. Geography may even appear in the titles of these novels, almost all of which are preserved with two titles: one consists of the lovers' names, as in *Daphnis and Chloe* or *Chaereas and Callirhoe*, while the other is based on the setting, as in Xenophon Ephesius's *Anthia and Habrocomes* (i.e., Ἐφησιακά). The latter form is, of course, modeled on the titles of histories, such as Xenophon's *Hellenica*. M. Philippides' argument that *Daphnis and Chloe* ought to be called the *Lesbiaca* has already been mentioned.

25. On this, quite naturally, see Anderson's chapter (in *Eros Sophistes*) on Achilles Tatius, which is entitled "Plato Eroticus." The first scholar to put the case for an ironic reading of *Leucippe and Clitophon* was Donald Durham, in "Parody in Achilles Tatius," *Classical Philology* 33 (1938), 1–19. Durham's specific contention that Achilles Tatius was mocking Heliodorus cannot be supported; shortly after his article appeared, the publication of a papyrus fragment showed beyond a reasonable doubt that Achilles Tatius predated Heliodorus, probably by at least a century. But we have already seen reason to suppose that by the late Antonine period, Achilles Tatius's floruit, there was plenty of at least superficially similar material ripe for burlesque.

26. For those who want to see the mystery religions as the genesis of the whole genre, this, of course, has been grist for the mill.

27. It is essential to bear in mind at this point that themes alone do not make a genre. If the cooking analogy may again be invoked, there are very important aspects yet to be considered, not necessarily related to the ingredients.

28. Note that when Heliodorus's Charicleia is affected with symptoms much like those experienced by Chloe in book 1 of *Daphnis and Chloe*, the former's parents, friends, and doctors are mystified as to the causes of this malady, but she herself is not.

29. This point is very well made by Mittelstadt, "Love, Eros."

30. There are, for example, two shipwrecks; and it is possible that the etiological myths are analogous to the learned digressions often found in other novels.

CHAPTER 9. THE NOVEL AND HISTORY

1. On the perhaps unduly neglected connection between storytelling and the origins of the ancient novel, see Alexander Scobie, "Storytellers, Storytelling, and the Novel in Graeco-Roman Antiquity," *Rheinisches Museum* 122 (1979), 229–259; also Sophie Trenckner, *The Greek*

Novella in the Classical Period (Cambridge: Cambridge University Press, 1958).

2. Thuc. 1.22.1.

3. Thuc. 1.22.4. The passage is notoriously hard to translate; the translation here (which is my own) is literal to the greatest possible degree, even at the expense of clarity, because the precise diction here is so important. Thucydides, like most classical authors, speaks of his audience "hearing" rather than "reading" the work at hand.

4. It may be apropos to reflect, just here, on the fact that the English word "idiot" comes from the Greek word ἰδιώτης, "private person" or "individual."

5. Martin Braun, *Griechische Roman und hellenistiche Geschichtsschreibung* (Frankfurt am Main: V. Klostermann, 1934). The "archaeology" of this subject should also include the work of Bruno Lavagnini, *Le origini del romanzo greco* (Pisa: F. Mariotti, 1921; reprinted as part of the same author's *Studi sul romanzo greco*, Messina and Florence: G. d'Anna, 1950); and J. Ludvíkovsky, *Recky Roman Dobroduzny* (Prague: Filosofika Fakulta University Karlova, 1925 [in Czech, with a summary in French]).

6. Perry, *Romances*, p. 175.

7. See Hägg, *Novel in Antiquity*, pp. 111–114. Though accepting the possible importance of the Hellenistic historians as models for the novelists, Hägg is in that book reluctant to assert that the novelists consciously modeled their work on historiography. See now, however, his article "*Callirhoe* and *Parthenope*: The Beginnings of the Historical Novel," in *Classical Antiquity* 6 (1987), 184–204.

8. There is no time for a detailed demonstration of this now; I refer skeptics to the first poem of Ovid's *Amores*. Tongue firmly in cheek, Ovid explains his inability to write martial epics by complaining that "laughing Cupid" steals a foot from every other line, so that what were intended to be dactylic hexameters become elegiac couplets, willy-nilly; and so perforce he must devote himself to erotic subjects.

9. Perry, *Romances*, p. 10.

10. One thinks here of Aristotle's famous dictum, early in the *Poetics*, that tragedy is more philosophical than history, because the former deals with universals, while the latter is confined to concrete particulars.

11. I notice that a similar observation has recently been made, in a discussion of certain vexed issues in the poetry of Catullus, by John Douglas Minyard, "The Source of the *Catulli Veronensis Liber*," *Classical World* 81 (1988), 343–353, esp. pp. 349–350.

12. Perhaps the best-known such study is that of Eva Brann, "The Music of the *Republic*," *Agôn* 1 (1967), 1–117.

13. For much of what follows, I am indebted to an essay by D. C. Earl,

"Prologue-Form in Ancient Historiography," in *Aufstieg und Niedergang der römischen Welt* 1.2 (1972), 842–856.

14. See Schmeling, *Chariton*, especially the first chapter, and Hägg, *Narrative Technique*.

15. There is some controversy about the date of 486/485 B.C. for the historical event purportedly depicted in the final books of Chariton. Still, regardless of the position one takes on the issue, Chariton's chronology seems utterly impossible.

16. See Epistle 66, "To Chariton."

17. The most salient example of such biographies is, of course, the *Life of Alexander* attributed to one ps-Callisthenes, the text history of which is inordinately complicated. These texts are not really relevant to the present study, for perhaps obvious reasons; but any full-fledged treatment of Greek prose fiction would have to account for them.

18. This may be a good time, by the way, to remind ourselves that the surviving texts are only a smattering of what seems to have been a thriving, if popularizing and subliterary, genre. How representative these texts are is subject to question, but the problem is really, of course, insoluble.

19. Cadmus, mythical founder of Thebes, is said to have been from Sidon.

20. See the third appendix in Perry, *Romances*, pp. 325–329.

21. This is not the way that Achilles Tatius's narrative technique is usually explained, as, for example, by Perry, in *Romances*.

22. We are, of course, skipping over *Daphnis and Chloe* in the chronological sequence. The reasons for doing so just now ought to be obvious.

23. In Gerald N. Sandy, "Classical Forerunners of the Theory and Practice of Prose Romance: Studies in the Narrative Form of Minor French Romances of the Sixteenth and Seventeenth Centuries," *Antike und Abendland* 28 (1982), 168–191.

24. Some readers may even have thought, upon glancing at Heliodorus's first sentence, of good old Snoopy: "It was a dark and stormy night."

25. Respectively, the opening words of the *Iliad*, "Sing the wrath," and the *Odyssey*, "Tell me of the man."

26. See J. R. Morgan, "History, Romance, and Realism in the *Aithiopika* of Heliodorus," *Classical Antiquity* 1 (1982), 221–265.

27. The allusion was first noted by Boissonade, in his edition of *Daphnis and Chloe*. See Valley, *Sprachgebrauch*, p. 102.

28. The Greek word σώφρων (*sôphrôn*) is notoriously hard to render

adequately. The adjective literally means "of sound wits"; but the noun, σωφροσύνη (sôphrosynê) is usually translated "moderation," "temperance," or "prudence."

CHAPTER 10. LONGUS'S PROSE IDYLL

1. The term "Lesbian" did not usually mean what it means today; but various poems, particularly from the Anacreontic school, suggest that a "Lesbian woman" was the paradigm of the erotic woman. It was no accident, then, that Catullus, a frequent translator and emulator of Sappho, chose the name "Lesbia" for his poetic lover.

2. Literature on the pastoral element of *Daphnis and Chloe* is extensive. Georg Rohde, in "Longus und die Bukolik," *Rheinisches Museum* 86 (1937), 23–49, argued that the pastoral element in *Daphnis and Chloe* was connected with Dionysus, one of whose cult titles, he argued, was βούκολος (boukolos, i.e., "cowherd"); this line of argument was picked up and amplified considerably by Wojaczek. Much more useful in this context are the following: Christie, "Longus and the Pastoral Tradition"; McCulloh, *Longus*, pp. 56–78; and especially two articles by M. C. Mittelstadt, "Bucolic-Lyric Motifs and Dramatic Narrative in Longus' *Daphnis and Chloe*," in *Rheinisches Museum* 113 (1970), 211–227, and "Longus, *Daphnis and Chloe*, and the Pastoral Tradition," *Classica et Medievalia* 27 (1966), 162–177. See also B. Effe, "Longos: zur Funktionsgeschichte der Bukolik in der römischen Kaiserzeit," *Hermes* 110 (1982), 65–84.

3. Wilamowitz, "Die griechische Literatur des Altertums," in *Die griechsiche und lateinische Literatur und Sprache*, 2d edition, Die Kultur der Gegenwart 1.8 (Berlin: Teubner, 1907), p. 185.

4. *RE* 31.1425; *IG* 12.2.68. On ancient Lesbos generally, see also *RE* 23.2107–2133.

5. Hunter (*Study of Daphnis and Chloe*) and McCulloh (*Longus*) are both much exercised on the subject.

6. Wojaczek, *Daphnis*, argues that the mythical persona of Daphnis was connected with Dionysus from the beginning, and that consequently all pastoral poetry is Dionysian. This is all grist for Merkelbach's mill, as may be imagined. Geyer, "Roman und Mysterienritual," points out that the cult title βούκολος can be attested only in Pergamum, where it had a particular point not applicable elsewhere. The name "Daphnis" had become all but generic, anyway, so that any attempt to build an argument around a mythical character of that name could hardly hold up

under scrutiny. Hunter's skepticism about any and all efforts to pin down a mythical Daphnis from which Longus's character is clearly derived is fully justified.

7. See the recent book by Andrew Ettin, *Literature and the Pastoral* (New Haven: Yale University Press, 1985). Certainly Vergil's Tenth Eclogue is a case in point.

8. The best-known pastoral prose piece is probably Dio Chrysostom's *Hunters of Euboea*. The distinction drawn here between the pastoral mode and the pastoral genre is taken from Ettin, *Literature and the Pastoral*.

9. On this, see Valley, *Sprauchgebrauch*, and Hunter, *Study of Daphnis and Chloe*.

10. Hunter, *Study of Daphnis and Chloe*, pp. 76–83.

11. I am very much indebted here to a paper by Maria-Victoria Abricka, "Notes on a 'Unified Field Theory' of Artemis," which I heard at a meeting of the North Carolina Classical Association in November of 1986, and a copy of which the author was kind enough to send me.

12. The scholarly literature on the *Phaedrus* is enormous and daunting to the nonspecialist. In what follows I have gleaned much of value from two recent studies: G. R. F. Ferrari, *Listening to the Cicadas: A Study of Plato's* Phaedrus, Cambridge Classical Studies (Cambridge: Cambridge University Press, 1987); Charles L. Griswold, Jr., *Self-Knowledge in Plato's* Phaedrus (New Haven: Yale University Press, 1986); and Josef Pieper, *Begeisterung und Göttlicher Wahnsinn* (Munich: Kösel-Verlag KG, 1962). I must also acknowledge a very special debt to a former graduate student of mine, David J. Miller, whose brilliant paper on Hesiod in the *Phaedrus* (written for me as a term paper) taught me volumes.

CHAPTER 11. LONGUS THE SOPHIST

1. Most "Western Civilization" courses of my acquaintance pass immediately from Nero to Constantine, with no more than passing notice taken of the Antonines.

2. See E. L. Bowie, "The Greeks and Their Past in the Second Sophistic," *Past and Present* 46 (1970), 1–41.

3. It is interesting to remark how prevalent a certain petulance toward the Romans is among Hellenists in our own day. For example, on p. 118 of Chase and Phillip's widely used Greek textbook, *A New Introduction to Greek* (Cambridge, Mass.: Harvard University Press, 1941), the authors caption a sealstone as follows: "a vigorous face, possibly one of the Romans who despoiled Greece and the East alike before bringing

that universal peace which proved to be sterile in the areas where once the πόλεις had lived their intense creative existence." More to the point, perhaps, is B. P. Reardon's dictum, in the first chapter of *Courants littéraires grecs*, that there is no such thing as Roman culture.

4. It should be noted, though, that Plutarch claimed scant knowledge of Latin; and, in the *Parallel Lives*, he rather consistently favors the great men of Greece over their Roman counterparts. Aelius Aristides, *Oratio* 15, Ἐις Ῥωμήν ("On Rome").

5. The notorious exception (which essentially proves the rule) was Judaea.

6. The best and most sympathetic treatment of the Greek literature of this period is by Reardon, in *Courants littéraires grecs*—despite that animus against the Romans. See also the relevant chapters in Albin Lesky's *Geschichte der griechischen Literatur*, 3d edition (Bern: Francke, 1971), and in W. von Christ, W. Schmid, and O. Stählin, *Geschichte der griechischen Literatur*, 6th ed., vol. 2.2: *Von 100 bis 530 nach Christum* (Munich, 1924).

7. Reardon's chapter on philosophy in *Courants littéraires grecs*, to which the following discussion is much and obviously indebted, is especially good on this point. He there suggests that the philosophical eclecticism characteristic of Galen and his contemporaries comes from a deep distrust of comprehensive systems of thought, a distrust which in turn emerges from a fundamental diffidence about the possibility of arriving at any final answers. See also Lacey, "Plato and the Second Century."

8. Those inclined to doubt this point—which cannot really be developed here without undue digression from the task at hand—are invited to read any ten pages of Seneca, and then read any ten pages of either Marcus Aurelius or Epictetus.

9. This outline of the cults is familiar enough, especially, thanks to Kérenyi and Merkelbach, to students of the ancient novel. A useful discussion can be found in Geyer, "Roman und Mysterienritual," pp. 184–186.

10. In my opinion it was precisely because Christianity combined the promise of eternal life with a compelling imperative for social and moral changes in the present that it posed a threat to the established order not posed by the other cults and was persecuted. Had the Christians confined themselves to worshiping a resurrected god, they might never have run afoul of Roman authority.

11. B. P. Reardon makes a similar point, from different perspectives, in three important articles on the Greek novel: "Aspects of the Greek

Novel," *Greece and Rome* 23 (1976), 118–131; "Novels and Novelties, or, Mysteriouser and Mysteriouser," in *The Mediterranean World: Papers Presented to Gilbert Bagnani* (Peterborough, Ont.: Trent University, 1975); and "The Greek Novel," *Phoenix* 23 (1969), 291–309.

12. Nietzsche, who had a keen appreciation for the tragic view of life, fulminated against what he called "Alexandrian" cheerfulness, which attempts to deny death. See *Die Geburt der Tragödie*, secs. 17 and 18. The dictum has often been applied to the ancient novels, in a way of which Nietzsche would surely have approved; but I have not yet found any indication that Nietzsche, despite his friendship with Erwin Rohde, had anything in particular to say about the ancient novels themselves. What his attitude would have been can easily be imagined, and Rohde's own fundamental lack of sympathy with the texts he studied may be apposite.

13. There is the matter of a story (possibly apocryphal) about Heliodorus, according to which he later converted to Christianity and became bishop of Tricca; later, however, having been ordered to burn all copies of *Theagenes and Charicleia,* he chose instead to resign his see. But then, even if we swallow the story whole, the point is that Heliodorus was not just any Christian but a bishop; and the alternative he was supposedly given to burning his novel was not excommunication but resignation of his see. We might further note that one of the most vehement diatribes against novels in antiquity was written by the arch-pagan, Julian the Apostate, in his *Epistles.*

APPENDIX 1: AUTHOR AND DATE

1. This is certainly the case with McCulloh, *Longus,* and Hunter, *Study of Daphnis and Chloe.* The former has a little to say about other Greek novels, next to nothing to say about the temper of the times, but rather a lot to say about the pastoral tradition. Hunter has a few words to say about the Second Sophistic, rather a lot to say about Longus's debt to the classical tradition, but almost nothing to say about the other Greek novels.

2. See L. Herrmann, "Velius Longus auteur de *Daphnis et Chloé,*" *Latomus* 40 (1981), 378–383.

3. The *Suda* is an anonymous Byzantine work, really a bibliographical dictionary, once wrongly thought to be the work of a man named Suidas. Photius was a Byzantine bishop and bibliophile, to whose *Bibliotheca* we owe references to (and sometimes synopses of) many lost texts from antiquity, especially ancient novels. Our only source for Iam-

blichus's *Babylonian Tale*, for example, is Photius's extended synopsis. The twelfth-century Byzantine romancers Theodorus Prodromus and Nicetas Eugenianus display some familiarity with *Daphnis and Chloe*; but it cannot be said that Longus was well known even then. Nicetas quotes 4.2–3 at 1.77–107 and refers to the story of Daphnis and Chloe at 6.439–450 of his *Drusilla and Charicles*; something about the tone of these passages makes one suspect that these are intended to be erudite (that is, recondite) allusions.

4. For good reason to be suspicious of most surviving biographies of those ancient authors not known to history outside of their literary productions, see a recent study by M. Lefkowitz, *Lives of the Greek Poets* (Baltimore: Johns Hopkins University Press, 1982). Lefkowitz argues convincingly that such biographies were mostly fabricated in antiquity, on the basis of inferences made from presumably autobiographical statements in the poems themselves.

5. Reeve, "Praefatio."

6. The *RE* has no listings under either "Logos" or "Logus" as proper names.

7. The earliest evidence for this line of argument that I can find is a reference to an essay in the *Nuntius Hebdomadico Florentino* (= *Novelle literarie*), 17 September 1779, given by Mitscherlich (an early editor; see the Annotated Bibliography), p. v. I have been unable to track down this reference, even given the vast resources of Harvard's Widener Library; I reproduce here what I have, in the hope that someone more adept than I in these matters can find what I could not. Similar arguments (without attribution) can be found in Harless's notes under the entry for Longus in his recension of Fabricius's *Bibliotheca*. Harless's position was given a favorable hearing by Maximilian Schoell, *Histoire de la littérature grecque profane*, 2d edition, vol. 6 (Paris 1824), p. 238, and by F. Jacobs, *Hirtengeschichten von Daphnis und Chloe* (Leipzig, 1832), in the preface. Antoine Kaíris, *Longus: Pastorales* (Athens: Sarizevanis, 1932), in his introduction, apparently meant to strengthen the argument by pointing out that Longus called the "books" of his text βίβλοι, not λόγοι; rather than prove the point, however, this seems only to add to the confusion.

8. Thus Reeve, p. v.

9. *IG* 12.2.88; see also *Supplementum* 76.41–80.

10. See the *Fasti Consulares* for that year; also the ninety-first entry under "Pompeius" in the *RE*.

11. In his *Römische Studien* (Leipzig: Teubner, 1922), p. 323.

12. The *RE* has eight listings under the cognomen "Longus," with

no two under the same *gentilicium,* while the *Prosopographia Imperii Romani* has 14 "Longi." Annibal Caro, in the preface to his famous Italian translation of *Daphnis and Chloe* (1786), suggested that the author was one of the Mussidii Longi; Herrmann's arguments in favor of Velius Longus have already been noted.

13. Wilamowitz, "Die griechische Literatur," p. 185. Wilamowitz was characteristically magisterial about all this, and did not say exactly why he thought this to be the case.

14. See S. A. Naber, "Adnotationes Criticae ad Longi Pastoralia," *Mnemosyne,* n.s. 5 (1877), 201. Naber arrives at his figure by some perhaps dubious arithmetic, since Strabo gives the distance in question by sea rather than by land, and expresses several of the segments of the journey in terms of sailing time rather than of actual distance.

15. H. J. Mason, "Longus and the Topography of Lesbos," *Transactions of the American Philological Association* 109 (1979), 149–163; and Peter Green, "Longus, Antiphon, and the Topography of Lesbos," *American Journal of Archaeology* 85 (1981), 195. Green accepts Mason's general arguments but has a different theory on the location of the estate.

16. See the introductions to the critical editions by Kaíris (*Longus: Pastorales*) and Georges Dalmeyda, ed., *Pastorales: Daphnis et Chloé,* Editions Budé (1934; Belles Lettres, 1960); there is also apparently a discussion of these matters in A. M. Scarcella, *La Lesbo di Longo Sofista* (Rome, 1968), but I have been unable to locate this book.

17. Dalmeyda, *Pastorales,* p. xii; n. 1 on p. xiii gives the ancient authorities.

18. See chap. 5.

19. Thus Otto Schoenberger, *Hirtengeschichten von Daphnis und Chloe,* Sektion für Altertumswissenschaft bei der deutschen Akademie der Wissenschaften zu Berlin, Bund 6 (1960; Berlin: Akademie Verlag, 1980), "Einführung," p. 10.

20. The point may not be self-evident but becomes clearer upon reflection. If I were a native of New York City, I would be unlikely to begin a story by saying that I happened to be in New York one day when, etc.

21. On this subject, I am very much indebted to an article by Ken Dowden, "Apuleius and the Art of Narrative," *Classical Quarterly* 32 (1982), 419–435.

22. See Lilian Furst, *Fictions of Romantic Irony* (Cambridge, Mass.: Harvard University Press, 1984). I had the privilege of exchanging observations about all this with Furst in person when she came to the cam-

pus of Purdue University in the spring of 1983 to deliver a series of public lectures on irony in literature.

23. See Reeve, "Praefatio," p. v; Hunter, *Study of Daphnis and Chloe*, pp. 3–15. For a review of other hypotheses, see Schoenberger, "Einführung," p. 10.

24. See H. Dörrie's review of Dalmeyda's Budé edition (*Pastorales*), in *Göttingische Gelehrte Anzeigen* 198 (1936), p. 348; Hunter, *Study of Daphnis and Chloe*, pp. 3–4.

25. Weinrich, "Anhang," and Mittelstadt, "Roman Narrative Painting"; see chap. 2. Mittelstadt tries to extend this similarity to cover the narrative structure of the whole novel.

26. Mittelstadt, "Roman Narrative Painting," p. 761.

27. The connection was first pointed out by H. Reich, *De Alciphronis Longique aetate* (diss., Königsberg, 1894); Reich's work was greeted with enthusiasm by E. Norden, who, in his *Die antike Kunstprosa*, vol. 1 (Leipzig: Teubner, 1898), p. 437, remarked that he had always felt that Longus was of second-century date but was glad to see it confirmed by Reich. See also G. Dalmeyda, "Longus et Alciphron," in *Mélanges Gustave Glotz* (1932), 1.277–278; Schoenberger, "Einführung," pp. 10–11; and Hunter, *Study of Daphnis and Chloe*, pp. 6–14. Hunter's detailed examination of the alleged evidence should lay Reich's thesis to rest once and for all. C. Bonner, "On Certain Supposed Literary Relationships," *Classical Philology* 4 (1909), 32–44 and 276–290, argued in favor of a common source for the similarities cited by Reich.

28. See *Leucippe and Clitophon* 8.7–10.

29. On Longus's language and diction, the standard work is Valley, *Sprachgebrauch*; see also Hunter, *Study of Daphnis and Chloe*, p. 85, and M. D. Reeve, "Hiatus in the Greek Novel," *Classical Quarterly*, n.s. 21 (1971), 514–539.

30. Hunter, *Study of Daphnis and Chloe*, p. 3; Reeve, "Praefatio," p. xiv, n. 4.

31. Hunter, *Study of Daphnis and Chloe*, pp. 3 and 90; Norden, *Antike Kunstprosa*, pp. 437–438.

32. Valley, *Sprachgebrauch*, takes it as an established fact that Longus belongs to the Second Sophistic and so does not discuss the issue in detail.

33. An important exception is Reardon, *Courants littéraires grecs*. Reardon's discussion has been very useful to the present study, as will become apparent later in this appendix.

34. Jungermann added the epithet to Longus's name on the title page of his 1605 edition of *Daphnis and Chloe*. He does not comment

upon or justify his addition to the superscription, but that does not necessarily vitiate the critical perception that underlay it.

35. By "the novel's historical context," I do not mean the mise-en-scène of the novel itself, or its fictive date but rather the historical circumstances under which it was written.

APPENDIX 2.

SCHOLARLY INTERPRETATIONS OF THE ANCIENT NOVEL

1. Erwin Rohde, *Der griechische Roman und seine Vorläufer* (Leipzig, 1876; Hildesheim: Georg Olms, 1960).

2. For the discussion that follows I am particularly indebted to the efforts of three previous scholars to make some sense out of the critical tradition surrounding the ancient novels: Giangrande, "Origins"; Perry, *Romances*; and Anderson, *Eros Sophistes*. After this portion of my discussion was already substantially complete, I discovered, to my great satisfaction, that Gareth Schmeling, in the relevant chapter of his *Chariton*, Twayne World Authors series 295 (New York: Twayne Publishers, 1974), analyzes the scholarship on the ancient novel very much as I do.

3. Please note that in this context the term "Orient" does not refer to the Far East, but to those nations and peoples who lived along the eastern Mediterranean and on to Mesopotamia and—to some extent—India. The term thus encompasses what had once been the Persian Empire at its greatest extent, before it was dismembered by Alexander and his successors.

4. *History and Romance in Graeco-Oriental Literature* (Oxford: Blackwell, 1938).

5. Braun's interest lay primarily, however, with the Hebrew tradition, and his remarks on the possible relationship between the Jewish romances about Joseph and Moses and the Greek novels are virtually obiter dicta.

6. Moses Hadas, "Cultural Survival and the Origins of Fiction," *South Atlantic Quarterly* 51(1952), 253–260; J. W. B. Barns, "Egypt and the Greek Romance," in *Mitteilungen aus der Papyrussammlung der Österreich*, Nationalbibliothek, ed. Gerstinger, n.s. 5 (Vienna 1956). In his *Eros Sophistes*, Anderson announced in a postscript (pp. 198–199) that the "true origins" of the Greek novel "have just been established," and that all (including *Daphnis and Chloe*) are of Eastern origin. He promised to reveal all in a forthcoming book, which has since been published: *Ancient Fiction: The Novel in the Graeco-Roman World* (London: Croom Helm; Totowa, N.J.: Barnes and Noble, 1984). Oddly, in *Eros Sophistes*

Anderson, like the present author, seems to understand the search for origins as something of a red herring (p. vii). One should note that Barns, "Egypt," also thinks that the Oriental "sources" of the Greek novels are older, rather than contemporary.

7. Parthenius was the author of what could only be described as an anthology of plots; see J. M. Edmonds and S. Gaselee, *Daphnis and Chloe: Love Romances of Parthenius* (Cambridge, Mass.: Harvard University Press, 1979). An introductory epistle, addressed to the Roman poet Gallus, offers the work as source material for erotic elegies. Since the work of Gallus (a contemporary of Catullus) survives only in one substantial fragment, and that just recently discovered, we have no way of knowing whether or not Gallus made use of the material that Parthenius provided him. Bruno Lavagnini, *Le origini del romanzo greco* (Pisa: F. Mariotti, 1921), reprinted in *Studi sul romanzo greco* (Messina: G. d'Anna, 1950); J. Ludvíkovsky, *Recky Roman Dobroduzny* (Prague: Filosofika Fakulta University Karlova, 1925), in Czech with summary in French.

8. Schoenberg's introduction to his critical edition of *Daphnis and Chloe* provides a useful synopsis of such arguments.

9. Just such a survey has been done by Hunter, *Study of Daphnis and Chloe*, pp. 22–31, who concludes as follows: "It is thus clear that although Longus has peppered his narrative with details from the legend of the Sicilian Daphnis, he has made no effort to use the legend as a constant narrative frame" (p. 31).

10. Theocritus's shepherd is evoked at 1.18, where Daphnis says, "Δάφνις δὲ μαραίνεται," which means, "Daphnis is wasting away."

11. At the same time, however, the resemblance between "Daphnis" and "Daphne" evokes from the outset the kind of etiological myth that Longus so thoroughly exploits. Longus's choice of names, then, is at the same time both casual and pointed. Nothing could be more typical of him.

12. The earliest form of this argument known to me is to be found in A. Chassang's *Histoire des romans et ses rapports avec l'histoire dans l'antiquité grecque et latine* (Paris, 1862). The same Martin Braun who wrote *History and Romance* (which, as its title implies, touched upon the thesis here under discussion), also wrote, in German, a study of the relationship between historiography and the novel: *Griechische Roman und hellenistische Geschichtschreibung*, Frankfurter Studien zur Religion und Kultur der Antike, 6 (Frankfurt am Main: V. Klostermann, 1938).

13. The *Cyropaideia*, or *Education of Cyrus*, is a highly romanticized biography of Cyrus, a pretender to the Persian throne.

14. Schwartz's essays were first published in 1896; a second edition, with a foreword by A. Rehm, was published in Berlin, by DeGruyter, in 1943. Weinrich, *Die griechische Liebesroman* (Zürich: Artemis, 1962).

15. Perry, *Romances*, p. 10; Perry uses "novel" and "romance" interchangeably throughout his book.

16. See the Preface.

17. Perry, *Romances*, p. 20.

18. This is the central thesis of his article "The Origins of the Greek Romance."

19. Perry, *Romances*, pp. 9–12.

20. Perry, *Romances*, pp. 96–98; Anderson, *Eros Sophistes*, p. 1. Rohde had dated *Daphnis and Chloe* to the sixth century A.D., a date which no one now accepts.

21. Karl Kerényi, *Die griechische-orientalische Romanliteratur in religionsgeschichtlicher Beleuchtung: Ein Versuch* (Tübingen: J. C. B. Mohr, 1927). See also his more recent work, *Der antike Roman: Einführung und Textauswahl* (Darmstadt: Wissenschaftliche Buchgesellschaft, 1971).

22. See R. E. Witt, *Isis in the Graeco-Roman World*, Aspects of Greek and Roman Life (Ithaca, N.Y.: Cornell University Press, 1971); and Friederich Solmsen, *Isis among the Greeks and Romans* (Cambridge, Mass.: Published for Oberlin College by the Harvard University Press, 1979).

23. Kerényi argued that the Isis episode was part of the ass/man story from the beginning; but few, if any, are now willing to accept that. This is a tangled issue, but one that (to my great relief) does not require treatment here. Apuleius was using a story that may be very old, a version of which—shorter, and without a trace of the Isis chapter—is preserved among the works of Lucian. Whether Apuleius's Isis book is the culmination of a carefully prepared program of symbolism, or merely an appendix, is still an issue for debate.

24. See the reviews of Kerényi's book by G. L. Hendrickson (*Classical Philology* 23 [1928], 292–293), Venceslao Ivanov (*Athenaeum*, n.s. 6 [1928], 269–273), Georges Seure (*Révue de Philologie*, 3d ser., 2 [1928], 289–290), and especially Rudolf Helm (*Philologische Wochenschrift* 48 [1928], 1475–1481), who calls Kerényi a prophet (p. 1481).

25. See the unsigned review in *Journal of Hellenic Studies* 48 (1928), 114, and especially A. D. Nock's review in *Gnomon* 4 (1928), 485–490.

26. Merkelbach, "Roman und Mysterium," *Antaios* 1 (1960), 47–60. In 1960, also, H. H. O. Chalk published his well-known study, "Eros and the Lesbian Pastorals of Longus," though obviously without having

read Merkelbach's work. Both scholars reach similar conclusions, though Chalk lays rather more emphasis on a syncretic cult that fused Dionysus with Eros, and is rather more sensitive to the explicitly literary claims that Longus makes for *Daphnis and Chloe* than is Merkelbach.

27. See Morton Smith's review of *Roman und Mysterium* in *Classical World* 57 (1964), 378; Robert Turcan, "Le 'roman initiatique': A propos d' un livre recent," *Révue de l'Histoire des Religions* 163 (1963), 149–199, esp. pp. 151–152; and Marisa Berti, "Sulla interpretazione mistica del romanzo di Longo," *Studi Classici e Orientali* 16 (1967), 343–358. Berti emphasizes and documents the literary, nonreligious origins of most of the symbols and images of which Merkelbach makes so much. The most devastating criticism of the initiation thesis, in this writer's opinion, is Geyer, "Roman und Mysterienritual." Geyer first points out the flimsiness of the evidence that links the mythical Daphnis to Dionysus and questions the evidence adduced by Merkelbach to show that the priesthood of Dionysus was organized along bucolic lines (a practice apparently limited to Pergamum, for rather particular reasons). She then goes on to examine two novels that she concedes to be allegorical and apologetic (the *Metamorphoses* and *Joseph and Asenaath*), isolates their distinguishing characteristics (dominant among which is what she calls the "Handlungskurve," the cycle of sin, suffering, and redemption), and demonstrates in great detail that none of these is operative in *Daphnis and Chloe*. Could it be that only a German can confound a German? It should probably be noted, however, that Geyer goes on to argue that the ancient novel was a generic descendant of the New Comedy.

28. See, in addition to *Courants littéraires grecs*, Reardon's "Greek Novel"; "Novels and Novelties, or, Mysteriouser and Mysteriouser"; and "Aspects of the Greek Novel."

29. See chap. 10.

30. Pp. 9–11 of Perry's *Romances* constitute a sort of *apologia pro vita sua*, in which Perry explains how he tried all the traditional approaches to understanding the genesis of the novel until he realized that he was getting nowhere and decided to try something new.

31. Perry, *Romances*, p. 44.

32. Perry, *Romances*, p. 175.

33. Perry, *Romances*, p. 29.

34. Perry, *Romances*, p. 47. Perry never explains exactly what he means by this phrase but uses it repeatedly, as though its meaning were self-evident. From the context, one might safely infer that Perry means the sort of person who today might read Harlequin romances.

35. This classification scheme is announced in the preface of *Romances*, p. vi; its justification is the main subject of Perry's second chapter, "The Form Romance in Historical Perspective."

36. For my own part, I find it ironic that Perry cites René Wellek and Austin Warren, *The Theory of Literature* (New York: Harcourt, Brace, 1949) in support of his sociological approach to literature, while the latter, in their chapter "Literature and Society," caution against pursuing the sociological perspective too far.

37. Anderson, *Eros Sophistes*.

38. I.e., in the Twayne World Authors series volume on Chariton cited above (*Chariton*). For the rehabilitation of Chariton, see also Tomas Hägg, *Narrative Technique*, and the relevant chapters by Anderson in *Eros Sophistes*, and Heiserman in *Novel before the Novel*.

39. Again, see Anderson's chapter on *Leucippe and Clitophon* in *Eros Sophistes*. In thinking about possible parody in all the Greek romances, I have sometimes wondered what might result if the libretto of one of Gilbert and Sullivan's operas were to be dug up in some distant future, when very little might still be known about the nuances of Victorian society and manners (and the English language). If we were to assume that all the characters in *Pirates of Penzance* were as much in earnest as they appear to be, and that the audience is expected to take seriously a band of cutthroat pirates who melt into helpless tears when they are told that their intended victim is an orphan, we might conclude that both the authors and their audiences were naive at best, at worst hypocritical.

40. Cervantes' last novel, *Persiles y Seguismunda*, was an avowed effort to emulate *Theagenes and Charicleia*. On Heliodorus's influence on modern literature, see Samuel L. Wolff, *The Greek Romance in Elizabethan Prose Fiction* (New York: Press of the New Era, 1912; repr., New York: B. Franklin, 1961); Carol Gesner, *Shakespeare and the Greek Romance: A Study of Origins* (Lexington: University Press of Kentucky, 1970); Sandy, "Classical Forerunners"; and M. P. Loicq-Berger, "Pour une lecture des romans grecs," *Les Etudes Classiques* 48 (1980), pp. 23–42.

41. Just such a tack is taken by Heiserman, *The Novel before the Novel*, who calls *Daphnis and Chloe* "a comedy of ideas" (pp. 130–133).

42. Note the increasing use of the term "serial novel" to denote comic books.

43. Scobie's first volume was *Essays on the Ancient Romance and Its Heritage*, Beiträge zur klassischen Philologie 30 (Meisenheim am Glan: Anton Hain, 1969), followed by *More Essays on the Ancient Romance*, published by the same publisher in 1973, as vol. 46 of the same series.

Scobie's particular interest is in the ancient novel's reworking of folk-tale motifs, on which he has done much valuable work.

44. Heiserman's own critical predilections (*The Novel before the Novel*) were toward psychoanalytical criticism, and he made several useful observations along this line. For the present purposes, his treatment of *Daphnis and Chloe* as a "comedy of ideas" was instrumental in causing me to rethink my own approach to Longus.

45. I see two problems in Anderson's *Eros Sophistes*, both of which conspire to keep it from being as important a contribution as it might have been: first, although he acknowledges that a working definition of humor is really necessary to control the scope of the discussion, he never provides it, so that "humor" becomes a rubberband concept, stretched to fit whatever aspects of style or theme are presently at hand; and second, he fails to recognize how thoroughly his own conclusions demolish Perry's "ideal/comic" taxonomy, which is inexplicably retained throughout *Eros Sophistes*.

46. Albert Henrichs, *Die Phoinikika des Lollianos*, Papyrologische Texte und Abhandlungen 14 (Bonn: Habelt, 1972). For a useful corrective to the allegorical reading proposed by Henrichs, a student of Merkelbach, see Gerald N. Sandy, "Notes on Lollianus' Phoenicica," *American Journal of Philology* 100 (1979), 367–376.

47. Sandy, "Notes," p. 372, remarks as follows: "When dealing with a text as fragmentary as the *Phoenicica*, it would be irresponsible to be dogmatic."

Annotated Bibliography
of Editions and Translations
of *Daphnis and Chloe*

The following is a list of all editions and translations of *Daphnis and Chloe* of which I am aware. There may be a few that have slipped through the net, but I believe this list to be essentially complete. Within each category (defined by language), the works are listed in chronological order, rather than alphabetical. An asterisk (*) designates those to which I have found a reference, but which I have been unable to verify; some of these listings are manifestly incomplete.

With older editions especially, I have attempted to reproduce the title as given on the title page, including uppercase and lowercase distinctions.

EDITIONS OF THE GREEK TEXT ALONE

Colombani, Raffaello, ed. ΛΟΓΓΟΥ ΠΟΙΜΕΝΙΚΩΝ, ΤΩΝ κατὰ Δάφνιν ΚΑΙ ΧΛΟΗΝ ΒΙΒΛΙΑ ΤΕΤΤΑΡΑ, *Longi Pastoralia de Daphnide et Chloe libri quatuor*. Florence, 1598. The editio princeps; note that it comes more than forty years *after* the publication of Amyot's famous translation (see below under "French").

Dutens, Ludwig, ed. ΠΟΙΜΕΝΙΚΩΝ ΤΩΝ ΚΑΤΑ ΔΑΦΝΙΝ ΚΑΙ ΧΛΟΗΝ ΛΟΓΟΙ ΤΕΤΤΑΡΕΣ. Paris, 1776.

Paciaudi, P. M., ed. Λόγγου Ποιμενικῶν τῶν κατὰ Δάφνιν καὶ Χλόην βίβλοι τέτταρες, *cum proloquio de libris eroticis antiquorum*. Parma, 1786. The *proloquium* is an interesting read.

*Coray (or Corais), A., ed. Paris, 1802.

*Amatius, Hieronymus, ed. Leipzig, 1803.

*Courier, Paul-Louis, ed. Rome, 1810. This is the famous edition, only a few copies of which were printed, in which Courier gave to the world the substance of his famous discovery, namely, the text of the lacuna in book 1. Courier was the first to find and collate manuscript F. (Manuscript V has a large gap in book I, which had previously been filled only by conjecture.) Shortly after he copied out the text of the lacuna, Courier spilled a bottle of ink over the manuscript, thus rendering his copy our only source for the affected passage. From that day to this, some have speculated that Courier defaced the manuscript intentionally.

*Passow, F., ed. Leipzig, 1811.

Seiler, Ernest Eduard, ed. *Pastoralia Graeca ad optimorum librorum fidem emendavit, adnotationes priorum editorum selectas ineditas R. Fr. Ph. Brunckii, God. Henr. Schaeferi, Franc. Boissonadii et suas adiecit Ernest Eduard Seiler.* Leipzig, 1843.

Hirschig, G. A., ed. *Erotici Scriptores.* Paris, 1856, 1885.

Hercher, Rudolf, ed. *Erotici Scriptores Graeci.* Vol. 1. Leipzig, 1858. The text of *Daphnis and Chloe* can be found on pp. 241–326.

*Piccolos, Nicolas S., ed. Paris, 1866.

Kaíris, Antoine, ed. *Longus: Pastorales. Edition critique.* Athens: M. S. Sarizevanis, 1932. A deluxe edition for bibliophiles; apparently the first such edition to contain the Greek text rather than a translation.

Reeve, Michael D., ed. *Longus: Daphnis et Chloe.* Bibliotheca Scriptorum Graecorum et Latinorum Teubneriana. Leipzig: Teubner, 1982.

BILINGUAL EDITIONS
Greek and Latin

Bonnvitius, Juda, and Nicola Bonnvitius, eds.; J. Cornario, trans. *Achillis Tatii de Clitophontis et Leucippes amoribus libri viii. Longi Sophistae de Daphnidis et Chloes amoribus libri iv.* Heidelberg, 1601, 1606.

Jungermann, Gottfried, ed. ΛΟΓΓΟΥ ΣΟΦΙΣΤΟΥ ΠΟΙΜΕΝΙΚΩΝ, ΤΩΝ κατὰ Δάφνιν καὶ Χλόην βιβλία τέτταρα. *Longi Sophistae de Daphnide et Chloe libri quatuor.* Hannover, 1605.

Moll, Petrus, ed. ΛΟΓΓΟΥ ΠΟΙΜΕΝΙΚΩΝ ΤΩΝ ΚΑΤΑ ΔΑΦΝΙΝ ΚΑΙ ΧΛΟΗΝ ΒΙΒΛΙΑ ΤΕΤΤΑΡΑ. *Longi Pastoralium de Daphnide et Chloe libri quatuor.* Frankfurt, 1660.

*St. Bernard, Io., ed. *Pastoralium de Daphnide et Chloe libri quatuor.* Paris, 1754.

Boden, B. G. L., ed. ΛΟΓΓΟΥ ΣΟΦΙΣΤΟΥ ΠΟΙΜΕΝΙΚΩΝ ΤΩΝ ΚΑΤΑ ΔΑΦΝΙΝ ΚΑΙ ΧΛΟΗΝ ΒΙΒΛΙΑ Δ. *Longi Pastoralium de Daphnide et Chloe libri iv, cum Laurentii Gambarae expositis.* Leipzig,

1777. This edition contains some of Gambara's peculiar adaptation of *Daphnis and Chloe* into Latin verse; see below under "Latin."

D'Ansse de Villoison, B. *Pastoralium de Daphnide et Chloe libri quatuor.* Paris, 1778.

Mitscherlich, C. G., ed. ΛΟΓΓΟΥ ΠΟΙΜΕΝΙΚΩΝ ΤΩΝ *κατὰ* ΔΑΦΝΙΝ ΚΑΙ ΧΛΟΗΝ ΒΙΒΛΙΑ Δ. *Pastoralium de Daphnide et Chloe libri IV, Graece et Latine. Accedunt Xenophontis Ephesiacorum de amoribus Anthiae et Abrocomae libri IV.* Scriptores Erotici Graeci 3. Biponti, 1794.

Schäfer, G. H., ed. *Longi Pastoralia Graece et Latine cum proloquio P. M. Paciaudi de libris eroticis antiquorum.* Leipzig, 1803.

*Paris, 1825. Cited by Reeve, p. xvi; see under "Editions of the Greek Text Alone," above.

Courier, P. -L., and G. R. L. de Sinner. *Pastoralia e codd. mss. duobus Italicis primum Graece integra edidit P. L. Courier. Exemplar Romanum emendatius et auctius typis recudendum curavit G. R. Lud. de Sinner.* Paris, 1829. The first such edition to take Courier's work into account.

Greek and English

Anon. *Longus, Literally and Completely Translated from the Greek with Introduction and Notes.* Athenian Society's Publications 4. Athens: Athenian Society, 1896.

Lowe, W. D., ed. *The Story of Daphnis and Chloe: A Greek Pastoral.* Cambridge: George Bell, 1908. Reprint. New York: Arno Press, 1979, in the series Greek Texts and Commentaries. This edition, like several others, does not contain the whole text of *Daphnis and Chloe*. Several passages felt to be deleterious to the morals of young readers, especially in book 3, were expunged.

Edmonds, John Maxwell, ed. *Daphnis and Chloe, by Longus, with the English translation of George Thornley, revised and augmented by J. M. Edmonds. The Love Romances of Parthenius, with an English translation by S. Gaselee.* Loeb Classical Library. London: W. Heinemann, 1916. Reprint. Cambridge, Mass.: Harvard University Press, 1979. Thornley omitted from his translation those same scandalous passages which Edmonds translated into Latin for the Loeb edition. The latest printing now has a version of these passages in English.

Greek and German

Jacobs, F. *Hirtengeschichten von Daphnis und Chloe.* Leipzig, 1832. Reprints. Munich: Müller, 1918 (ed. H. Floerke); Heidelberg: H. Meister, 1945; Hamburg: E. Hauswedell, 1961.

Schoenberger, Otto. *Hirtengeschichten von Daphnis und Chloe. Griechisch und deutsch.* Schriften und Quellen der alten Welt, herausgegeben von der Sektion für Altertumswissenschaft bei der deutschen Akademie der Wissenschaften zu Berlin, Bund 6. Berlin: Akademie Verlag, 1960, 1973, 1980. An excellent and informative introduction.

Greek and French

Dalmeyda, Georges, ed. *Pastorales. Daphnis et Chloé.* Editions Guillaume Budé. Paris: Belles Lettres, 1934, 1960. The introduction has much of value, including an interesting defense of a new translation independent of Amyot.

TRANSLATIONS
Latin

Gambara, Lorenzo, trans. *Expositorum ex Longo libri iv heroico carmine.* Rome, 1569, 1581. This peculiar work is more of a paraphrase, in Latin dactylic hexameters, than a translation.

French

Amyot, Jacques, trans. *Les amours pastorales de Daphnis et de Chloé, escriptes premièrement en grec par Longus, et puis traduictes en françois.* Paris, 1559. Reprints. Paris, 1594, 1596, 1609, 1718, 1745; Amsterdam, 1749; London, 1764; Bouillon, 1776; London, 1779, 1780; Paris, 1795, 1800, 1803. (Some copies of this 1803 reprint have been found with an addendum inserted giving the text of Courier's discovery.) Amyot provides an interesting example of a translator whose fame eclipsed that of the original author.

*Lecamus. Edition of Amyot, date uncertain.

Lyonnoise, Dame Louise Labé. *Histoires et amours pastoralles de Daphnis et Chloé. Ensemble un débat judiciel de Folie et d'amours.* Paris, 1578. The *débat judiciel* is (as Abraham Lincoln said of a certain poet) "For those who like that sort of thing, this is just the sort of thing they would like."

Marcassus, P., ed. *Les Amours de Daphnis et Cloé [sic].* Paris, 1626. This edition, too, is more a paraphrase than a translation.

Courier, P.-L., ed. *Longus, Daphnis et Chloé. Traduction de Amyot. Révue et complété par P.-L. Courier.* Paris, 1809. Reprints. Paris, 1829, 1872 (ed. Charavay), 1873, 1875 (ed. A. S. Pons), 1876, 1878, 1880 (ed. Chassang), 1892 (illus. Luigi Rossi and Conconi), 1902, 1911 (ed.

Gaschet), 1919 (illus. Carlegle), 1925 (ed. Marsan); Paris: A. Lemerre, 1928; Chelsea: Ashendene Press, 1933; Monaco: Editions du Rocher, 1946.

Italian

Manzini, Giovanni Battista, trans. *Gli amori innocenti di Dafni e della Cloë.* Bologna, 1643. Reprint. 1647.

Gozzi, Gaspar, trans. *Gli amori pastorali di Dafni e Cloe.* Venice, 1766.

Caro, Annibal, trans. *Gli amori pastorali di Dafni e di Cloe di Longo Sofista.* Crispoli, 1786, 1794; Parigi, 1800; Milan, 1812.

Ciampi, Sebastiano, ed. *Gli amori pastorali di Dafni e Cloe descritti de Longo Sofista, volgarizzati de Annibal Caro col supplemento tr. de Sebastiano Ciampi. Nuova e cor. ed. illus. con xxv incisioni.* Milan, 1863. Ciampi, it will be noticed, undertook to do for Caro's authoritative and popular translation what Courier himself did for that of Amyot: revise and supplement it in light of Courier's discovery.

English

Daye, Angell, trans. *Daphnis and Chloe, excellently describing the weight of affection, the simplicitie of love, the purport of honest meaning, the resolution of men, and the disposition of Fate, finished in a pastorall, and interlaced with The shepherd's holidaie.* London, 1587. Reprint. London, 1890 (ed. Joseph Jacobs). This is actually a translation of Amyot's French, not Longus's Greek. Daye translates and paraphrases freely; one may note that the title page does not actually say, in so many words, that this is a translation. A better comment on Longus's obscurity could hardly be imagined.

Thornley, George, trans. *Daphnis and Chloe, a most sweet and pleasant pastoral romance for young ladies, done into English by Geo. Thornley, gent.* London, 1657. Reprints. London and Edinburgh: Ballantyne Press, 1893; London: Simpkin, Marshall, Hamilton, Kent and Co., 1922 (ed. George Saintsbury); New York: Pantheon Books, 1949 (illus. Maillol). Note the intended audience; and note, too, that while Thornley represents himself as translator, Longus's name is not mentioned on the title page.

Anon. *The Power of Love, or, The Lives and pastoral amours of Daphnis and Chloe.* Dublin, 1763.

*Cragg, Jacob, trans. 1764.

LeGrice, trans. *Daphnis and Chloe, a pastoral novel now first selectly translated into English from the original Greek of Longus.* Penzance, 1803.

Note the spurious claim to be the "first" translation into English.

Smith, Rowland, trans. *The Greek Romances of Heliodorus, Longus, and Achilles Tatius*. London, 1855. Reprint. London: George Bell, 1889. Smith's edition used the translation of LeGrice. In fact, since LeGrice's name never appears on the 1803 edition, it is only through Smith's attribution that we know who the translator was.

Anon. *Daphnis and Chloe, from the Greek of Longus*. With an Introduction by Jules Claretie. Illustrated by Raphael Collin. Boston and Paris: n.d. This collector's edition, undated, is manifestly a translation of Amyot-Courier, not of the Greek; it seems to be early twentieth century.

Anon. *Longus: Daphnis and Chloe, with literary and artistic notices*. Illustrations by M. Scott. Philadelphia: G. Barrie, 1902.

Moore, George, trans. *The Pastoral Lives of Daphnis and Chloe*. London: Heinemann, 1924. 2d ed., 1927. Reprint. In The Works of George Moore, Uniform Edition, 1933; New York: Limited Edition Club, 1934; Paris: Editions Verve, 1961 (illus. M. Chagall); New York: Braziller, 1977 (with Chagall's illustrations).

Lindsay, Jack, trans. *Daphnis and Chloe*. London: Daimon Press, 1948.

Hadas, Moses, trans. *Three Greek Romances: Daphnis and Chloe, by Longus; An Ephesian Tale, by Xenophon; The Hunters of Euboea, by Dio Chrysostom*. Garden City, N.Y.: Doubleday, Anchor Books, 1953.

Turner, Paul, trans. *Daphnis and Chloe: A New Translation, with Introduction*. Penguin Classics. Harmondsworth, Middlesex: Penguin Books, 1956. 2d ed. Baltimore: Penguin Books, 1968. Unexpurgated edition published at Harmondsworth, 1968.

Collins, Christopher, trans. *Daphnis and Chloe*. Illustrated by Felix Hoffman. Barre, Mass.: Imprint Society, 1972.

German

Anon. *Lustgarten der Liebe von steter brennende Liebe zweier liebhabende junge Personen Daphnidis und Chloe*. Frankfurt, 1615. Another of those translators who fail to acknowledge the original. The translation is very free.

Anon. *Daphnis und Chloe, aus den griechischen des Longus übersetzt*. Berlin, 1765.

*Passow, F., trans. 1820. This would seem to be the translation given to Goethe by Eckermann. Eckermann mentions Passow, but I have been unable to locate a copy, or any precise bibliographical material.

(Note that he issued a Greek text in 1811.) This is a pity; one would like to know what Goethe read.

Mauersberger, Arno. *Daphnis und Chloë: Ein antiker Liebesroman.* Sammlung Dieterich 44. Leipzig: Dieterich, 1964. 2d ed. 1970.

Spanish

Valera, Juan, trans. *Dáfnis y Cloe, las pastorales de Longo. Tradicción directa del griego, con introducción y notas por un aprendiz de helenista.* Madrid, 1880. Reprints. Seville, 1883; Madrid: Bibliotheca Nueva, 1927.

Montes de Oca, Francisco, trans. *Dáfnis y Cloe, Longo. El asno de oro, Apuleyo.* Sepan Cuantos 1. Mexico City: Porruá, 1975.

Portuguese

Boiteux, Lucas Alexandre, trans. *Daphnis e Chloé, pastoral de Longus; traduzida do francez por L. A. B.* Bibliotheca Positiva. Rio de Janeiro: Typ. do Jornal do Commercio, Rodrigues e Co., 1936.

Dutch

Roelants, Leo, trans. *Daphnis en Chloé, uit het Fransch van P. L. Courier vertaald door Leo Roelants.* Hoogstraten: Moderne Vitgeverij, 1943.

Russian

Merezhkovskii, Dmitri, trans. *Dafnis i Khloia, povest' Longusa.* St. Petersburg: Pirozhkova, 1904. A colleague in the field of Russian literature once told me that this translation was well known in its time.

Polish

Parandowski, J., trans. *Dafnis & Chloe. Longus.* Warsaw: Czytelnik, 1962.

Hebrew

Chrisman, Mordecai, trans. *Dafnis u-Helo'yah: sipar Yevani 'atik.* Tel Aviv: M. Shoham, 1919–1920.

Bronovsky, trans. Δάφνις καὶ Χλόη. Tel Aviv: Ketsin hinukh rashi, 1969.

Selected Bibliography

Works marked with an asterisk (*), though not specifically cited in the notes, were of value or interest in preparing this study. Some deal with topics not directly treated herein. Works marked with a double asterisk (**) were not found; I report whatever I know of them, in the event that some more fortunate or more diligent reader may be able to locate them.

Monographs and articles bearing exclusively or predominantly on the establishment of a sound text of *Daphnis and Chloe* have been omitted. (Those interested in such matters will find a useful bibliography in M. D. Reeve, *Longus: Daphnis et Chloe* [Stuttgart: Teubner, 1982], in the "Praefatio.") An exception has been made for an exchange of articles between Reeve and Douglas Young, over the latter's intriguing thesis that the peculiarities of this text's transmission can be accounted for by supposing that Longus himself issued a revised edition of *Daphnis and Chloe*.

WORKS ON LONGUS

**Asser. *De Longi Sophistae usu grammatico.* 1873.

Berti, Marisa. "Sulla interpretazione mistica del romanzo di Longo." *Studi Classici e Orientali* 16 (1967), 343–358.

*Blanchard, J. M. "La pastorale de Daphnis et Chloé: histoire de la mimesis." *Quaderni Urbinati di Cultura Classica* 20 (1975), 39–62.

*Borthwick, E. K. "A Note on some Unusual Greek Words for Eyes." *Classical Quarterly* 30 (1980), 252–256.

*Calder, William M. "Longus 1.2: The She-goat Nurse." *Classical Philology* 78 (1983), 50–51.
*Castiglioni, L. "Stilo e teste del romanzo di Longo." *Rendiconti del Istituto Lombardo* 61 (1928), 203–223.
Chalk, H. H. O. "Eros and the Lesbian Pastorals of Longus." *Journal of Hellenic Studies* 80 (1960), 32–51.
Christie, Frederick C. "Longus and the Development of the Pastoral Tradition." Ph.D. diss., Harvard University, 1972. Summarized in *Harvard Studies in Philology* 77 (1973), 246–248.
*Cresci, L. R. "Il romanzo di Longo Sofista e la traduzione bucolica." *Atene e Roma* 26 (1981), 1–25.
Dalmeyda, G. "Longus et Alciphron." *Mélanges Gustave Glotz*. Paris, 1932.
Deligiorgis, Stavros. "Longus' Art in Brief Lives." *Philological Quarterly* 53 (1974), 1–9.
*Dörrie, H. *De Longi Achillis Tatii Heliodori memoria*. Ph.D. diss., Göttingen University, 1935.
———. Review of Dalmeyda's Budé edition of *Daphnis and Chloe*. *Göttingische Gelehrte Anzeigen* 198 (1936), 348.
Effe, B. "Longos: zur Funktionsgeschichte der Bukolik in der römischen Kaiserzeit." *Hermes* 110 (1982), 65–84.
*Figueiredo Farinha, O. de. "Dáphnis e Cloe, romance de Longo." *Classica* 4 (1978), 79–81.
Forehand, W. E. "Symbolic Gardens in Longus' *Daphnis and Chloe*." *Eranos* 74 (1976), 102–111.
Geyer, Angelika. "Roman und Mysterienritual: Zum Problem eines Bezugs zum dionysischer Mysterienritual im Roman des Longos." *Würzberger Jahrbücher für die Altertumswissenschaft*, n.s. 3 (1977), 179–196.
Green, Peter. "Longus, Antiphon, and the Topography of Lesbos." *American Journal of Archaeology* 85 (1981), 195.
Herrmann, L. "Velius Longus auteur de *Daphnis et Chloé*." *Latomus* 40 (1981), 378–383.
*Hubeaux, J. "Le Dieu Amour chez Properce et chez Longus." *Académie Royale de Belgique, Classe de Lettres et des Sciences Morales et Politiques* 5.39 (1953), 263–290.
Hunter, R. L. *A Study of Daphnis and Chloe*. Cambridge Classical Studies. Cambridge: Cambridge University Press, 1983.
Kestner, Joseph W. "Ekphrasis as Frame in Longus' *Daphnis and Chloe*." *Classical World* 67 (1974), 166–171.
Levin, Donald Norman. "The Pivotal Role of Lycaenium in Longus' *Daphnis and Chloe*." *Rivista di Studi Classici* 25 (1977), 5–17.

McCulloh, William. *Longus.* Twayne World Authors series 96. New York: Twayne Publishers, 1970.

MacQueen, Bruce D. "Longus and the Myth of Chloe." *Illinois Classical Studies* 10 (1985), 119–134.

Mason, H. J. "Longus and the Topography of Lesbos." *Transactions of the American Philological Association* 109 (1979), 149–163.

Merkelbach, Reinhold. "*Daphnis und Chloe*: Roman und Mysterium." *Antaios* 1 (1960), 47–60.

Mittelstadt, M. C. "Longus and the Greek Love Romance." Ph.D. diss., Stanford University, 1964. Summary in *Dissertation Abstracts* 25 (1964/65), 1202–1203.

———. "Longus, *Daphnis and Chloe*, and the Pastoral Tradition." *Classica et Mediaevalia* 27 (1966), 162–177.

———. "Longus, *Daphnis and Chloe*, and Roman Narrative Painting." *Latomus* 26 (1967), 752–761.

———. "Bucolic-Lyric Motifs and Dramatic Narrative in Longus' *Daphnis and Chloe*." *Rheinisches Museum* 113 (1970), 211–227.

———. "Love, Eros, and the Poetic Style." In *Fons Perennis: Saggi critici di filologia classica raccolti in onore del Prof. Vittorio d'Agostino.* Turin: Amministrazione della *Rivista di Studi Classici*, 1971.

Naber, S. A. "Adnotationes Criticae ad Longi Pastoralia." *Mnemosyne*, n.s. 5 (1877), 201–205.

*Philippides, Marios. "A Note on Longus' *Lesbiaka*." *Classical World* 71 (1978), 460–461.

———. "The 'Digressive' *Aitia* in Longus." *Classical World* 74 (1980), 193–199.

*Reeve, Michael D. "Author's Variants in Longus?" *Proceedings of the Cambridge Philological Society* 195 (1969), 75–85.

Reich, H. *De Alciphronis Longique aetate.* Diss., Königsberg, 1894.

Rohde, Georg. "Longus und die Bukolik." *Rheinisches Museum* 86 (1937), 23–49.

Scarcella, A. M. "La donna nel romanzo di Longo Sofista." *Giornale Italiana di Filologia*, n.s. 3 (1972), 27–36.

**———. *La Lesbo di Longo Sofista.* Rome, 1968.

Turner, Paul. "*Daphnis and Chloe*: An Interpretation." *Greece and Rome* 7 (1960), 117–123.

Valley, Gunnar. *Über den Sprachgebrauch des Longos.* Uppsala: Berling, 1926.

*Young, Douglas. "Author's Variants in the Manuscript Tradition of Longus." *Proceedings of the Cambridge Philological Society* 194 (1968), 65–74.

*————. "Second Thoughts on Longus' Second Thoughts." *Proceedings of the Cambridge Philological Society* 197 (1971), 101.

WORKS ON THE ANCIENT NOVELS

Anderson, Graham. *Eros Sophistes: Ancient Novelists at Play.* American Classical Studies 9. Chico, Calif.: Scholar's Press, 1982.

————. *Ancient Fiction: The Novel in the Graeco-Roman World.* London: Croom Helm; Totowa, N.J.: Barnes and Noble, 1984.

Barns, J. W. B. "Egypt and the Greek Romance." In *Mitteilungen aus der Papyrussammlung der Österreich.* Nationalbibliothek, n.s. 5. Vienna, 1956.

Bonner, Campbell. "On Certain Supposed Literary Relationships." *Classical Philology* 4 (1909), 32–44.

Braun, Martin. *Griechische Roman und hellenistische Geschichtschreibung.* Frankfurter Studien zur Religion und Kultur der Antike 6. Frankfurt am Main: V. Klostermann, 1938.

————. *History and Romance in Graeco-Oriental Literature.* Oxford: Blackwell, 1938.

Chassang, A. *Histoire des romans et ses rapports avec l'histoire dans l'antiquité grecque et latine.* Paris, 1862.

*Corbato, C. "Da Menandro a Caritone. Studi sulla genesi del romanzo greco: i suoi rapporti con la commedia nuova." *Quaderni Triestini sul Teatro Antico* 1 (1968), 5–44.

Dowden, Ken. "Apuleius and the Art of Narrative." *Classical Quarterly* 32 (1982), 419–435.

Durham, Donald. "Parody in Achilles Tatius." *Classical Philology* 33 (1938), 1–19.

Garcia Gual, Carlos. *Los orígenes de la novela.* Colección Fundamentos 16. Madrid: Ediciones ISTMO, 1972.

Gesner, Carol. *Shakespeare and the Greek Romance: A Study of Origins.* Lexington: University Press of Kentucky, 1970.

Giangrande, Giuseppe. "The Origins of the Greek Romance," *Eranos* 60 (1962), 132–159.

*Gulick, C. B. "The Origins of the Novel." *Harvard Graduate's Magazine* 33 (1924), 205.

Hadas, Moses. "Cultural Survival and the Origins of Fiction." *South Atlantic Quarterly* 51 (1952), 253–260.

Hägg, Tomas. *Narrative Technique in Ancient Greek Romances: Studies of Chariton, Xenophon Ephesius, and Achilles Tatius.* Stockholm: P. Aström, 1971.

————. *The Novel in Antiquity*. Berkeley and Los Angeles: University of California Press, 1983.

*Heinze R. "Petronius und der griechische Roman." *Hermes* 34 (1899), 494–519.

Heiserman, Arthur. *The Novel before the Novel: Essays and Discussions about the Beginnings of Prose Fiction in the West*. Chicago: University of Chicago Press, 1977.

Helm, Rudolf. *Der antike Roman*. 2d ed. Studien zur Altertumswissenschaft 4. Göttingen: Vandenboeck, 1956.

Huet, Msgr. Pierre-Daniel. *Lettre à M. Segrais de l'origine des romans*. Paris, 1678.

Kerényi, Karl. *Die griechische-orientalische Romanliteratur in religionsgeschichtlicher Beleuchtung: Ein Versuch*. Tübingen: J. C. B. Mohr, 1927.

————. *Der antike Roman: Einführung und Textauswahl*. Darmstadt: Wissenschaftliche Buchgesellschaft, 1971.

Lavagnini, Bruno. *Le origini del romanzo greco*. Pisa: F. Mariotti, 1921. Reprinted in *Studi sul romanzo greco*. Messina: G. d'Anna, 1950.

*Levin, Donald Norman. "To Whom Did the Ancient Novelists Address Themselves?" *Rivista di Studi Classici* 25 (1977), 18–29.

*Littlewood, R. "Romantic Paradises: The Role of the Garden in the Byzantine Romance." *Byzantine and Modern Greek Studies* 5 (1979), 77–95.

Loicq-Berger, M. P. "Pour une lecture des romans grecs." *Etudes Classiques* 48 (1980), 23–42.

Ludvíkovsky, J. *Recky Roman Dobroduzny*. Prague: Filosofika Fakulta University Karlova, 1925. In Czech, with summary in French.

Merkelbach, Reinhold. *Roman und Mysterium*. Munich: Beck, 1962.

*Perry, Ben Edwin. "Literature in the Second Century." *Classical Journal* 50 (1955), 295–298.

————. *The Ancient Romances: A Literary-Historical Account of Their Origins*. Sather Classical Lectures 37. Berkeley and Los Angeles: University of California Press, 1967.

Rattenbury, R. M. "Chastity and Chastity Ordeals in the Ancient Greek Romances." *Proceedings of the Leeds Philosophical and Literary Society* 1 (1926), 59–70.

Reardon, B. P. "The Greek Novel." *Phoenix* 23 (1969), 291–309.

————. "The Second Sophistic and the Novel." In *Approaches to the Second Sophistic*, ed. G. Bowersock, 23–29. University Park, Pa.: American Philological Association, 1974.

————. "Novels and Novelties, or, Mysteriouser and Mysteriouser." In

The Mediterranean World: Papers Presented to Gilbert Bagnani. Peterborough, Ont.: Trent University, 1975.

———. "Aspects of the Greek Novel." *Greece and Rome* 23 (1976), 118–131.

*———, ed. *Erotica Antiqua: Acta of the International Conference on the Ancient Novel.* Bangor, Wales, 1977.

Reeve, Michael D. "Hiatus in the Greek Novel." *Classical Quarterly,* n.s. 21 (1971), 514—539.

Rohde, Erwin. *Der griechische Roman und seine Vorläufer.* 4th ed. Reprint. Hildesheim: Georg Olms, 1960.

*Sandy, Gerald N. "Recent Scholarship on the Prose Fiction of Classical Antiquity." *Classical World* 67 (1974), 321–359.

———. *Heliodorus.* Twayne World Authors series 647. Boston: Twayne Publishers, 1982.

———. "Classical Forerunners of the Theory and Practice of Prose Romance in France: Studies in the Narrative Form of Minor French Romances of the Sixteenth and Seventeenth Centuries." *Antike und Abendland* 28 (1982), 168–191.

**Scarcella, A. M. "Metastasi narratologica del dato storico nel romanzo erotico greco." *Materiali e contributi per la storia della narrativa grecolatina* 3 (1981), 341–367.

*Schissel von Fleschenberg, Otmar. *Entwicklungsgeschichte des griechischen Romanes im Altertum.* Halle: Niemeyer, 1913.

Schmeling, Gareth. *Chariton.* Twayne World Authors series 295. New York: Twayne Publishers, 1974.

———. *Xenophon of Ephesus.* Twayne World Authors series 613. Boston: Twayne Publishers, 1980.

Schwartz, Edward. *Fünf Vorträge über den griechischen Roman.* 2d ed. Berlin: DeGruyter, 1943.

Scobie, Alexander. *Essays on the Ancient Romance and Its Heritage.* Beiträge zur klassischen Philologie 30. Meisenheim am Glan: Anton Hain, 1969.

———. *More Essays on the Ancient Romance.* Beiträge zur klassischen Philologie 46. Meisenheim am Glan: Anton Hain, 1973.

———. "Storytellers, Storytelling, and the Novel in Graeco-Roman Antiquity." *Rheinisches Museum* 122 (1979), 229–259.

Todd, Frederick. *Some Ancient Novels.* London: Oxford University Press, 1940.

Turcan, Robert. "Le 'roman initiatique': A propos d'un livre récent." *Révue de l'Histoire des Réligions* 163 (1963), 149–199.

Turner, Paul. "Novels, Ancient and Modern." *Novel* 2 (1968), 15–24.

**Villemain, M. *Essai sur les romans grecs.*
*Warren, F. M. *History of the Novel prior to the Seventeenth Century.* New York, 1895. Reprint. Folcroft, Pa.: Folcroft Press, 1969.
*Wehrli, F. "Einheit und Vorgeschichte der griechish-römischen Romanliteratur." *Museum Helveticum* 22 (1965), 133–154.
Weinrich, Otto. *Der griechische Liebesroman.* Zurich: Artemis, 1962.
Wolff, Samuel. *The Greek Romance in Elizabethan Prose Fiction.* New York: Press of the New Era, 1912. Reprint. New York: B. Franklin, 1961.

STUDIES OF ANCIENT LITERATURE AND THOUGHT

Bowersock, Glen, ed. *Approaches to the Second Sophistic: Papers Presented at the 105th Annual Meeting of the American Philological Association.* University Park, Pa.: The American Philological Association, 1974.
Bowie, E. L. "The Greeks and Their Past in the Second Sophistic." *Past and Present* 46 (1970), 1–41.
Christ, W. von, W. Schmid, and O. Stählin. *Geschichte der griechischen Literatur.* 6th ed. Vol. 2.2: *Von 100 bis 530 nach Christum.* Munich, 1924.
Cichorius, Conrad. *Römische Studien.* Leipzig: Teubner, 1922.
Ettin, Andrew. *Literature and the Pastoral.* New Haven: Yale University Press, 1985.
Ferrari, G. R. F. *Listening to the Cicadas: A Study of Plato's Phaedrus.* Cambridge Classical Studies. Cambridge: Cambridge University Press, 1987.
Furst, Lilian. *Fictions of Romantic Irony.* Cambridge, Mass.: Harvard University Press.
Griswold, Charles L. *Self-Knowledge in Plato's Phaedrus.* New Haven: Yale University Press, 1986.
*Heil, G. "Mythos als Gegenstand der Sprachreflexion." *Die Altsprachliche Unterricht* 23.2 (1980), 26–42.
Johnson, Robert A. *He: Understanding Masculine Psychology.* King of Prussia, Pa.: Religious Publishing Co., 1974.
Kaibel, G. "Dionysios von Halikarnass und die Sophistik." *Hermes* 20 (1885), 497–513.
Kennedy, George. *The Art of Persuasion in Greece.* Princeton, N.J.: Princeton University Press, 1963.
———. *The Art of Rhetoric in the Roman World, 300 B.C.–A.D. 300.* Princeton, N.J.: Princeton University Press, 1972.
———. "The Sophists as Declaimers." In *Approaches to the Second Sophistic,* ed. G. Bowersock, 17–22. University Park, Pa.: American Philological Association, 1974.

Lacey, Philip. "Plato and the Intellectual Life of the Second Century A.D." In *Approaches to the Second Sophistic*, ed. G. Bowersock, 4–10. University Park, Pa.: American Philological Association, 1974.

Lefkowitz, Mary. *Lives of the Greek Poets*. Baltimore: Johns Hopkins University Press, 1982.

Lesky, Albin. *Geschichte der griechischen Literatur*. 3d ed. Bern: Francke, 1971.

Moors, Kent F. *Platonic Myth: An Introductory Study*. Lenham, Mass.: University Press of America, 1982.

Norden, Eduard. *Die antike Kunstprosa*. 2 vols. Leipzig: Teubner, 1898.

Pieper, Josef. *Begeisterung und Göttlicher Wahnsinn*. Munich: Kösel-Verlag, 1962.

Pinciano, Alonso López. *Philosophia Antiqua*. Milan, 1595.

Reardon, B. P. *Courants littéraires grecs des duxième et troisième siècles après J.-C.* Paris: Belles Lettres, 1971.

Rohde, Erwin. "Die asianische Rhetorik und die zweite Sophistik." *Rheinisches Museum*, n.s. 41 (1886), 170–190.

Russell, D. A. *Greek Declamation*. Cambridge: Cambridge University Press, 1983.

Schmid, W. *Der Atticismus in seiner Hauptvertreten*. 4 vols. Stuttgart: Kohlhammer, 1887–1897.

Schoell, Maximilian. *Histoire de la littérature grecque profane*. 2d ed. Paris, 1824.

Solmsen, Friederich. *Isis among the Greeks and Romans*. Cambridge, Mass.: Published for Oberlin College by Harvard University Press, 1979.

Wilamowitz-Moellendorff, Ulrich von. "Die griechische Literatur des Altertums." In *Die griechische und lateinische Literatur und Sprache*. 2d ed. Die Kultur der Gegenwart 1.8. Berlin: Teubner, 1907.

———. Review of André Boulanger's edition of Aristides. *Litteris* 2 (1925), 126. Reprint. *Kleine Schriften* 3 (1969), 421.

Witt, R. E. *Isis in the Graeco-Roman World*. Aspects of Greek and Roman Life. Ithaca, N.Y.: Cornell University Press, 1971.

Wojaczek, G. *Daphnis: Untersuchungen zur griechischen Bukolik*. Meisenheim am Glan: Anton Hain, 1969.

Zaslavsky, Robert. *Platonic Myth and Platonic Writing*. Lenham, Mass.: University Press of America, 1981.

Index